AN AMERICAN ICON IN PUERTO RICO

Transnational Girlhoods

EDITORS: Claudia Mitchell, *McGill University*; Bodil Formark, *Umeå University*; Ann Smith, *McGill University*; Heather Switzer, *Arizona State University*

Girlhood Studies has emerged over the last decade as a strong area of interdisciplinary research and activism, encompassing studies of feminism, women and gender, and childhood and youth and extending into such areas as sociology, anthropology, development studies, children's literature, and cultural studies. As the first book series to focus specifically on this exciting field, *Transnational Girlhoods* will help to advance the research and activism agenda by publishing full-length monographs and edited collections that reflect a robust interdisciplinary and global perspective. International in scope, the series will draw on a vibrant network of girlhood scholars already active across North America, Europe, Russia, Oceania, and Africa, while forging connections with new activist and scholarly communities.

AN AMERICAN ICON IN PUERTO RICO
Barbie, Girlhood, and Colonialism at Play

Emily R. Aguiló-Pérez

berghahn
NEW YORK · OXFORD
www.berghahnbooks.com

First published in 2022 by
Berghahn Books
www.berghahnbooks.com

© 2022, 2023 Emily R. Aguiló-Pérez
First paperback edition published in 2023

Library of Congress Cataloging-in-Publication Data
Names: Aguiló-Pérez, Emily R., author.
Title: An American Icon in Puerto Rico: Barbie, Girlhood, and Colonialism at Play /
    Emily R. Aguiló-Pérez.
Description: New York: Berghahn Books, 2022. | Series: Transnational Girlhoods;
    volume 4 | Includes bibliographical references and index.
Identifiers: LCCN 2021057365 (print) | LCCN 2021057366 (ebook) |
    ISBN 9781800733862 (hardback) | ISBN 9781800733879 (ebook)
Subjects: LCSH: Girls—Puerto Rico—Social conditions. | Barbie dolls—Social
    aspects—Puerto Rico. | Play—Social aspects—Puerto Rico. | Group identity—
    Puerto Rico.
Classification: LCC HQ799.P9 A48 2022 (print) | LCC HQ799.P9 (ebook) |
    DDC 305.23082/097295—dc23/eng/20211230
LC record available at https://lccn.loc.gov/2021057365
LC ebook record available at https://lccn.loc.gov/2021057366

British Library Cataloguing in Publication Data
A catalogue record for this book is available from the British Library

ISBN 978-1-80073-386-2 hardback
ISBN 978-1-80539-111-1 paperback
ISBN 978-1-80073-387-9 ebook

https://doi.org/10.3167/9781800733862

For my parents, Carmen and Fernando

CONTENTS

ILLUSTRATIONS

Figures

Tables

Preface

Who is Barbie, and how do we feel about her? For a very extended period of my childhood, Barbie dolls were my favorite toys.[1] I remember spending hours every afternoon after school creating different scenarios and going through the house to look for objects I could use as accessories for my dolls. From the age of six to probably eleven I was a rather shy, or perhaps private, girl, especially when it came to playing with my dolls. Thus, most of my play with Barbie dolls occurred by myself. Although a lot of play with Barbie is composed of using the doll as a fashion prop where children try different clothes on her, experiment with her hair, and use her as a sort of mannequin, Barbie play oftentimes takes the form of creating scenes and narratives. In my case, every day had a different narrative, with different dolls, and in different settings. At least one of my dolls was a teacher, one a dancer, and various others were singers. These were all things I wanted to be when I grew up, so I vicariously lived my dreams through my dolls. Having different outfits and being able to dress them according to the occasion, place, or profession I selected contributed greatly to the play. Other dolls already had a profession, and I would play along with these established roles most of the time.

Those of us who avidly played with Barbie can still remember the feelings of holding the doll, changing her clothes, brushing her hair, and assigning her a name, a role, and with it a personality. We created stories that ranged from having fun with friends to participating in family situations, or from mirroring issues happening at school to dramatizing the plots of our favorite TV shows. Other times we created our own shows or soap operas with our dolls. The narratives I came up with were very different and relied upon my mood or my current interests. Singing had always been an interest of mine since I was very little, so it played an important role in my play. However, *where* things happened and *what* happened in those places were constantly changing. Sometimes the narrative would take place at the doll's school; in this case, since for me all my Barbie dolls were adults, other toys came into play so they could be the students. Other times, a wedding would take place, an event that I could perform once I finally had a wedding dress for my dolls; however, since there were only two Ken dolls, my dolls had to become actors in a soap opera in order for many "weddings" to occur. As such, many of the narratives were centered on boy dilemmas, although friendship and family were also featured.

Barbie is a cultural icon that has been present since 1959, enjoying popularity as a toy among girls ever since.[2] She has become a great part of children's culture—be it by the doll's presence or by its absence in children's lives (Aguiló-Pérez 2014). In my conversations with many adult women, as is also apparent in the scholarship about Barbie, I have encountered a plethora of responses to the doll. Some have voiced their love for Barbie because it takes them back to their childhood when they played with the doll for hours. Others have admitted they played with Barbies, although they did not tell their friends at the time they were doing so because Barbie was "for babies"; in their conversations with me, they express gladness in knowing that I played with them as well, as it provides a sense of comfort for them to know they were not alone in playing with the doll.

Others, however, react negatively to Barbie. For instance, in a news article titled "Barbie Fucks It Up Again," author Pamela Ribon (2014) criticizes a book called *Barbie: I Can Be a Computer Engineer* (Mattel 2010) that was published at the time. In it, Barbie designs a game to show kids how computers work, but she is only the designer; the boys are the developers: "I'm only creating the design ideas," Barbie says, laughing. "I'll need Steven and Brian's help to turn it into a real game!" (2010: n.p.). The story continues with Barbie infecting both her computer and Skipper's with a virus. Barbie, as a computer engineer, should be capable of solving this problem, yet she resorts to asking the boys for help. Ribon (2014) argues that the book continues the portrayal of Barbie (and, thus, girls) as not completely intelligent. The book has since been pulled from the website of its publisher, Random House Kids, and Mattel has offered a public apology. Yet, the reality is that it *was* written, and someone thought it would be a reasonable depiction of Barbie as an engineer. I found out about *Barbie: I Can Be a Computer Engineer* when a friend shared Ribon's 2014 article on Facebook. Accompanying the link was my friend's commentary, in which she articulated her hatred for the doll and explained that she would never allow her daughter to play with Barbie because the doll sends the wrong message to girls. Her reaction, like that of many others, was to limit her daughter's access to the doll because of its antifeminist messages.

Yet, reactions to the doll can also be mixed. As some of the testimonies I examine in this book illustrate, women and girls may remember some aspects of Barbie with fondness while also recognizing moments of tension and dissatisfaction with the doll. This is not unique to the participants described here, of course. At the time I was finishing the manuscript for this book, I was also teaching a seminar course titled "Examining Girlhood Studies through Barbie." Every week we focused on a different aspect of Barbie's history in girlhood, including her creation, her body, her whiteness, and her heteronormativity. In these discussions, some students (of various genders) expressed their love for the doll, while others wanted to take her apart—both literally and figuratively—because they just did not like her. Others had mixed feelings. They had enjoyed playing with Barbie during their childhood and still liked the doll, yet they would dive into the discussions of Barbie by critically examining her and pointing out all the ways the doll has been problematic. Still, there were a few students who had loved Barbie so much and who had such fond memories with her that they found it difficult to criticize her.

Barbie's iconic presence in children's lives and in popular culture is what makes her such a fascinating artifact to study. The doll has been a popular toy since it was introduced in 1959. Those who have studied the Barbie phenomenon note that no other toy has generated so much media interest. For over thirty years Barbie has been a topic that continues to garner attention, and the release of the 2018 Barbie "Sheroes" line, which tried to inspire girls around the world, exemplified this hot topic in girlhood cultures and girlhood studies. In fact, in March 2018 I was one of three professionals interviewed on the Wharton School of the University of Pennsylvania's *Knowledge@Wharton* podcast, where we discussed the Sheroes line and the various reasons behind Mattel's move to create these dolls as a response to years of criticism of Barbie as a role model for girls. With this line, Mattel aimed to appease mothers' anxieties by celebrating women in history. The Sheroes Barbie line also received widespread attention due to its inclusion of a Frida Kahlo doll. Multiple online articles discussed important aspects such as ableism, copyrights, and capitalism. Notably, the podcast *Latino USA* created an episode devoted to the discussion of the Frida Kahlo Barbie and a number of the issues surrounding her.

Beyond this line of dolls, Barbie—the toy, the brand, the cultural icon—has been the subject of documentaries, TV programs, and other media over the years. But most recently she was the subject of a 2018 Hulu documentary titled *Tiny Shoulders: Rethinking Barbie*, as well as an episode of the Netflix series *The Toys That Made Us* (episode 2). What these examples illustrate is that, for a number of reasons, Barbie is a topic of interest for a wide audience. For adults, especially feminist women, the doll becomes a subject of internal debate. Women often feel a sense of shame in admitting they had any relation to Barbie. Reid-Walsh and Mitchell (2000) note that Barbie has always been controversial, and her most ardent critics are women. In cultural conversations, the doll has occupied a position of contradiction, where women who identify as feminists also negotiate the fact that they played with Barbie. In a way, Barbie has become an icon that represents antifeminism while also evoking feelings of nostalgia, thus creating an interesting tension that provides a platform to explore and come to understand feminist issues such as sexuality, race, equality, accessibility, class, motherhood or gender roles, femininity, performance, and queer theory. Driscoll notes:

> No product for girls, no dominant toy of any year, no feminist account of popular culture, and no transitionally marketed representation of the body can entirely escape its relation to Barbie in the Western public sphere; nor can any contribution to intellectual inquiry about girls, girlhood, feminism, embodiment, or commodity culture entirely avoid Barbie. (2008: 45)

In academic scholarship about Barbie there have been both concerns about the effects of girls playing with Barbie and enjoyment in the long spectacle of the Barbie archive. Barbie is a fashion doll. Her purpose, according to creator Ruth Handler, was to act as a prop for girls to dress up and try different outfits on. This, however, is not the only way girls actually play with Barbie. They create narratives, often complex ones, about a range of topics and situations, including those centered on their own lived experiences. Despite the fact that Barbie was created devoid of any specific educational goal, different postulations on the doll express concern about what girls may learn through their interactions with Barbie culture. The numerous layers of subjects that emerge in the conversation about Barbie and her long-lasting presence in girlhood culture makes her an object that offers insight into experiences of girlhood worthy of examination.

Whether women's and girls' experiences with the doll have been positive or negative, Barbie has generally played a role in childhood, especially in Western cultures (Driscoll 2008; Rand 1995). As such, a number of scholars have written about individuals' childhood experiences with the doll and their negotiations with how Barbie contributed, and still contributes, to their own identities (McDonough 1999; Rand 1995; Reid-Walsh and Mitchell 2000; Rogers 1998). In many ways, Barbie contributes to women's identities and how they continue to view the doll, either in relation to their own childhood experiences or as adults who do not want to promote Barbie play among their own offspring. For this reason, I decided during my doctoral studies that I wanted to examine individuals' views on Barbie and their experiences with the doll either currently taking place (girls) or through memories of their play (teenagers and adults). This was the easy part. As soon as I began "announcing" to friends, peers, family, professors, and others that Barbie would be the subject of my research, they would share countless stories about their own childhoods playing with Barbie or not being allowed to play with Barbie, or even sharing stories of their own children and their relationship with the doll. One friend, a white woman, talked about how she would play for hours, utilizing the little round divider typically placed in pizza boxes as a miniature table for her dolls. In contrast, another friend, a Black woman, shared with me that her mother did not buy Barbie dolls because they lacked diversity. A different acquaintance, a white woman, shared that her feminist mother did not like Barbie, but she allowed the doll in the house with one condition: she had to have a career.

While these stories were fascinating and varied, I knew the scholarship on Barbie had explored similar approaches, especially in the United States. What new perspectives could my research offer? I considered my own childhood in Puerto Rico and my deep play with Barbie: Why was she so prominent in my girlhood? Moreover, why was she not a big part of my sisters' childhoods? Did my mother ever consider not allowing Barbie into our home? These questions, then, extended to consider how big or small a role Barbie dolls had played for women in Puerto Rico and whether the dolls still played any role in Puerto Rican girls' lives. When Barbie has been examined in relation to Puerto Rico, it has mostly been about the Puerto Rican doll, which came out in 1997. Aguilar (1997), Navarro (1997), Negrón-Muntaner (2002), and Rivera-Brooks (1997) wrote about the markedly divided opinion on the Puerto Rican Barbie doll at the time it was produced. As they explain, while Puerto Rican Barbie was received enthusiastically in Puerto Rico, it caused a heated debate among Puerto Ricans on the U.S. mainland. Many of the latter objected to her light skin, among other aspects, and the description about Puerto Rico's history it provided, which I discuss later in this text. Puerto Rican Barbie has been one of its kind because it was the first time Puerto Rico was featured in the "Dolls of the World" Barbie line, and she has not been featured since. Thus, she pertains mainly to a specific generation of girls who grew up with her in the mid-1990s. There has also, to this point, never been a study of the experiences with Barbie for those who grew up in the Puerto Rican archipelago.

In paying attention specifically to the experiences of Puerto Rican women and girls, this book aims to extend the research on Barbie to places where the scholarship has yet to explore the memories that adult women have of their own play or nonplay with Barbie dolls and the social and cultural implications these memories may have on their adult lives. In addition, it continues exploring Barbie's role in Puerto Rican girlhoods by presenting the perspective of girls who played with Barbie at the time of my study, played with Barbie at some point in their lives, or rejected Barbie. I use the term "Puerto Rican girlhoods" as a plural because I explore the individual experiences of eighteen Puerto Rican women and three girls across various generations. Yet, these experiences do not just represent one type of girlhood experience in Puerto Rico but instead illuminate how Barbie played a role in their individual formations, what these experiences share with one another, and how they divert from each other.

Reflections on My Position as Researcher/Participant

At the genesis of my research and throughout the entire process of the study, I was aware of my position within the discussion about Barbie. Like many media and cultural studies scholars, I approached this project from the standpoints of both a fan and a critic of Barbie. Throughout my girlhood I loved the doll, and I never had negative experiences with her. I do not recall ever receiving problematic messages from her, about looks, class, race, or other topics. At that time, I did not critically analyze the messages and ideologies that surrounded me. Yet, whereas my experiences with Barbie were positive, I understood as a researcher that my own experiences did not represent everyone else's. Moreover, as a scholar, I had become more attuned to the ways that Barbie could be problematic for girls and the range of interactions girls had with the doll. Having understood this, I was prepared to hear about a multitude of narratives and opinions toward the doll.

While I had an idea of what I might hear, I did not have predetermined themes—these emerged organically. What fascinated me was the possibility of weaving together all the narratives around common themes and discovering how new sections in my discussion were being created. One section was especially very important for me: "More Than a Doll: Barbie's Significance in Girlhood and Womanhood," in this book's conclusion, came together after I realized that the relationship of some of my participants with Barbie went beyond that of a child and a favorite toy. I had not planned for this section, yet after reviewing my data, I began piecing together these narratives where Barbie was a companion through girls' difficult times; she served as an outlet when no one else was able to or when real life was just too arduous to confront. Thus, though I aimed to find what Barbie's influence was in Puerto Rican girlhoods, I never knew how important a role she played in the life of some girls.

In my position as researcher, I also had to hold back from agreeing or disagreeing with participants, or from even voicing my opinion about a topic they were discussing. For instance, when one participant talked about body image, she expressed certain ideas that are very ingrained in our culture—one being the idea that if you are not thin, you are not beautiful, or, in other words, "She has a pretty face, but . . ." I wanted to respond by saying something like, "Women with curves *are* beautiful." However, I understood that my position as the researcher was not to pass judgment or to tell my participants what to think. Instead, I was there to *listen* to them because my main goal was to learn about their perceptions and experiences outside of my own. I also felt it was important to maintain respect, especially with participants I had not met before. Questioning something they said, disagreeing with them, or voicing my opinions could have jeopardized the rapport we had built and their openness to continue sharing sometimes difficult memories.

In my continuous reflections about the study described in this book, I point to my own development as a qualitative researcher. As I underwent the process of transcribing interviews, I noticed several moments that needed a follow-up question or an elaboration on a point the participant had made. I only became aware of these instances as I listened to the recorded interviews and realized that I wanted to know more about specific topics, but I either did not think about it in the moment of the actual interview or did not feel comfortable asking more at the time (e.g., I did not want to make a participant who did not like Black Barbie dolls uncomfortable by asking her to expand on her stance). My assessment of my own practices indicates that I need to become more aware of these moments.

Finally, this project helped me, as a researcher and participant, unearth my experiences in relation not only to Barbie but also to girlhood in general. Moreover, it pushed me to explore perceptions of Barbie that are not my own, to examine discourses about race, and to continuously learn and unlearn a lot of what I had come to understand about the United

States–Puerto Rico relationship. In each chapter I aimed to talk not only about my participants' experiences but also my own, and thus I became "researched," which is an important aspect of memory-work approaches (Onyx and Small 2011). Nevertheless, I was careful not to become the central figure in my research. First and foremost, I wanted to honor the experiences of other women and girls. At the same time, I also tried to be reflexive in the perspectives I was providing and my own understandings of the topics at hand. I asked questions about how I was talking about topics and how I could best explain ideas that are closely tied to the culture. It was important for me to analyze not only what was happening among my participants but also what my place in the process was. This happened through the practice of self-reflection that occurred simultaneously as I analyzed the data.

Notes

1. In this instance and throughout the rest of this book, when I refer to Barbie dolls I include Barbie and her friends (e.g., Ken, Skipper, Teresa, Midge), unless specified. I use the name Barbie because she is the most prominent of the dolls and she is the face Mattel® uses to promote this product line.
2. Barbie has been part of all children's lives, including the lives of female, male, nonbinary, transgender, and other children. I use the term "girl" in this book because of my focus on girlhood in Puerto Rico. All participants in my research, both adults and children, self-identified as girls or women. Therefore, I discuss Barbie's role in girls' lives, understanding that the doll is not exclusively a "girl" toy, while also acknowledging that Mattel's marketing efforts have been mostly directed at girls.

ACKNOWLEDGMENTS

First and foremost, I want to thank all of my participants who shared stories with me. Without you there would be no study, and I would not have been able to trace the experiences of Puerto Rican women and girls with Barbie. I thank you from the bottom of my heart for sharing your anecdotes—however painful, shameful, funny, or wonderful they were—with me. Thank you to everyone else who shared stories, articles, pictures, and anything related to Barbie—it's wonderful to know that so many people cared about my work and always thought of me when Barbie came up.

This book is based on my doctoral dissertation, and as such I would be remiss not to thank the members of my committee, who were more than I could have ever asked for in a team. Jacqueline Reid-Walsh, who is always supportive, encouraging, and enthusiastic for my academic and professional endeavors, thank you for guiding me through my entire doctoral career. I thank Daniel Hade, Christine Thompson, and Courtney Morris for facilitating discussions on childhood, media, merchandising, gender, and race, among other topics, that informed my research.

I must thank the peer reviewers of my manuscript who provided insightful, concrete, supportive, and constructive comments. They helped me look at some aspects more deeply and encouraged me to be more assertive in my writing. The revisions and additions I made based on their comments resulted in a much stronger book. I am also profoundly grateful to my editor at Berghahn Books, Amanda Horn, who was so patient and generous with me. The fears of publishing my first academic book were sometimes paralyzing, and they were exacerbated by going through the process during a global pandemic. Having a thoughtful, understanding, and excellent editor was invaluable. So, thank you so much!

Parts of this research would not have been possible without the opportunities I had to examine Barbie artifacts at the Strong National Museum of Play through their research fellowships. Thank you Christopher Bensch, Patricia Hogan, and the staff members who helped me during my two weeks of work. I thank Mr. Luis Felipe Orama at the Museo de Muñecas Barbie in Quebradillas for the opportunity to look around and learn more about Barbie's fans in Puerto Rico. Thank you to the library at the University of Puerto Rico Río Piedras, specifically the Center for Puerto Rican studies at Lázaro Library for allowing me to use the microfilms and helping me in my search for Barbie in Puerto Rican newspapers.

To my family—immediate and extended—who celebrated every accomplishment with me and were always happy with my success. Thank you so much! To my students in the spring 2020 semester, thank you for your patience, and for asking me about my book and making me feel like a rock star for writing one! And to the students in my spring 2020 ENG 400 course, thank you for the stimulating and intelligent conversations about Barbie, dolls, girlhood, gender, race, and the body—and for teaching me so much about pop culture. I had a blast teaching the course and learning from you. Finally, and more importantly, I want to thank and dedicate this work to my siblings: Fernando, Camille, and Frances; siblings-in-law: Frances E. and Enrique; and my niblings: Gael Alejandro, Fernando Enrique, Paola Rose, and Sofia Paloma. I am so lucky to have you in my life. I love you! Thank you, Adam for encouraging me to go for it and submit the book proposal. It would have taken me so long to summon the courage to do it otherwise, so I am grateful for your constant support. I truly cannot thank my parents, Carmen and Fernando, enough for taking me to some of my interviews during the data collection period. My mother also oftentimes served as a research assistant—looking for my childhood artifacts and sending me materials I needed—and sent me care packages, and also listened to me blabber about my work, grad school, the job market, pre-tenure life, and all the ups and downs of academia. ¡Gracias, gracias, gracias!

INTRODUCTION

The Transnational Doll
from Our Childhoods

As I write the pages of this book, a variety of Barbie doll companions sit on my bookshelves. Some are from my childhood, others I received as gifts during grad school, and others I acquired through the years in my continued research about Barbie. They are joined by Barbie paper dolls, Barbie PEZ dispensers, and miniature Barbie cake toppers. Some traveled with me, while others became part of my life more recently, but they all serve as reminders of my girlhood and that of many Puerto Ricans. With this I do not intend to make a blanket generalization about Puerto Rican girls to claim that they all play(ed) with or even own(ed) a doll. However, it is not far-fetched to state that Barbie has been a constant presence in many Puerto Rican girls' lives. During the 1990s, Puerto Ricans had "the highest per capita number of Barbies in Latin America" (Negrón-Muntaner 2004: 224); 72 percent of Puerto Rican children at the time owned at least one Barbie doll compared to 49 percent in Chile, which was the second highest in Latin America. One reason for Puerto Rico's high numbers, and especially the stark difference between the first and second highest numbers, is the island's political and economic ties to the United States.

Notes for this section can be found on page 25.

Puerto Rican girlhoods cannot be separated from Puerto Rico's colonial history, as it has been a U.S. territory since 1898. As such, the constant back-and-forth movement of people between Puerto Rico and the United States is a central part of Puerto Rican identity (Duany 2002). Hence, transnationality often defines what it means to be Puerto Rican. While as a territory Puerto Rico is part of the United States (and there are many political and economic ramifications this territorial status entails), there is sovereignty in the culture and traditions found there. Thus, there are cultural borders that Barbie must permeate. Barbie, who is a U.S. icon and who embodies what many in the United States believe to be "real American" values—whiteness, heterosexuality, and social and financial capital—then becomes an even more complex figure in Puerto Rican childhoods. For many, she is the very thing Puerto Ricans must reject: the veneration of a U.S. icon in a U.S. colony. Nevertheless, Barbie is a transnational object (Grewal 2005; Hegde 2001; MacDougall 2003; Negrón-Muntaner 2002) that has permeated national borders as well as cultural ones. In this regard, Barbie in Puerto Rican girlhoods fits the more literal definition for transnationalism that speaks to operating across national boundaries. Many movements between Puerto Rico and continental United States are caused by economic necessities, as populations move in search of better opportunities to thrive financially. Consequently, Puerto Ricans have become transnational subjects of two lands. In the cases presented in this book, Barbie as an object often served as a companion for some of the participants as they moved to or from—between—Puerto Rico and the continental United States.

Yet not all transnational experiences take place by physically moving from one place to another. Ann Smith (2017), in her introduction to *The Girl in the Text* (the inaugural book in the Transnational Girlhoods series), suggests redefining the term "to include the process of weakening borders other than those between nation-states" (9). So, if we consider that transnationalism goes beyond physical borders, Barbie in Puerto Rico is an excellent place to examine this notion. I posit, then, that Barbie can be transnational not just in the ways she travels across the world and is adopted into local cultures but also, perhaps even more so, in the ways she affords transnationalism without requiring physical movement. Yes, for some of my participants Barbie was a travel companion when their families moved from Puerto Rico to the continental United States or vice versa, but for many, Barbie was a vehicle for transnational imagination, through which they could travel back and forth. For some girls, transnationalism transpired in their homes in the form of Barbie play, negotiating language, culture, and ideologies. For other girls, playing with the doll provided a space to imagine upward mobility that only seemed possible to them by moving to the continental United States.

An American Icon in Puerto Rico: Barbie, Girlhood, and Colonialism at Play presents an examination of Barbie's arrival and subsequent place in Puerto Rican girlhoods with a lens toward the doll's role as a transnational object in transnational contexts. The book highlights the complicated relationships that women and girls in Puerto Rico have with Barbie. In Puerto Rico, Barbie is an embodiment of contradictions. As a toy produced in the United States and brought to the island during times of economic changes, Barbie is simultaneously a representation of dreams and opportunities for financial upward mobility and a reminder that not everyone can have those opportunities. She is both a representation of idealized (white) beauty standards that girls are conditioned to look up to and a distorted image of beauty that girls reject. Barbie in Puerto Rico is both a welcomed icon of U.S. culture and a contended symbol of colonial power. Concurrently, through Barbie, this book looks at the contradictions and complexities that are also part of girls' lives, specifically in Puerto Rico.

Memoirs of Puerto Rican Girlhoods

There is no clear or single way to map the experiences of being a girl in Puerto Rico. Yet, examples of girlhood experiences have been documented in literature through memoirs produced by Puerto Rican women writers like Esmeralda Santiago and Judith Ortiz Cofer. Their accounts focus on issues often encountered in Puerto Rican girlhoods, such as girls finding their own identities (where language, culture, and race play important roles), facing puberty, and inhabiting the borderlands between girlhood and womanhood.

Adding to the already difficult experiences and biological changes in a girl's life, Santiago (1993, 1999) and Ortiz Cofer (1990)—just like some participants of this study—had to navigate other complicated issues, including moving to a new place. In *When I Was Puerto Rican* (1993), Esmeralda Santiago chronicles her life as a young girl living in Macún, a *barrio* in Puerto Rico, and her move to Santurce, a developing metropolis closer to the island's capital and a stark contrast to Macún. Moving to this new environment made Santiago (1993) an object of jokes among her more "sophisticated" peers, who considered her a *jíbara*—a term usually referring to the people of the interior mountainous regions of Puerto Rico—for the dialect she used, for never having heard of Santa Claus, and for not "knowing how to use the pencil sharpener screwed to the wall of the classroom" (39). The term has a negative connotation here, as Santiago's peers used it to refer to her as someone who is ignorant or uncultured due to a lack of education. Her second memoir, *Almost a Woman*, begins with her experiences as a thirteen-year-old living in Brooklyn. Santiago (1999) writes about having to face the trials and tribulations of entering the teenage years along with the difficulties of being an "Other" in a new place. In some ways she was experiencing the situations of her past in Santurce, but on a much greater scale. She narrates her journey as she stands on the bridge between girlhood and womanhood—*casi mujer* (almost a woman)—and the bridge between Puerto Rican culture and the new world she has entered, being prevented from crossing over by her family's conservative traditions.

Speaking from the point of view of her child self in *Silent Dancing: A Partial Remembrance of a Puerto Rican Childhood*, Ortiz Cofer (1990) negotiates two different cultures: her homeland, Puerto Rico, and her host city, Paterson, New Jersey, and the constant migration from one place to the other. Her experiences resemble those of many Puerto Ricans who spent their childhoods migrating between the island and Los Nueva Yores, Puerto Ricans' way of referring to the United States.[1]

Some of my participants experienced this movement during their childhoods; those who did, spent one to three years in the United States, though most of their childhood occurred in Puerto Rico. Among many things, Ortiz Cofer (1990) had to negotiate her identity in both places; she was too *gringa* when she spoke Spanish and too Latina when she spoke English. Similarly, for Santiago (1999) there was an added pressure to recognize her often-conflicting identities in this new world. She had to avoid sustaining her mother's disapproval for embracing "Americanness" too readily and simultaneously find ways to elude being mocked by her American classmates for her old-fashioned ways, which were perceived as direct products of her Latina roots.

Ortiz Cofer (1990) also writes about the important women in her life—her mother, her grandmother (whom she called Mamá), and the women from the stories her grandmother told her—who taught her different lessons about womanhood and being a woman in a patriarchal society. Growing up in a Catholic family, Ortiz Cofer (1990) learned what many

Puerto Rican girls continue to learn to this day: that the only birth control is abstinence, that you need to marry unless you want to be a *jamona* (an old wench, a mature woman who has not married), and that dating too much makes you a *puta* (a whore, a woman that is too easy). Comparably, Santiago (1999) discovered through the stories about other women what it means to be a (good) girl and later a (good) woman. She learned quickly that white Americans' only exposure to Puerto Rican culture was *West Side Story*, where a girl had the option of being bad, like Anita, or good, like Maria. The same binaries appeared in her own culture, where her mother urged her to live carefully so she is not perceived as too loose but also not too naïve: "I decided to never become one of those calculating *putas*, but neither would I become a *pendeja*, who believed everything a man told her" (Santiago 1999: 15). One cannot consider these binaries of "good" versus "bad" girlhoods without also thinking about the ways that racialized bodies are often assigned the latter descriptor. Data shows that adults perceive girls of color, particularly Black girls, as less innocent and in need of less protection than white girls (Bernstein 2015; Epstein, Blake, and González 2017), something that I examine more deeply in chapter 2. This adds a layer of complexity for Puerto Rican girls, whose innocence is never presumed because of their skin color. Further, and chapter 4 discusses, racial identity in Puerto Rico often characterizes Blackness in negative ways.

Like many Puerto Rican girls, Santiago (1999) and Ortiz Cofer (1990) describe girlhoods full of binaries, contradictions, and conflicting ideologies. Their stories, briefly described here, serve as blueprints for understanding certain Puerto Rican girlhoods and for making sense of the stories shared in this book.

Methodologies and Ethics

How does one begin to explore the role of such an iconic doll in any context? Originally, when planning the project that developed into this book, I was curious about how Puerto Rican girls interacted with Barbie. Did they play with the doll? Did they create complex narratives? Did they reenact their own lived experiences through the doll? I wanted to understand girlhood through girls. Fortunately, I found that, when recruiting participants, a good number of women wanted to be part of the study. Thus, what resulted was an intergenerational examination of girlhood experiences with Barbie, beginning with the first generation to play with Barbie when the doll was initially produced and continuing to girls in the present. The study described in this book engaged in memory-work with adult women and girls in order to learn about their interactions with Barbie and the social and cultural implications these memories had on their girlhoods and, if applicable, on their adult lives. I explored the childhood experiences of Barbie play of eighteen adult participants, who all identified as having interacted with Barbie to varying degrees, and the experiences of three preteen girls who at the time played with Barbie. These interactions included both the presence and absence (the acceptance and rejection) of Barbie in each girl's childhood. Working with both adults and children afforded this project a more extensive insight into the experiences of girls from different generations playing with or even rejecting Barbie dolls. By doing so, I was able to describe and interpret the role of Barbie play and Barbie culture in some girls' identities as well as the meaning those experiences had in adulthood.

The group represents only a small sample of girlhood experiences. They neither stand in for larger discussions of Puerto Rican girlhoods nor do they (or I) claim to speak for all Puerto Rican girls and women. As people learned about my research through conversations, social media, or word of mouth, some reached out to me, wanting to share their stories. What began as a vision for mostly individual stories ended up becoming a collective endeavor. When compiling the schedule for interviews, I noticed that I could group some of the participants together based on their relationships to each other. From the beginning, I knew that I would carry out a group interview with the women in my family in order to capture our familial interactions. Yet, when childhood friends, colleagues, and mother/daughter pairs signed up, the possibilities for sharing individual and collective stories increased.

Before each interview began, I reminded participants that they could stop the interview at any point and that they did not have to respond to anything they did not feel comfortable answering. The majority of the interviews lasted between forty-five and sixty minutes. During individual and group interviews, I asked participants about various aspects of their experiences with Barbie, including, but not limited to, the narratives they created when they played, the roles they assigned to their dolls, and their access to Barbie merchandise. As each round of interviews concluded, I transcribed and translated the audio recordings to English using participants' pseudonyms that they either chose or asked me to assign them.

Because my study required participants to reconstruct past and present lived experiences, I prepared myself to be sensitive to the emotions that memories might trigger and to respond accordingly. To do so, I drew from methods and approaches employed in examining and eliciting memories (Crawford et al. 1992; Haug et al. 1987; Mitchell and Reid-Walsh 2002). It was important to me that I always remained sensitive to participants' emotions and reactions to questions, especially about race and class. If I perceived any discomfort on their part, I either rephrased the questions or moved on to other questions. Once adults shifted from talking about their experiences as children to sharing their perspectives as adults, I was able to ask direct questions about topics that may be uncomfortable and may not arise organically. For instance, I asked, "Did you care about the color of her skin?" or, "Do you think she was too thin or that she was a role model?" Because women were working through their memories and needed to think and reflect upon their interactions with Barbie from many years ago, asking these types of questions directly was beneficial. However, in my interviews with girls, I approached this differently. I did not ask these direct questions because I was more interested in their genuine responses, preferring that over talk about specific subjects like race, gender, or body image just to answer my own research questions. I aimed to allow girls to guide the interview, and I raised questions mainly when they brought up topics. For instance, one of my questions intended to find out if the color of Barbie's hair and/or her skin was something important for my participants. Instead of directly asking these questions to girls, I waited until they mentioned Barbie's hair or skin to ask them about them more in depth.

It was also important to me that participants were allowed to choose the location for the interviews. First and foremost, I wanted my participants to feel comfortable and safe, and I also wanted to meet them in a place that was convenient for them, as it was important for me to develop a trusting relationship with them. By letting them choose the time and place, I allowed them to be part of the research process, which helped disrupt the researcher-participant hierarchy common in positivist research. Offering the choice to select the setting of our encounter let them know that their voice was valued in every step of the research process. This also allowed me to capture more personal experiences that may not have happened otherwise. For instance, when participants invited me into their homes, I was able to carefully look at some of their Barbie objects to see how they were placed within the home and to get a sense of where play happened.

These objects served the important purpose of illustrating participants' interactions with Barbie. Participants maintained a personal relationship with the artifacts they shared with me, and in whichever form they were shared, they were part of the participants' stories and their lived experiences during childhood—and in some cases even adulthood. Some participants provided pictures of their Barbie dolls, Barbie houses, and other Barbie objects, while others still kept some of their objects and were able to share them with me. For the interviews with girls, I invited the mothers and daughters to bring Barbie dolls or anything related to Barbie so we could talk more about it together. Some of the interviews with girls took place in their homes, where they showed me many of their Barbie artifacts and at times also demonstrated a typical episode of doll play. Even in interviews that did not take place at girls' homes I was able to get a sense of their Barbie artifacts and what transactions occurred between girl and object. For an interview with two sisters, for instance, their mother brought a plastic bin that stored the girls' dolls and doll accessories. The girls also brought a Barbie DVD and a Barbie book. The sisters talked about these items during the interview, and I was able to look through the artifacts as they told stories.

Having these artifacts, either in person or in photographs, allowed me to develop a deeper understanding of their significance in my participants' lives, and they served to bring up stories and memories of Barbie play. Many adults that I interviewed no longer had these artifacts in their possession, but some were able to provide pictures of them. These pictures offered a visual representation of the three-dimensional artifacts of childhood play. They still served to elicit memories and deep conversations about the stories created through Barbie, the stories of the participants' childhood, and Barbie's significance in their lived experiences.

In addition to individual and group interviews, I engaged in the study of about three hundred Barbie artifacts at the Strong National Museum of Play in Rochester, New York. Through this research I closely examined and documented the different ranges of Barbie dolls that have been produced from the doll's conception up until a decade ago. These dolls represent the different eras of Barbie throughout which my participants have engaged. I examined the types of dolls produced, the changes Barbie has undergone, the colors of her clothes, the types of accessories and products that accompanied the dolls, among other aspects. Finally, part of the data was informed by document research. In the time spent at the Strong Museum, I also studied various texts about Barbie (Gerber 2009; Sarasohn-Kahn 1996; Tosa 1998) and original documents (transcripts, photographs, preliminary reports) from a research study about the role of dolls for women growing up in the 1910s and 1930s, specifically mothers and daughters. The documents from said study provided a model for approaching and structuring my own study of familial relationships. Additionally, during my time in Puerto Rico I examined local newspapers and magazines from 1959 to 1962 to understand the context of the time when Barbie arrived in the island.

As a researcher, I needed to consider my approach to examining the data as well as any bias or subjectivity I would potentially bring to the study. While total objectivity in research is often highly encouraged, Glesne explains that complete objectivity is "neither possible nor desirable" in qualitative research (2011: 152). Throughout the study I kept in mind that my subjectivity could still inform my research as long as I remained critical about it. This especially emerged naturally through my own memory-work—as a participant of my own research—where I not only described my memories of Barbie play but also reflected on them and how they continue to shape my own understandings. This was also a critical aspect of my interpretations of the experiences that participants shared through groups and individual interviews when they exercised memory-work. I also considered and continuously reflected upon how I was representing my participants through the presentation of the data. To avoid misrepresentations, I aimed to contextualize and situate my participants' testimonies as much as possible. In addition, I quoted them extensively rather than paraphrasing them in order to avoid changing the meaning of their expressions.

Working with Memories

Based on the memories that emerged during my interviews and conversations with participants, I looked at the construction and performance of their own identities in relation to Barbie.[2] To achieve this, I drew from methods of qualitative inquiry, which allowed for a deeper understanding of the various experiences that women had with the doll. By studying the experiences of women and girls from various generations, I was able to more deeply examine the role Barbie played and continues to play in Puerto Rican girlhoods.

Guided by memory-work (Haug et al. 1987; Mitchell and Reid-Walsh, 2002), the participants were encouraged to share stories from their childhood and to think about what those memories meant to them as girls and

as adults. In addition, participants were encouraged to bring personal Barbie artifacts to share during interviews, such as dolls, photographs, books,
magazines, or any other Barbie item from their childhood. By employing
artifactual memory (Brown 1998; Reid-Walsh 2013) as a method of data
collection, I was able to collect stories triggered by the artifacts and also
examine the objects of play. In one specific case, the artifacts comprised a
plethora of Barbie dolls that the participant began collecting as an adult.

Memory-work was developed by German feminist and socialist Frigga
Haug and others and published in *Female Sexualization: A Collective Work
of Memory* (1987), and its underlying theory is that "subjectively significant events, events which are remembered, and the way they are subse-
quently constructed, play an important part in the construction of self"
(Crawford et al. 1992: 37). This is an important differentiation between
memory-work and other types of accounts, such as testimonials or confes-
sionals, centering on the word "work." Mitchell and Reid-Walsh explain,
"The person remembering is the one who 'works back' or 'works through'
the memory" (2002: 62). In this "exercise" the person remembering is
willfully pulling out memories and questioning them, with the goal being
why it was, not *how* it was. Naturally, the process of memory-work relies
on *memories*, and memories can be unreliable. Yet, those who employ the
method are less concerned with the unreliability of memories. Instead,
they are interested in the process that recalling memories involves. Crawford et al. argue that

> the memories are true memories, that is, they are memories and not inventions
> or fantasies. Whether the memories accurately represent past events or not, how-
> ever, is irrelevant; the process of construction of the meanings of those events is
> the focus on memory-work. (1992: 51)

Those who draw on their own memories do so from the assumption that
our past has something to tell us about our present selves, about our individual subjectivities, about what made us what we are. What is important, then, is the value and meaning each author places on their memories
rather than the exactness of the memories themselves. In this research
involving memory-work, there is a deliberate remembering about a deliberate phenomenon. Memory-work is a feminist social constructionist
method because it disrupts the barriers between the subject and object
of research. The basis for knowledge is the women's everyday experience.
Accordingly, the researcher positions herself as part of the group, becoming "researched" as well, while the participants become researchers, "thus

eliminating the hierarchy of 'experimenter' and 'subject'" (Onyx and Small 2011: 775). In addition, memory-work requires an environment that is open, one in which the participants feel safe sharing their memories and they can trust those around them (O'Reilly-Scanlon and Dwyer 2005). Thus, just like most feminist and girlhood research, the building of rapport between researcher and participants is imperative.

Memory-work is often employed in girlhood studies research because it allows women to think about their own childhood and look at it through a critical and informed lens. The method has been used in different ways to investigate various phenomena. It can be used to explore other people's memories of certain events or activities, while it can also be used to explore the researchers' own experiences. As previously mentioned, Reid-Walsh and Mitchell (2000) employed memory-work to understand how adult women feel about Barbie and how their play may have shaped who they are today.[3] For Reid-Walsh and Mitchell (2000), these accounts are significant simply because the women are admitting to playing with Barbie in a field where that is highly criticized. The accounts shared by some of the women showed the significance of Barbie play in their adult life. Their play with Barbie had somewhat foreshadowed their conventional or unconventional professions: "a teacher constructed school tableaux for Barbie; the architecture professor and the Internet critic similarly presaged their unconventional professions through their play with the doll" (Reid-Walsh and Mitchell 2000: 186). This was a significant aspect of my research, which was dependent upon the questions I asked participants.

Some of my women and girls in this project had an idea of the types of issues their Barbies faced, their professions, relationships, and other general ideas, even if they could not completely remember the narratives they created. Yet, because one of my questions aimed to trigger their memories by asking "What did the dolls mean to you?" I was able to find out more about the participants through their answers. Furthermore, these questions served to elicit more memories about their play than directly asking them, "What type of narratives did you create?" By thinking and reflecting on their childhood with dolls, the participants provided an insight to how these experiences contributed to their sense of self, both as children and as adults.

Memories can be deemed unreliable for various reasons. Sometimes our memories can stem from a reworking of what we actually *do* remember and what we *want* to remember: discussing an interview he remembers seeing when he was little that helped him deal with his own sexuality,

Muñoz admits, "My memory and subjectivity reformatted that memory, letting it work within my internal narratives of subject formation" (1999: 4). Nevertheless, whether his memory was accurate or not, whether he was remembering an actual event or a reworking of a memory, he understood that he needed that memory to be part of his self (Muñoz 1999: 5). As Rand (1995) argues, we should not take memory accounts exactly as they appear to be. We select what we want to remember often due to its significance while we also choose (consciously or inadvertently) what we want to forget. Instead of focusing on the veracity or accuracy of the memories, I am more interested in the implications these memories have in the women's construction of identity. As seen in Muñoz's (1999) case, the fact that this was a memory of something he believed had really happened contributed to his formation and to his later acceptance of being a queer Latino. In the same vein, my participants—as well as myself—could be remembering aspects of Barbie play that may or may not have happened or that could have happened slightly differently; yet, what is important to take away here is *how* they remember them, *why* they remember them, and what their significance is for their (our) lives. In discussing what to ask of participants during their memory-work, Haug suggests that participants should avoid recounting sequences or biographical stories as they allow the author to "reconstruct herself" (1997: 4). Her concern is not so much with the reconstruction of the memory itself but rather the reconstruction of the "self," *who* the participant makes herself to be. While it may be inevitable to have some participants reconstruct who they were/are, it is important to examine what these reconstructions of the self may be telling about the person's identity and experiences.

Sometimes the emotions attached to the memories can distort the ability to question what is being remembered, i.e., the *why*. This may happen especially if we think of memories as exclusively carrying or being a product of nostalgia, and if we simultaneously associate nostalgia solely with sentimentality. However, the resistance of thinking through memories or the emotions that are carried with them can be a site of exploration in itself, and a place to further examine the meanings and constructions of self that are attached to them. Atia and Davies propose that "nostalgic thinking can be a force that complicates, rather than one that simplifies" (2010: 181). In this sense, what can be transformative about nostalgia is "what can allow it to be useful, creative and generative, even radical, rather than its popular designation as sentimental" (Strong-Wilson et al. 2013: 5).

Working with Girls and Adults: Possibilities and Challenges

Giving girls a voice is an important aspect of girlhood studies, as noted by Mitchell and Reid-Walsh (2008) in their essay titled "How to Study Girl Culture." They offer insightful observations about the world and their own lived experiences. Especially when critically studying a children's toy such as Barbie, which has undergone excruciating examinations since her creation, their voices are crucial. Elizabeth Chin's (1999) ethnographic work with ten-year-old poor and working-class Black children in New Haven, Connecticut, presents a model for Barbie research in which girls' agency is central. In her study, the girls' interactions with dolls complicate the toy industry's idea that ethnically correct dolls serve as a progressive solution to representation and inclusion in toys and children's lives. The girls in her study subverted the ways in which they were supposed to play with the dolls and modified them to fit their own narratives and experiences. In terms of play with Barbie dolls, Hohmann (1985) studied the play performance of a seven-year-old girl named Jennifer. He notes that Jennifer incorporates other aspects of her life where she is not usually in control but can now control through her dolls. As he observed, Jennifer acted out scenes of her life where her little sister behaves inappropriately and is scolded or punished for it. For Hohmann, Jennifer's play is significant because through Barbie play Jennifer was able to both learn and demonstrate her knowledge of "an adequate behavior within the social environment of the two sisters" (1985: 116). It also gave Jennifer the opportunity to "express a variety of problems which occur within her family" (1985: 120). Through Barbie play, Jennifer was able to perform a close imitation of her life.

These studies in which children are involved and, more importantly, are provided with a voice offer a window to their lived experiences that is critical to understanding children's and, more specifically, girlhood culture. Hohmann (1985) took on the role of participant observer, but this was mainly possible because he had been Jennifer's babysitter in the past, thus they had built trust prior to his study. Chin (1999) had access as an observer because she was part of the community in which she was working, as she lived in the same neighborhood as some of her participants. In my own undertaking, I wanted to understand women's and girls' experiences with Barbie in order to understand their interactions with and relationship to Barbie dolls and Barbie play. As a result, I employed the same methods of data collection for both adults and girls: interviews and artifactual data. Rather than trying to interpret girls' experiences with Barbie through their play, I wanted to have conversations with them about their opinions and experiences with Barbie. In doing so, girls were able to have a more active voice in the study of their cultures and play practices. In some cases, the location enriched the conversation as it allowed girls to not only show me their dolls but also briefly demonstrate how they play(ed) with them. Christensen suggests that "in order to hear the voices of children in the representation of their own lives it is important to employ research practices such as reflexivity and dialogue" (2004: 165). Following the same ideas for the interviews with adults, I asked the girls what they liked about Barbie, what they disliked, and what their overall views were on the doll and other Barbie artifacts. This led to other critical discussions of Barbie through the perspective of girls. The girls were able to voice their own concerns, issues, and opinions about Barbie dolls, which provided perspectives that complemented those of the adults. This project did not solely discuss girls in hypothetical scenarios, but rather invited girls to share their experiences.

I also took into account my position as researcher. I am an adult Puerto Rican woman who is also a former Barbie player. I share parts of my background with some of the participants in this study, but there is a range of differences between us, from slight disparities to major ones. At every step of the research process, I examined my own position as researcher and as participant, my relationship to girlhood (my own and my participants'), and how these affected the study. Finally, my research addressed an important question in girlhood studies: "Whose girlhood?" This study specifically focused on Puerto Rican girlhoods, which is not a singular but rather a "multiplicitous" experience that varies by age, race, class, and location, among others. There were, of course, certain limitations in the participant sample; therefore, my study was not able to account for every type of experience with Barbie among Puerto Rican women and girls.

In my work with adults, I examined childhood from the past and additionally how the experiences from childhood informed women's identities as adults. Mitchell and Reid-Walsh (2002) discuss the importance and usefulness of memory-work in research about childhood. Writing on nostalgia and memories of cowboy/cowgirl play and nostalgia marketing strategies of the toy industry and their contribution to memory-work studies, they explore memory as phenomenon and method of data collection in the context of researching children's popular culture. These concepts and methods are applicable for looking at adults' memories—how they construct and use them both as a way of inquiring and as a method of feminist research. The questions Mitchell and Reid-Walsh pose speak to the complexity of the relationship between the rememberer and the experience being remembered, and also to the complexity of childhood in relation to adulthood. They ask an important question about the validity of working with adults within childhood studies: "Why work with adults if we are really interested in children and childhood?" (Mitchell and Reid-Walsh 2002: 48).

Working with adults' memories can be as fraught as working with children, though in different ways (Mitchell and Reid-Walsh 2002). In many cases, despite some participants being able to recall the solicited aspects of their childhood, others could not recall or recalled very little of their childhood play. Nonetheless, they assert, these participants usually had the most to say about their childhood play during discussions. This could perhaps be a result of memories triggered by objects brought up in conversation or by other participants' accounts about their childhoods. To this effect, the combination of the methods of memory-work and interviews (individual and in groups) become greatly useful for my research, as the different conversations can help trigger memories or remind participants of specific events from their childhood. For this research, my participants were encouraged to bring Barbie artifacts to both the individual and collective interviews so we could explore them together. In this sense, group interviews became more helpful with eliciting memories, since we often remember certain aspects of the past when we are reminded of them by someone else's experiences.

Nevertheless, "remembering, forgetting, and even resistance to remembering . . . are all central to the study of memory" (Mitchell and Reid-Walsh 2002: 56). Furthermore, these different aspects of remembering, not remembering, or resistance can provide even more insight to the person's experiences, in the case of this research, with Barbie. Similarly, participants' rejection or lack of interaction with Barbie (or perhaps choosing not to remember interactions with Barbie) may offer key information about women's perceptions of Barbie, or even themselves both as adults and as children in relation to the doll. In this lies the usefulness of working with adults when researching childhood and, more importantly, with women's memories to examine their girlhood experiences and to collaborate on how these experiences influenced their identities.

Meet the Participants

In the brief descriptions that follow, participants have been assigned pseudonyms that will be used hereafter in order to keep their identities anonymous. In describing the location of where my participants grew up or where they are from, I provide general geographic areas rather than specific places. The information provided in the descriptions was gathered through my interviews and conversations with participants. Some of them I had known before, thus my own knowledge of their lives (which I corroborated with them) also contributed to their descriptions. The ages provided are from the time of the interviews, which took place during May and June 2015 and February 2016.

Individual Interviews

Carla. Age thirty-three, grew up and still resides in a small town in southwestern Puerto Rico. She describes herself as an artisan, a teacher, and many things at the same time. Carla estimates that around sixty Barbie dolls went through her home between 1987 and 2000. She remembers playing with Barbie until age fifteen.

Marisa. In her early sixties, raised in a town in northwestern Puerto Rico. She has lived in the southwest for more than twenty years. The short visit and conversation took place in her house where her daughter's surviving collection, comprising thirty-eight Barbie dolls, is still displayed.

Alondra. Age thirty-two, had about fifty Barbie dolls. She spent most of her childhood in northeastern Puerto Rico, but she has also lived in the continental United States and Brazil. Currently, she lives in northeastern Puerto Rico, where she has been for the last ten years. She remembers Barbie as her favorite toy. She believes Barbie play strengthened her skills as a writer and storyteller and that it was a great preparation for her interest in theater. Alondra played until she was about ten years old. Our interview occurred through email communication because we could not travel to meet one another in person. Her written answers were very detailed, and

Table 0.1. Table with participants' names and ages.

Gen. Born in the '50s (First Barbie)	Gen. Born in the '60s	Gen. Born in the '70s	Gen. Born in the '80s	Gen. Born in the Early '90s	Gen. Born in the Late '90s to Early 2000s	Gen. Born in the Late 2000s
63 – Lourdes 62 – Carmen 62 – Marisa 59 – Patricia	None	45 – Lisa 40 – Autumn 40s – Susan	32 – Carla 32 – Camille 32 – Alondra 30 – Frankie 30 – Isabel 30 – Jessica 29 – Mariela 29 – Emily 28 – Elsa	25 – Gabriela 25 – Frances	None	11 – K.C. 9 – Annie 8 – Sharon

we followed up with one another a couple of times when I needed more information or clarification.

Group Interviews

I was a researcher and participant for three group interviews. The first was my family group, composed of my mother, my aunt, and my two sisters. Within this group formation we collectively thought about the ways in which each person's play was different from the others' and how, even among sisters who grew up in the same house, the relationship with Barbie may have been different. The conversations and dynamics that emerged in this group interview inspired my choice to examine and document Barbie's role in familial relationships. This family interview took place in the San Juan metropolitan area. Some participants were present in person—Emily, Carmen, and Lourdes—while Camille and Frances joined via Skype from their respective homes in the continental United States.

The second group in which I took part consisted of two of my childhood friends, with whom I played Barbie multiple times. Because we all knew each other and played together, the conversations and memories ranged from individual experiences to shared experiences with Barbie. The third group consisted of five women, none of whom knew one another during childhood but who became friends as adults. All of the participants in this group are educators. The experiences shared by each participant were individual—their own childhood experiences—yet it was interesting to realize that some of our experiences were similar. We each explored our individual childhood memories of Barbie, yet as a group of adults we also talked about our perceptions about the doll in the present. The familiarity between the participants, and between the participants and myself, served as an asset to the process. While everyone shared their individual memories, some of the childhood experiences described happened with various members of the groups together. Therefore, in these cases, participants helped one another in constructing collective memories and making sense of both their individual and shared experiences.

Below, I describe the participants from the first three groups (group 1: family; group 2: childhood friends; group 3: colleagues). I was twenty-nine years old at the time of these interviews, and I consider myself a participant in groups 1, 2, and 3.

Group 1: Family

Carmen. In her early sixties, lives in a small town in southwestern Puerto Rico. She mainly grew up in the south of Puerto Rico, although she did live in Florida for about two years when she was a child. She is Emily, Camille, and Frances's mother. She owned one Barbie, which she describes as having black hair and wearing a blue-and-red outfit. For Carmen, the greatest pleasure gained from playing with Barbie was being able to sew her outfits and make accessories for the doll. She remembers playing with Barbie and other dolls (such as a Thumbelina and paper dolls) until she was about thirteen or fourteen years old. At some point as an adult her Barbie disappeared, a fact that Carmen still talks about with sadness.

Lourdes. Also in her early sixties, Carmen's older sister (the second of three girls). She also grew up in the south of Puerto Rico and spent a couple of her early years in Florida. As an adult, Lourdes moved to the San Juan area, where she still resides. Lourdes is Emily, Camille, and Frances's aunt. Just like her sister Carmen, Lourdes only owned one Barbie doll. She remembers having played with Barbie until she was thirteen years old.

Camille. Age thirty-two. She is Carmen's eldest daughter (the second of four children), Lourdes's niece, and Emily and Frances's sister. Similar to her mother and aunt, Camille enjoyed Barbie mostly because of the doll's clothes. The time she spent with the dolls was mostly for playing dress-up.

Although she did not play much with Barbie dolls, she interacted with other Barbie products.

Frances. Age twenty-five. Frances is the youngest of Carmen's children and Camille and Emily's little sister. Frances was active in the conversation that took place among the family members mostly by describing how she saw other people play with Barbie and how that influenced her own decisions about playing with the doll. Growing up, Frances did not like Barbie dolls and barely played with them.

Group 2: Childhood Friends

Jessica. Age thirty. She was born in the San Juan area and lived most of her life since she was six years old in southwest Puerto Rico. This is where she started playing with Barbie. Jessica remembered that what she liked most was setting everything up under her bunk bed and creating spaces that looked like a house for Barbie. She interacted with Barbie until she was around thirteen years old.

Mariela. Age twenty-nine. She spent most of her childhood in the west side of Puerto Rico. It was in fourth grade that she began playing with Barbie. Her play was very imaginative; she adopted objects from around the house to create furniture and other artifacts for Barbie play. Mariela played with Barbie dolls until she was almost fourteen or fifteen years old. She had her dolls until she moved to the San Juan area when she was a junior in high school.

Group 3: Colleagues

Isabel. Age thirty. She grew up as the only girl among her cousins in a small western town on the island. Her interactions with Barbie happened through doll play and through other Barbie products. Isabel could not remember when she stopped playing with Barbie dolls, but she has many memories from when she was about eight to ten years old.

Frankie. Age thirty. The youngest of four sisters, Frankie grew up in a southwestern town in Puerto Rico, although her early childhood years were spent in the United States. She is the youngest of four sisters. Her family moved back to Puerto Rico when she was ten years old, at which time she stopped playing with Barbie dolls.

Lisa. Age forty-five. Born in New York, Lisa moved to Puerto Rico when she was three years old. There she grew up in two towns on the west side. Lisa stated that her Barbie era was short, possibly between the ages of seven and ten. When she was ten, she preferred playing volleyball and doing more physical activities.

Elsa. Age twenty-eight. Elsa was not present for the entirety of the interview, but she contributed some comments that I include in chapter 4. She played with Barbie in her childhood. Elsa was born in Puerto Rico, yet during her girlhood she moved around to many countries, including Germany, Italy, the United States, and finally back to Puerto Rico when she was ten.

The other set of group interviews comprises discussions with mothers and daughters. For these next three groups, my role was solely of a researcher and not a participant, although I interjected at certain points in the conversations. Below I describe each participant in the last three groups (group 4: mother and adult daughter; group 5: mother and child daughter; group 6: mother and two daughters).

Group 4: Mother and Adult Daughter

Patricia. In her later fifties, a retired teacher who enjoys painting and making dolls out of clay. She was born and raised in New York until the age of eleven, when she moved to Puerto Rico. Her parents and family members are Puerto Rican. She is Gabriela's mother and a former teacher. During her childhood she owned a total of about ten Barbie dolls (and friends), though her current Barbie collection contains 233 dolls. She fell in love with Barbie when she was four years old and saw a Barbie commercial. She played for hours in her room every day, and her play with Barbie went on until the age of sixteen. When her husband threw out all of the Barbie dolls and outfits her mother had given her, and which she still kept at age thirty-two, she decided to begin collecting them.

Gabriela. Age twenty-five. Gabriela grew up in the south of Puerto Rico. She is Patricia's only daughter. Her mother still keeps Gabriela's old Barbies, which amount to 131 dolls. She indicated that when her mother would buy her a Barbie, she would use it for a couple of weeks and then grow tired of her. She did reiterate many times during the interview that she loved playing with Barbie. She played with Barbie dolls until she was twelve years old. Gabriela and Patricia's interview took place in their home, where they were able to show me their collections of Barbie artifacts.

Group 5: Mother and Child Daughter

Autumn. Age forty. She is Sharon's mother. She grew up on the east coast of the United States and moved to Puerto Rico as an adult, about ten years ago. Her family is not Puerto Rican. She works as a professor at a university in Puerto Rico. Although Autumn is not Puerto Rican and did not grow up in Puerto Rico, her experiences from the perspective of the mother of a girl born and being raised in Puerto Rico are important to be considered when talking about her daughter's experiences of girlhood.

Sharon. Age eight. She is Autumn's oldest daughter. She was born in Puerto Rico and has been raised in a town in the west of the island. This interview also took place in their home, which allowed Sharon to show me her various dolls and even demonstrate how she sometimes plays with her brother with their different toys.

Group 6: Mother and Two Daughters

Susan. In her forties, has interacted with Barbie both as a girl playing with the doll and as a mother of two girls: K.C. and Annie. As a mother and educator, Susan had some reservations about the doll; however, she enjoyed her childhood play with Barbie: "I loved them very much, and I looked at them and brushed their hair and kept them well. They were special."

K.C. Age eleven. She is Susan's oldest daughter, who is growing up in a southwestern town in Puerto Rico. K.C. was mostly shy and quiet during the group interview, but she shared some of her experiences with Barbie, especially with a book about professions she brought to the interview.

Annie. Age nine. She is Susan's youngest daughter and K.C.'s sister. Annie was the more talkative of the sisters, sharing with us her various experiences with Barbie play, her favorite aspects about the doll, and even her concerns about the effect Barbie's body could have on people.

Overview

An American Icon in Puerto Rico explores certain experiences that Puerto Rican women and girls had with Barbie; however, it does not seek to generalize and argue that these experiences are *the* experiences of girls in Puerto Rico or that they are even representative of the population at large. It is important to note, for example, that the participants whose experiences brought this book to life are all cisgender girls and women. Thus, there are certainly experiences that this book could not illustrate and discuss. Rather, this book offers a window into some interactions with Barbie, and especially how they differ and overlap across generations, showing how Barbie's transnationality crossed not only geographical borders but also generational ones.

In chapter 1, "Girlhood, Dolls, and Barbie: Spaces of Innocence?" I lay the groundwork for understanding how dolls, and then more specifically Barbie, serve as sites for interrogating constructions of girlhood and girls' identity formations. Though Barbie was not necessarily conceptualized as an embodiment of childhood (she began as a teenager but was later marketed as a career woman), Mattel pounced on parents' moral panic about girls "growing up too fast" and framed some of their doll lines as the perfect solutions to maintain girls' innocence. The chapter thus examines ideologies around childhood innocence, comparing societal constructions of whiteness as inherently innocent with the adultification of Blackness (Black girls, specifically). The chapter explores definitions of "girlhood" that expand the term beyond particular age ranges and instead posit it as fluid according to context.

Chapter 2, "The Politics of Barbie in Puerto Rico: A New Icon Emerges," introduces readers to Barbie's arrival to Puerto Rico in the early 1960s and the socioeconomic and political contexts that created the "perfect" conditions for her entrance into the island. A system of tax cuts for US companies, cheap local labor, and the United States' strong colonial hold over Puerto Rico contributed to a high influx of imported US products to the island, including Barbie dolls. The chapter moves into examining the colonial relationship between the United States and Puerto Rico through the conflicting discourses that arose following the production of the Puerto Rican Barbie in 1997. It situates Barbie's presence in the island and among Puerto Ricans in the continental United States and showcases the conflicting views on the doll. It also compares the responses from adults at the time to responses from those who were girls in the late 1990s.

For some, Puerto Rican Barbie was a symbol of national pride; for others, she was a symbol of colonization. Drawing from the experiences of some of the participants, the chapter ends with an exploration of girls' mobility between Puerto Rico and the United States as part of their identities, and it examines one participant's case in which Barbie was used to negotiate colonizing practices. Barbie's world centers on fashion and luxury. Presenting this from the standpoint of Puerto Rico's sociopolitical status, I explored how girls may use Barbie to dream about upward mobility and how they might see the United States as the only option to attain this. The women in this study, who belong to the generation that grew up in the 1950s and 1960s, owned only a few Barbie dolls and artifacts. This generation also exemplified the historical moment the island was living at the time. From the 1940s to the 1960s Puerto Rico went through what is dubbed the "great migration" due to the economic recession. Their dreams of emulating Barbie and their admiration for her clothes could have been a result of their imagined transnational movement into the United States, the land of opportunity, from where Barbie came.

Chapter 3, "Fashioning a Self: Experiences of Body and Feminine Identities with Barbie," describes my participants' relationship with Barbie. It analyzes the various themes their play involved, the roles they assigned to the dolls and themselves, and other aspects of play. It takes into consideration participants' Barbie artifacts, which included such things as dolls, pictures, and magazines. The chapter examines participants' opinions about Barbie and how Barbie influenced the participants' views of femininity and gender expectations. From some participants' perspectives, Barbie was the ultimate girl, and if you were a girl, you had to have one. This complicated some girls' relationship with the doll, as they felt they did not fit Barbie's constructions of girlhood and femininity. Therefore, identity was also established with the rejection of the doll. Moreover, in this chapter I examine the participants' perceptions regarding Barbie's body, a site of contestation in and of itself, and its effects on their own experiences and interactions with the doll.

Barbie embodies a very specific brand of femininity, which is often held as "ideal." She is an affluent, heterosexual, white woman with an impossible body. As a result, it is difficult for many girls to see themselves reflected in the doll. In chapter 4, "Accessing Barbie: Conversations about Class and Race," I examine how participants talked about race and class through the doll. The chapter begins with a discussion of Barbie, the material girl, and how Barbie is constructed as a symbol of affluent femininity.

This takes place through the wide array of products that girls are encouraged to acquire in order to have a "true" Barbie play experience. Participants in this study identify this issue because they experienced the ways in which Barbie and her products can become explicit markers of class and affluence. The chapter continues with a discussion of racial constructions on the island and the discourse employed to talk about them. These serve as a framework for examining some of the participants' responses to white Barbie and their interactions with Black Barbie dolls or other dolls of color. In many ways, these participants' responses were manifestations of the discourses about race in Puerto Rico, which often position Blackness as less beautiful than whiteness. Historically, the Barbie brand has had a problem with racial and ethnic diversity, which I briefly explore in this chapter in order to contextualize how girls and women negotiated Barbie's whiteness and the ways that Mattel continuously centered the white doll as *the* Barbie, even when the brand included dolls of color.

Drawing from conversations between mothers, daughters, and/or sisters, from ages eight to sixty-two, the final chapter, "All in the Family: Barbie's Place in Familial Dynamics," examines familial female relationships in the context of Puerto Rican girlhoods. The chapter presents an analysis of conversations between female family members about their decisions to play with Barbie or not. It pays particular attention to the influence of Barbie's race and her status as a symbol of femininity in the participants' decision-making process. It also examines how Barbie helped to foster familial relationships.

Readers of this book can understand Barbie's position as a transnational object beyond the United States, Canada, and Australia, where much of the research has focused. Its primary goal is to provide a better understanding of some Puerto Rican girls' and women's identities in relation to Barbie. What was the impact of Barbie in the girlhoods of a group of Puerto Rican women and girls from different generations? Girls' individual experiences vary from one another and within their own selves. In other words, one person may experience Barbie in various ways—loving the doll while also hating her, wanting to be like the doll while also feeling shame for this desire, playing with the doll while abhorring her white affluent femininity. Moreover, Barbie's presence in girls' lives is also shaped, in part, by girls' familial relationships. The stories presented in this book show how Barbie can become part of a girl's life through a parent's desire to pass down Barbie traditions and, at the same time, how parents' opinion about the doll can influence how much impact Barbie can have in a girl's life. Engaging with scholarship in cultural studies and girlhood studies, *An American Icon in Puerto Rico* shows that Barbie's role in Puerto Rican girlhoods was complex and multidimensional.

Notes

1. I know this from my own experiences hearing people around me refer to the United States as such. Ortiz Cofer also uses this term and explains its usage in her memoir (1990: 14).
2. For the purposes of my research, when I refer to Barbie I am talking about all the members of the Mattel Barbie brand, so when discussing Barbie with my participants in a broader sense I included other Barbie artifacts, such as magazines, books, trading cards, sticker books, fashion plates, etc., in addition to the doll itself.
3. One part of their article "Just a Doll? 'Liberating' Accounts of Barbie-Play" discusses women's confessions to Barbie play. One woman seemed apologetic in her confession, especially because she considered herself to be a feminist but also liked the traditional gender roles (e.g., cooking, cleaning, having children, decorating, and organizing parties); moreover, this confession was made in her women's studies class, making it more difficult to confess. This was a memory that she had buried, yet somehow it surfaced during class discussion; as she noted, "This was the first time I noticed that I did grow up to be somewhat ashamed of such 'girls' culture' items such as Barbies, playing house, and soap operas" (Reid-Walsh and Mitchell 2000: 179). The other woman who confessed to playing with Barbies did so by rationalizing her behavior. In her opinion, Barbie can be a good role model for girls: "Barbie today includes doctors, astronauts, and diplomats from all races and nationalities. Barbie today goes on to university to get her degree" (Reid-Walsh and Mitchell 2000: 179).

CHAPTER 1

Girlhood, Dolls, and Barbie
Spaces of Innocence?

The way we see it, girls are growing up too fast. From every angle, today's girls are bombarded by influences pushing them toward womanhood at too early an age—at the expense of their innocence, their playfulness, their imagination.

—Mattel (2005), "Save Girlhood" Campaign

In 2005, Mattel, the creators of Barbie and American Girl Dolls launched a short-lived campaign encouraging parents to buy their daughters dolls in an effort to "save" them from growing up too fast. At a time of moral panic brought about by the proliferation of social media, Mattel "worried" about the dangers girls could incur if they engaged with it, including being pushed "toward womanhood." This was a curious take, especially because throughout the 1980s and 1990s Mattel had marketed Barbie as a career woman, aiming to inspire girls to dream of being astronauts, rock stars, teachers, doctors, dentists, firefighters, and presidents, among many others. But Mattel was also (and perhaps more) concerned about the dangers the corporation was running into as sales of their staple "girl" toys had declined. In 2005, Barbie's declining sales contributed to Mattel's

---

Notes for this section can be found on page 46.

first-quarter profit drop of 28 percent, and sales of the fashion doll world-wide were down 15 percent (Vincent 2005). In the third quarter of 2005, Barbie sales in the United States had dropped 30 percent (Cabot 2005). But the campaign was built on an emotional appeal to parents' fears about their children, and especially daughters, outgrowing "wholesome" child-hood toys such as dolls. For Mattel, there was a vested financial interest in prolonging children's interactions with toys such as dolls and offering them as solutions for dissuading girls from becoming "too adult too soon."

On Defining Girlhood(s) and Girls

Adults often have romanticized ideas about childhood, seeing it as an era of innocence and bliss, where children are free to play, imagine, and enjoy activities without the worries and concerns that often burden (and are at-tributed to) adults. It is surprising to some, then, to learn that children in the past were often seen as "sinful." Adults ascribed to religious doctrines about the original sin, which saw every human being as being born already tainted by Adam and Eve's disobedience and therefore in need of salvation (Gubar 2021). Historian Robin Bernstein (2011) explains that, at a cer-tain point, "childhood was understood not as innocent but as innocence itself; not as a symbol of innocence but as its embodiment. The doctrine of original sin receded, replaced by a doctrine of original innocence" (2011: 4). Yet, while ideas about what constitutes childhood change, depending upon time period and culture, many of them posit the child as in need of protection from some external danger. More specifically girlhood (or as I will discuss, *white* girlhood) is constructed as a period of innocence that must be contained and protected.

Girlhood is a complex term to define, as noted by Reid-Walsh: "The term 'girlhood' has had a history as an ideologically loaded term in West-ern culture" because its "different denotations and connotations make for a fuzziness of meaning" (2011: 92). The concept has been defined as "the state of being a girl; the time of life during which one is a girl. Also: girls collectively" (Oxford English Dictionary). Thus, Reid-Walsh (2011) explains, the term can refer to a developmental stage, but it can also define girls as a collective group. Driscoll (2002) notes that girls are socially constructed as female children or young women. Cultural differ-ence plays a critical role defining who is considered a girl and what con-stitutes girlhood, especially according to its cultural context. For instance,

27

in "Princess Culture in Qatar: Exploring Princess Media Narratives in the Lives of Arab Female Youth," Kristen Pike specifies that she employs the term "girl" even though her participants were between eighteen and twenty-four years old because in Arab countries the term "woman" refers to "married females" (cited in Aguiló-Pérez 2016). Girlhood, then, can be multiplicitous in the age range it covers, the experiences related to it, and the cultural, political, and social contexts that give way to its meanings. But girlhood is not constrained by age and developmental bounds. Gottschall et al. posit girlhood as a "continuous process of becoming, or assembling with the material and discursive resources that are at hand in any particular space and time" (2013: 31), informed by "girls' affective engagements with media images" (2013: 35). Speaking about Black girlhood, specifically, Ruth Nicole Brown defines it as the representations, memories, and lived experiences of being and becoming in a body marked as youthful, Black, and female "not dependent on age or physical maturity" (2009: 1). Thus, girlhood is not static, it is not (solely) defined by a specific period of time, but rather it is continuously becoming.

In my own usage of the word within informal settings I have referred to adults collectively as girls (e.g., "a girls' night out" or "my girlfriends") or singularly when speaking directly to a friend (e.g. "Girl, your hair looks great today!"). Scholars have noted how the term "girl" can be a form of infantilizing women, especially in the workplace (and more so when men are the ones calling women "girls"), while the term has also been adopted by adults collectively, especially within groups that foment female empowerment. The Guerrilla Girls, formed in 1985, are a group of anonymous feminists who work against sexism and racism in the art world through activism and the creation of educational material. In response to the questions "Why do you call yourselves 'girls'? Doesn't that upset a lot of feminists?" the Girls note that they wanted to be shocking: "Calling a grown woman a girl can imply she's not complete, mature, or grown-up. But we decided to reclaim the word 'girl,' so it couldn't be used against us" (Guerrilla Girls 1995: par. 7). In the early 1990s riot grrrl culture, an underground feminist hardcore punk movement, adopted and adapted *girl* not only to identify themselves as a female movement but also to signify the sound of a growl. Moreover, members of the movement often referred to themselves and women in general as girls. Similarly, the mid-1990s British music group Spice Girls famously embraced "Girl Power!" as their slogan and their primary message to girls. The fact that the Spice Girls were adults adopting the word *girl* rather than *ladies* in their name and in their motto caused "Girl Power" rather than "Woman Power" to become an act of inclusion toward girls of all ages, not exclusively adults. Not surprisingly, the majority of the fan base consisted of girls. By implementing the term *girl*, these various movements provided a definition of girlhood that extended to adults.

Driscoll (2002) meaningfully narrates her own negotiations with girlhood, pointing to the fact that she was not considered a girl anymore in her thirties but that she might still be called "girl" or even refer to herself as girl. She adds that her engagement with "girl" things and "girl" behaviors connect her even further to girlhood because girlhood is something that she has experienced, and "it doesn't truly seem to have been completed" because, as she explains, "I'm still not sure when I stopped being a girl, if I did" (2002: 2). In many ways, adults continue to actively engage in what is considered girls' culture, whether they are consumers or producers. Reid-Walsh notes that, "if participating in the popular culture of girls or in commercialized girl culture is considered an aspect of girlhood, then the age rises even further to include middle-aged women" (2011: 93). There are many ways in which adult women participate in the culture of girls. Notably, it takes place within the princess culture promoted in Disney princess films (Hains 2015; Pike 2015) and, more relevant to my research, within Barbie products, especially collector's items. The latter will become more evident in my discussion of two adult participants who created collections of Barbie dolls.

Yet, it is important to remember that girlhood, in every sense of the multiple definitions given to the word, is profusely layered with complexities and difficulties ranging from changes in the body to confronting racism to being denied humanity. Not everyone gets to be seen as *girl* within ideas of innocence, and much of the moral panic that has exacerbated with social media, and which Mattel has commodified, was positioned toward white girls. While we often think of childhood as a time of innocence, not every child is assigned this characteristic. US ideologies about childhood that included innocence and protection were rooted historically in the nation's founding principles (Wright 2016). By the mid-nineteenth century, a number of cultural forces had combined to construct childhood as a territory of innocence. However, "that innocence was raced white" (Bernstein 2011: 4), as Black children were not afforded the privilege of innocence at the time (Wright 2016). In other words, white children were assumed to be innocent; their childhood automatically made them that way. Furthermore, "the white child's innocence was transferable to surrounding people

29

and things, and that property made it politically usable" (Bernstein 2011: 6). It also means that any nonwhite kids—especially Black children—did not have that same assumption of innocence extended to them and in fact were often seen as "corrupting" forces that might harm white children who were exposed to them. Robin Bernstein argues that "in the second half of the nineteenth century, pain functioned as a wedge that split childhood innocence, as a cultural formation, into distinct black and white trajectories. White children became constructed as tender angels while Black children were libeled as unfeeling, noninnocent nonchildren" (Bernstein 2011: 33). Further, toward the end of the nineteenth century and the beginning of the twentieth, even purportedly progressive programs that aimed at protecting children sustained this binary construction of Black and white childhoods. As Simmons describes of girlhood in New Orleans, predominantly white "progressive moral reform movements such as the Woman's Christian Temperance Union sought governmental regulation," expressing much concern over the working-class white girls and young women who lived in the city (2015: 160).

For Black girls at the time, their childhood was not "carefree" or blissful. Rather, they were forced to be vigilant in order to protect themselves from mistreatment and violence, which denied them periods of innocence and ease that white girls enjoyed. Even the literature directed at Black girls was not focused on preserving their innocence; rather, it was "intended to 'instruct them aright,' that is, to teach Black children to grow into responsible, law-abiding citizens through edifying tales and moral lessons" (Wright 2016: 56). This is not characteristic only to past centuries. In early 2015, the African American Policy Institute released *Black Girls Matter: Pushed Out, Overpoliced, and Underprotected*, a study on the treatment of Black girls in schools. The institute found that Black girls tend to be disciplined at a much higher rate than white boys and white girls and schools are less likely to intervene in situations of sexual harassment or sexual violence against Black girls. Today, adults view girls of color, and especially Black girls, as less innocent and more adult-like than white girls. A report published by the Center on Poverty and Inequality at the Georgetown University Law Center points to the adultification of Black girls in the United States as one explanation for why they are disciplined much more often and more severely than white girls, not only in schools but also in the juvenile justice system (Epstein, Blake, and González 2017). Black girls, then, continue to be denied opportunities to be children—and are not allowed to be girls—in the same ways that white girls are afforded.

Relatedly, speaking of her own childhood, scholar Omaris Zamora examines the ways that she internalized her Blackness as almost sinful, "always on the wrong side of both biblical and social 'law,'" and so because of her Blackness she was not granted innocence (2020: 2). Black Caribbean or Dominican girls, she adds, are thought of as "*willful*," "deviant," and "too fresh for our age" (Zamora 2020: 2). The adultification of Black girls, and the denial of their innocence, is no different in Puerto Rico. In 2017, eleven-year-old Alma Yariela Cruz Cruz, a Black special education student, was charged with five counts of alleged aggression toward other children. According to the charges, Cruz pushed other students, allegedly threatened to push two of them down the stairs, and was rude to them (Ramos Oliver 2017: par. 2). Cruz, her mother, and her legal representation voiced that she was finally standing up for herself and defending herself after two years of racial bullying and verbal assault from her peers. The school's principal never took action to stop the bullying or to intervene when Cruz was the victim. Yet, when Cruz took action to defend herself, the principal expelled her and called the police, giving way to the girl being legally processed.

Considering girlhood specifically in Puerto Rico, the data (mainly on childhood) speaks to the most difficult aspects of childhood: those who live below poverty levels have little to no access to health services and education, and they also lack healthy and informative sexual education. In the prologue for the 2010 report *Nuestros Niños Cuentan* (Our children count), supported by the Puerto Rican chapter of the National Council of La Raza (NCLR), the authors discuss that "children do not always receive the attention they deserve in the research and public policies" (Rivera-Hernández and Andino Ortiz 2010: ii).[1] According to the 2000 Census, 58 percent of children (male and female) under the age of eighteen live in poverty (Rivera-Hernández and Andino Ortiz 2010: i). They add that "a recent analysis demonstrated that 59,000 children between the ages of four and 17 suffer some type of mental health condition" (2010: i). Similar data are reflected in *Kids Count 2015 Data Book: State Trends in Child Well-Being* (Annie E. Casey Foundation 2015). Their research found that 463,000 children in Puerto Rico lived in poverty, amounting to 57 percent of the children population (Annie E. Casey Foundation 2015: 42). The numbers are disconcerting and provide an indication of the unforgiving circumstances in which a great part of the population experiences childhood. Taking into consideration that a major part of the population lives in poverty, one needs to reflect on the implications of this issue in other important aspects of childhood and development. Living in poverty likely means limited access to education and basic needs such as healthcare, food, water, and appropriate living conditions. These are perilous conditions to experience the already difficult phase that is childhood development.

These issues are complicated when concerns about matters related to girls are involved. Rivera-Hernández and Andino Ortiz's report informs that unplanned pregnancies among single female adolescents are a source of concern in Puerto Rico. Furthermore, they note that the probabilities that adolescent mothers and their children will spend most or part of their lives in poverty are high. They are also concerned with the number of births among girls under the age of fifteen, which increased from 350 in 1990 to 444 in 1994, although they had decreased by the year 2000 (Rivera-Hernández and Andino Ortiz 2010: 40). As these data suggest, girlhood often involves a number of situations that add to the complexities and difficulties of navigating this phase of life. Besides this data and the statistics about childhood in general and the research about children and education, girlhood in Puerto Rico has remained unexplored. The research that exists focuses primarily on studying Puerto Rican girlhood in the United States rather than on the island (see, for example, Lobenstine et al. 2001). As could be surmised, the experiences in each place—while possibly similar in some aspects—are often different, beginning with the most basic reason: that Puerto Ricans in the archipelago are the majority population while Puerto Ricans in the continental United States are considered minorities. Some of the experiences of growing up in a Puerto Rican household on the island or in the United States, however, can be very similar. Lobenstine et al. (2001) present a study in which mothers and daughters collaborated in order to examine their experiences of possible selves.[2] While the project's aim was not to study Puerto Rican girlhood specifically, a majority of participants were born in Puerto Rico or were of Puerto Rican descent. One participant offers an account that, though not illustrative of every Puerto Rican girl's experience, partly describes being a girl in a chiefly patriarchal society:

> I was born in Puerto Rico, moved to the US at the age of five. I grew up with a very traditional, strict macho father. Talking about sex, drugs and alcohol was very simple, "never do it." Things were hidden well in the home front. . . . So I grew up very ignorant in these topics. My dad was a machista, he would say, "Women should stay home take care of the children, clean the house and have food ready for him." I knew I didn't want this in a marriage or in my life. Even

though my dad was strict and harsh, he was very loving and caring. My dad was my inspiration; I learned a lot from him. (Lobenstine et al. 2001: 7)

The girl's experiences with machismo described above reflect ideologies that continue to place girls in domestic spheres and see them mostly as mothers in training. When the differentiation between boys and girls as separate entities emerged in the nineteenth century, boyhood consisted of boys being "doers, adventurers, explorers, creatures of action, guile, mischief, intellect, and leadership" (Hateley 2011: 87). Meanwhile, girl-hood was considered to involve little action and more emotion, girls were thought of as docile and unimaginative, and they were mostly perceived (and represented) as domestic beings, raised to become mothers (Hateley 2011). In his famous work *Emile* ([1762] 1921), Jean-Jacques Rousseau offered this distinction between boys and girls in relation to types of roles they should enact during their play and in their daily lives:

> Boys and girls have many games in common, and this is as it should be; do they not play together when they are grown up? They have also special tastes of their own. Boys want movement and noise, drums, tops, toy-carts; girls prefer things which appeal to the eye, and can be used for dressing-up—mirrors, jewellery [*sic*], finery, and specially dolls. The doll is the girl's special plaything; this shows her instinctive bent towards her life's work. ([1762] 1921: 293)

He continues, "Little girls always dislike learning to read and write, but they are always ready to learn to sew. They think they are grown up, and in imagination they are using their knowledge for their own adornment" (Rousseau [1762] 1921: 293). These characteristics presented in girl char-acters across a myriad of children's literature mirrored the reality of girls' real lives, which were chiefly limited to the realms of their homes.

Discussing girlhood, Simone de Beauvoir ([1949] 2009) explains that girls were required to stay home and that their few activities outside were closely watched over. Furthermore, girls were not encouraged to organize their own fun and pleasure, while boys were allowed these independent activities. Research on play shows that these characteristics of girlhood and boyhood remain present in the behaviors each gender shows during play. A review of the literature on gender and play shows that, for the most part, girls do most of their playing inside. In addition, it shows that girls' play tends to be sedentary, quieter, and passive as it involves arts and crafts, playing with dolls, and talking in small groups, often as a result of the gender roles imposed by the adults in their lives (Boyle, Marshall, and Robeson 2003; Johnson, Christie, and Wardle 2005; Frost, Wortham, and

Reifel 2012). This is not surprising since, historically, girls have been assigned domestic roles as part of their "play" or leisure time in order to educate them on their female duties. In their play with dolls, even when boys
were included, both genders performed their play in socially prescribed
ways (Forman-Brunell 2011). While girls pretended to be little mothers to
their dolls, boys often personified more authoritative roles such as doctors
or preachers.

Studying Girlhood through Dolls:
Dolls and the Construction of Identity

Historically, children have often been given gender-specific toys, alongside
the message that the toy was preparation for the roles they were expected
to fulfill as adults: for girls the role was motherhood and domestic duties
(thus their toys consisted of dolls, play cookware, decorating sets, etc.),
and for boys the toys were building blocks or cars, sports gear, and building sets (Lipkin 2009). In nineteenth-century America, girls were urged
toward usefulness rather than pleasure in their play, which assumed the
role of natural training in the established values they would need as future
wives and citizens (Forman-Brunell 2011). Most of a girl's time was spent
attending school, praying, and performing nonleisure activities, thus
the time spent with dolls was very limited. Still, this limited time with
dolls continued to be educational since dolls served utilitarian purposes:
girls would sew clothes for them—learning a valued skill to contribute
to the household—and, naturally, they played "mother" with them. In
the decades following the Civil War, however, dolls gradually began to
serve more modern purposes rather than utilitarian ones. According to
Forman-Brunell (2011), doll play went beyond simply practicing sewing
skills and instead emphasized the display of high fashion. In addition,
adults expected girls to imitate (female) rituals of high society through
their doll play. They were encouraged to reenact housewarming and tea
parties and urged by adults to recreate funerals. Following this type of
play, texts that depicted doll fiction emerged, providing girls with both an
outlet and a way of playing with their dolls. These texts, often written from
the perspective of a doll who loves her girl owner (friend), also portrayed
powerful feelings of love between girl and doll, which bordered between
maternal and romantic and which was reciprocal and passionate. Then, by
the early 1890s, "the growing importance of mothering and child study

had influenced popular ideas about doll play for girls" (Forman-Brunell 2011: 232). From then on, the images that portrayed doll play often depicted mothering love between girl and doll, and girls cradling their babies with maternal sentimentality. Forman-Brunell notes that contemporaries rhetorically asked, "Is it not the harmless, childish joy that develops and educates the young girl's maternal instinct, and in so doing helps to elevate her to the pinnacle of true womanhood?" (2011: 232).

As objects of girls' material culture, dolls possess different meanings among producers, the adults who purchase them, and the girls who receive them. Producers, parents, and the experts who advise them have long agreed that dolls are designed to provide an important focus for socialization and preparation for womanhood. However, "intention and reception do not always correspond" (Lloyd 2015: 39). Children often practice dramatic play with dolls by using a variety of props and objects, combining multiple roles and themes, and creating a pretend scenario (Leong and Bodrova 2012). Doll play, then, can be looked at through the lens of dramatic play as it occurs as a social practice between doll and player, and at times between player and other player(s). Doll play, including (and more specifically) Barbie play as delineated in this project, incorporates the aforementioned characteristics suggested by Leong and Bodrova (2012). The research on dramatic play mostly refers to pretend play that involves at least two parties. For instance, Marsh notes that "play can be an individual practice but often the impetus for playful activity in childhood is social" (2010: 4). Drawing on the argument that play is fostered by the desire to engage with the community, Pelletier (2008) suggests that,

> rather than being removed from real life, secluded within a 'magic circle', play is ritualistic, concerned with establishing and maintaining social norms and policing borders between social inclusion and exclusion. It is used to frame play as a social practice, embedded in social rituals, with its own "instrumental" behaviors, and within the broad functioning of society. (2008: 4)

While the roles and themes, conflicts, and negotiation to solve arguments during doll play can take place between the players, doll play among my participants took place mostly as an individual and private activity. Thus, within my research, these characteristics surfaced in the actual play among the dolls and objects themselves rather than between the players. As will be illustrated in later chapters, I drew from these standpoints on play to understand the relationship between girls and Barbie, to examine the meanings they placed on their interactions with the doll, and to recognize how doll play with Barbie, mostly dramatic, allowed girls to explore their identities.

A major part of girls' play with dolls situated them in a domestic role, usually that of a mother, as this was the way they were taught to play with them or how girls were depicted in texts that involved doll play. Yet, while these play practices are exhibited in current play, they are not naturally inherent in each gender. Rather, these are the practices that toy creators have produced through their marketing strategies. Moreover, these are practices fostered by parents and other adults to establish different roles for each gender, teaching children that they are expected to have very different societal roles. Some scholars argue that dolls reinforce norma-tive notions about gender and femininity (Forman-Brunell, 2012). Social constructions of girlhood (and femininity) suggest that females belong to the domestic sphere—more specifically, the role they are supposed to fulfill as adults is motherhood. These constructions are inherent, and often overtly depicted, in the merchandise for girls (and boys), advertisements, literature, and toys (Lipkin 2009). Weida states, "Advertisements and television programming centered on dolls and action figures often poses narrowly gendered and heteronormative models of adulthood to young people" (2011: 2). For a long time, advertisements for children's toys have, for instance, delineated the play spaces that children can inhabit and the objects with which they can interact. Girls are mostly portrayed playing with dolls, kitchen sets, and cleaning supplies, to name a few. In contrast, boys are mostly depicted with tools, cars, guns, and sports gear.

Yet, scholars also "point to the ways in which dolls and the girls who play with them negotiate, revise, and disrupt the cultural categories of girlhood" (Forman-Brunell 2012: 4). For instance, Weida suggests that "play enables children to reconfigure meanings and iconography different from those intended by the marketers and/or feared by parents, demon-strating that what is intended may not ultimately designate those messages and images ultimately constructed by young people" (2011: 2). Many girlhood studies scholars support examining gender issues through mate-rial culture, especially through dolls (see Driscoll 2002; Forman-Brunell 2011; Hains 2012; Reid-Walsh and Mitchell 2000).[3] As the scholarship about dolls indicates, dolls are not simply mere objects of play in girls' lives that come in contact with girls as symbols of femininity. They serve as spaces where a diverse set of meanings emerge according to how girls interact with the dolls. Further, they become spaces where girls negotiate and perform their own ideologies about girlhood and femininity.

An important reason that supports the study of girlhood through dolls is the central function these objects have in children's lived experiences. As Lloyd suggests, "Dolls tell the historical narrative of everyday life, of political and social attitudes, and of the role of the sexes" (2015: 37). They can contribute to the construction of feminine identity, but they can also serve as an outlet for anger and violence (Aguiló-Pérez 2017). As I have previously noted, dolls can be used "in subversive, dark, and even sexualized ways to push against patriarchal ideas of femininity and constructions of gender roles" (see Bernstein 2015; Lloyd 2015) (in Aguiló-Pérez 2017). Girls, for instance, may change their dolls' appearances to look "less feminine," or they may imagine sexual scenarios between dolls of the same sex in order to resist ideas of heteronormativity.

Scholars have highlighted the importance of studying the objects that are deeply embedded in children's culture, such as dolls and action figures, making the argument that "the critical analysis of the characteristics between girls and dolls/action figures provides valuable insights into the continuities and changes of gender identities in American cultures" (Wagner-Ott 2002: 246). From an early age, gender roles and gender identities are made clear to children through the use of toys and the categorization of toys for girls and toys for boys. One way in which girls are indoctrinated and trained for their future domestic roles is through the use of dolls, specifically baby dolls (de Beauvoir [1949] 2009; Lipkin 2009; Forman-Brunell 2011). Yet, with the creation and popularity of the fashion doll, especially Barbie, the "training" offered by baby dolls changed.

Barbie as a Site of Interrogation

One crucial aspect of the study described in this book is identifying girls' and women's construction of their own feminine identities through their experiences of play with Barbie. Barbie dolls have usually been the center of great criticism due to their appearance. As many have argued, the dolls' so-called perfect body poses as a negative influence on little girls who presumably grow up wanting to look just like the doll, creating or at least making girls more susceptible to body issues and low self-esteem. Cultural studies scholars, such as Lord (1994), Rand (1995), duCille (1994, 1999), Steinberg (1997), Gilman (1998), and Lipkin (2009), among others, argue about the detrimental effect that Barbie, fashion, baby, and toddler dolls have on girls in relation to gender identity. Lipkin notes that in doll play, domesticity is pervasive: "Girls have the option of a multitude of dolls to choose from . . . but preparation for motherhood is a central tenet: Dolls are made to be fed, have diapers changed, are in need of strollers, bibs, high chairs, and more. Girls are taught to take pride in nurturing at this early age, and that this is their expected role" (2009: 9). Conversely, Barbie is marketed as a young woman who can do anything on her own and who can achieve any goal she establishes for herself. When comparing Barbie dolls to baby dolls as role models in girls' lives, Rogers cites Darlene, a professional librarian at a university library: "Baby dolls, which had encouraged us all to be and stay in the image of motherhood, may have been replaced with Barbie, the career girl" (1999: 16). Here, it becomes clear that Barbie sends a message that is very different from the message baby dolls send. While baby dolls encourage girls to delimit their goals to domestic roles—taking care of babies, completing chores around the house, serving as wife and mother—Barbie may show girls that their goals can be found outside the domestic. Girls can have careers just as Barbie does, and therefore she serves as a more positive role model for girls. However, Darlene also finds Barbie problematic in that she may send the message that girls can be "anything-else-that-you-wantta-be-as-long-as-you-are-an-anorexic-and-sexy-girl," and she questions whether this has "sent a better or worse message to our children" (Rogers 1999: 16).

Wohlwend notes the different ways in which the player, which in most cases is a girl, constructs identities through doll play:

> Dolls elicit performances of imagined characters for doll players in relation to the doll (e.g. baby dolls elicit pretend mothers). But dolls can also be proxies that allow children to pretend an imagined self through the doll (e.g. Disney Princess dolls elicit portrayals of players as princess characters). (2015: 92)

Girls have used Barbie dolls to pretend an imagined self through them and to construct an identity of who they see themselves to be, or who they would like to be. Through Barbie play, many of my participants were able to create a self, explore who they were, and even navigate complex topics that were not being discussed with them.

The idea that girls perform an imagined self and create identities through doll play has been adopted by Mattel, Barbie's producer, in many of their advertisements for the doll (for example, their "We Girls Can Do Anything" campaign in the 1980s). More recently, in a commercial titled "Imagine the Possibilities," Mattel employs this idea by capturing through hidden cameras "real reactions to girls imagining everything they might one day become" (Barbie 2015). The girls imagine themselves as professors, veterinarians, soccer coaches, and businesswomen, revealing at the end that they were imagining themselves through Barbie play. Many of my participants and those who knew about my research shared this video with me through social media platforms, stating that they identified with the message of the commercial as they experienced imagining what they could be through their own play with Barbie.

Barbie was introduced by Mattel, Inc. in 1959 and was initially considered innovative for being a "teenage" doll. However, it was not truly representative of a grown-up infant figure. She appeared in the wake of the popular concretization of the idea of the teenager, teenybopper, and teen. According to Driscoll, Barbie was never *just* a fashion doll. Although fashion was part of her life, it usually functioned in terms of Barbie's career, which in some cases was in fact fashion itself. Finally, Driscoll (2008) discusses the importance of Barbie in scholarship, noting that no other toy has generated so much media interest. Barbie has become "a standard for scholarly discussion of the relations between popular culture, dominant ideologies, and childhood development as much as she has always been a centerpiece for the popular media" (Driscoll 2008: 45). In academic scholarship about Barbie, there have been both concerns about the effects of girls playing with Barbie and also enjoyment in the long spectacle of the Barbie archive.

Despite her many flaws, Barbie can be used in a more positive and progressive way to instill other values to girls. Barbie can serve as a model of independence, autonomy, assertiveness, and choice. Cox comments that "if Barbie has indeed provided a behavioral model for a segment of the population, the values instilled by her miniature utopia will play an increasing role in the lives of those children who buy her version of the American Dream" (1977: 307). Since the doll has been so influential for so many years, it is important to apply her influence in a different form: instead of *only* emphasizing her troublesome figure and the message it might instill, the focus should be shifted to the possibilities Barbie creates for girls and how these may inform girls better about the roles they can have in society. While a vast number of scholars have condemned Barbie for "educating" girls to be obsessed with looks and depicting a mostly white, middle-class, heterosexual femininity, Tosa (1998) argues that it is society that shapes a doll's role and the messages it transmits to girls:

> The doll's role in the game of life is merely reflective of the society that produced her. A doll has no pretense of her own. She is not "born" autonomous and whole. She is our puppet, passive, accepting, content to be shaped and molded in our hands as we imitate gods in the rites of creation. Thus, we really cannot accuse a doll of being "non-educational"; she is the product of the same culture of which she is a mirror, along with countless other toys and games of questionable educational merit. (1998: 22)

Mitchell and Reid-Walsh also shift the conversation about Barbie toward a more positive one, arguing that "Barbie exists as a perfect cultural site for interrogating the margins, borders, and contradictions of our lives as girls and women" (1997: 87). They acknowledge the usual negative connotations that accompany Barbie, especially in scholarship, yet what they want to do is provide Barbie as a cultural site "in her own right." In this essay, Mitchell and Reid-Walsh focus less on the doll itself and more on the texts about her that include print and play paraphernalia.[4] They ask the following question: "What do these artifacts mean in the development of the nineties' girls who will become young women at the turn of the century?" (Mitchell and Reid-Walsh 1997: 91).[5] The authors view these Barbie texts as ways to offer a challenge to both feminists and their daughters in terms of interpretations. As they note, Barbie has always been controversial, and while in earlier years these critics were men, now their most ardent critics are women. However, although the doll has occupied a position of contradiction, the authors suggest that she can also be positioned as Barbie-as-interrogator thanks to the texts. They ask: "What does it mean that Barbie exists as feminist historian through collector cards that allow girls and their mothers to 'recover' women's history? What does it mean that Barbie addresses eating disorders, or makes it possible for a daycare centre to be enlarged? How do little girls connect these texts?" (Mitchell and Reid-Walsh 1997: 98). They argue that by extending the text of Barbie to include other artifacts that define Barbie as a cultural text, Barbie is moved toward a site of interrogation.

There is a vast literature on Barbie, which ranges from blog posts to newspaper articles, from quantitative to qualitative research about Barbie play, from textual analysis of Barbie books to artwork and photography projects of Barbie, among the many Barbie-related works that can be found. Many have drawn from their own lived experiences to critically examine Barbie's role in their lives and how those experiences may represent the experiences of many women and children with the doll. When this literature has involved adults' memories, it includes some works by authors who have written about their own experiences (see duCille, 1999; McDonough, 1999; Rand, 1995), while others have written about other people's experiences gathered through interviews and informal conversations. Lord (1994), McDonough (1999), Rand (1995), and Rogers (1998) have published extensively on Barbie and the various problematic aspects the doll presents. Their work draws from a variety of sources, including interviews and informal conversations with girls, educators, toy producers and marketers, academics, Barbie collectors, and women who used to play Barbie. In *Forever Barbie: The Unauthorized Biography of a Real Doll*, Lord (1994) offers a detailed account of the creation of the Barbie doll. Lord chronicles Barbie's history and her relevance as a cultural icon. She draws on interviews with toymakers, an eclectic group of Barbie collectors, visual artists, and feminists who disagree on Barbie's impact on young girls. The author sees Barbie, who has had myriad careers, as a female role model. Similarly, Rogers (1998) in *Barbie Culture* presents extensive research on Barbie and the culture that surrounds her. The author presents diverse (and often opposing) opinions about the doll given by adults who used to play with it, and also offers the opinion of educators who have experienced Barbie culture in their own classroom. In *The Barbie Chronicles: A Living Doll Turns Forty*, McDonough (1999) collects an eclectic Barbie literature that comes from a variety of authors. The contributions in this anthology discuss a range of topics, such as puberty, sexual awakening, body image, torture play, boys playing with dolls, breast cancer and its influence on a girl's view of Barbie's breast, race and lack of diversity in Barbie dolls, and the embrace of and rejection to the doll. It includes critical essays that reflect on each author's own experiences with the doll, research on Barbie in terms of race and gender roles, and even creative nonfiction such as poems about Barbie. Erica Rand's critical work in *Barbie's Queer Accessories* explores various topics of feminism in relation to Barbie, including class, race, and gender. She takes a look at the corporate marketing strategies used to create Barbie's versatile yet predominantly white image. Rand (1995) compares the values inherent in the Barbie life—for instance heteronormativity—as well as her unattainable body figure against the naked, queered, transgendered, and trashed versions created and favored by many young owners and collectors of the doll.

Dittmar, Halliwell, and Ive (2006) address body image influences in their study of 162 girls, ages 5 to 8. The participants were exposed to images of either Barbie dolls, Emme dolls (US size 16), or no dolls, and then they completed assessments of body image. Girls exposed to Barbie reported lower body esteem and greater desire for a thinner body shape than girls in the other exposure conditions. However, this immediate negative impact of the Barbie doll was no longer evident in the oldest girls. The authors suggest that their findings imply that, even if dolls cease to function as aspirational role models for older girls, early exposure to dolls epitomizing an unrealistically thin body ideal may damage girls' body image, which would contribute to an increased risk of disordered eating and weight cycling.

Others have focused on the perceptions that girls have about Barbie. These include a range of topics such as children as consumers and also Barbie's image. For instance, Engin (2013) addresses how preteen girls interact with and within the world of Barbie. Her data was gathered through participant observation in girls' games. She analyzes Barbie in children's culture, aiming to answer such questions as: How much do children follow cues from Mattel as they play with and think about Barbie? To what extent does Barbie's popularity come from the doll itself rather than from Mattel's successful marketing strategies? She suggests that Mattel's strong marketing strategies have made Barbie one of the rare exceptions to the idea that "nothing lasts forever" (Engin 2013: 36). She argues that while Barbie has been criticized for the negative ideologies she embodies and for perpetuating hegemony in multiple ways, she will continue to do so because "she is the perfect doll for the all consuming-global kid/citizen [sic] and moves with a snowball effect in penetrating the households with young children" (2013: 36). Kuther and McDonald (2004) present two qualitative studies with young adolescents that gather their experiences and perspectives about the doll. The first study, which involved focus groups with twenty sixth-grade girls, suggested they have ambiguous feelings about the doll and the feminine sexualized image Barbie represents. The second study gathered essay responses from fifty seventh- and eighth-grade boys and girls about their experiences with and opinions on Barbie dolls. The participants reported both positive and negative feelings toward the doll and its influence on girls' development. Finally, Collins et al. (2012) discuss the outcomes of "Reinventing Barbie," a workshop they designed for middle-school girls to discuss, critique, and reflect on the construction of female bodies and feminine identities in popular culture by remaking Barbie dolls. The girls reconstructed Barbies based on their reflections, and then they came together to discuss their dolls as expressions of their visions for transforming the feminine. In this specific instance girls were prompted to transform Barbie according to their ideas about femininity—something I explored with my own college students in a course about Barbie. This kind of transformation to a doll (or an object of play) can allow children, and adults, to examine their current ideologies and also consider the role that the object had in their own development. For some of the girls in depicted this book, as I will expand upon later, this transformation was a necessity to make Barbie someone with whom they could identify or to make the doll fit their play better.

A reason why girls might transform Barbie is because of the lack of diversity presented when they were growing up. Scholars have focused on issues of race and ethnicity, even with the creation of dolls of color, because there has been a lack of realistic representations of nonwhite dolls among the Barbie line. Despite efforts to bring ethnic and racial variety to the Barbie brand, the central figure in everything that is related to the doll is Barbie—the white, tall, blue-eyed blond girl. In addition, the multi-ethnic dolls in the Barbie line still present problems of representation. DuCille (1994), for instance, offers a critical look at Barbie and issues of race, multiculturalism, and capitalism. Drawing on research and her own experiences, duCille questions Barbie's position in these issues and Barbie as a commodity. She argues that Mattel has made Barbie's multiracialism a commodity, describing the colored Barbie doll (i.e., Jamaican, Puerto Rican, Chinese, Mexican, and Native American Barbie, among others) as "carbon copies of an already grossly stereotypical and fantastically female original, . . . a sterling example of the universalizing myopia of mass production" (1994: 115). As will be apparent in my discussion of race, this was an aspect of Barbie that some of my participants noticed. They pointed out how all the dolls looked the same, even if there was a variation in the color of their skin and the ethnicity they were representing. However, some participants negotiated white Barbie's place as the central figure (and the mold for all other dolls) by changing the doll's looks. Chin (1999) offers examples of how girls subvert Barbie's whiteness by modifying her appearance to meet their needs. In this research, Chin (1999) also discusses why, even though Mattel created a line of exclusively Black dolls, these still presented problems of representation. Native American Barbie dolls have presented similarly deep problems. Not only are certain ethnicities underrepresented, but when they exist, they are "depicted predominantly in time-worn stereotypes as primitives from the past" (Schwarz 2005: 296).

At the same time that these issues are present in Barbie and other dolls, research has also shown that Barbie play (or doll play) can serve as a site of research that liberates women. Reid-Walsh and Mitchell (2000) focus on the accounts of former Barbie players as they discuss what it means for them now as adults to think of themselves as former Barbie doll players. The doll has been highly criticized and considered an antifeminist toy mostly because of its physical attributes, and it has been considered responsible for girls' body image issues. Some of the women Reid-Walsh and Mitchell (2000) discuss argue that Barbie is not to blame for these issues; rather, criticism should be placed upon the way girls are raised and the values they are taught at home. For two women, for example, playing with Barbie consisted of inventing lives and situations, making outfits, and being what they wanted to be through their dolls. For them, the focus was not on the doll's body but rather on the choices the doll presented for them.

Studying Barbie as a Transnational Object

A significant amount of the work around Barbie mainly focuses on experiences in the global north. In this sense, the research is limited, since Barbie is a global phenomenon that has traversed borders and is present in many parts of the world. It is only more recently that there has been a growth in studies that examine Barbie in a global context, either by placing the research in a location outside the United States or Canada or by focusing on the multicultural line of Barbie "Dolls of the World." Magee (2005) offers a new perspective on the study of Barbie dolls as she extends her research to the "Dolls of the World" line and focuses her analyses on Mattel's Ghanian Barbie and other "Dolls of the World" in a post–Cold War American society. She notes that while many scholars have commented on the ideologies that Barbie exemplifies and promotes, few have given attention to this specific line of the Barbie brand, and those who have have focused on how these dolls promote American-like consumption in other parts of the world. Magee (2005) asserts that the largest market for the Ghanian Barbie and other dolls is in the United States, therefore her work addresses this gap through an examination of their American consumption as well as commenting on the complex issues of ethnicity and nationhood that the dolls raise. Thus, her work is not outside the United States, but it covers a new aspect of Barbie that has not received much attention.

Other works, however, have studied the Barbie phenomenon outside the United States, in places such as Pakistan, India, and Mexico. For instance, Sohail, Naz, and Malik (2014) address the problematic whiteness and the beauty standards Barbie poses especially in a different culture. Their study explores Barbie phenomena in an urban Pakistani context with a postcolonial perspective to find out the ways that Barbie affects female Pakistani children. They worked with thirty young girls ages eight to eleven and thirty parents, presenting them with a survey and question-naires as well as interviewing them. According to Sohail et al. (2014), the doll is idealized and liked by much of the population, pointing to their conclusion that a blond doll representing Western culture has a strong impact on the young minds of female children, including serious health threats, as they idealize their doll and develop low self-esteem. Hegde presents a critical look at Barbie as a commodity, which stemmed from her experience at an airport store in India, where she noticed a selection of Barbie dolls "shimmering in fantastic gold and tinsel exotica" (2001: 129). She draws examples from the play experiences of her fourteen-year-old daughter and the complications that Indian Barbie presented in her play scenario. Hegde (2001) suggests that global circulation of products like ethnic Barbie creates a transnational space of contestation over questions of consumption, identity, and cultural authenticity. Mattel's version of global representation only serves to confine and demarcate cultural boundaries in girls' local world of play and friendship. Barbie, she argues, survives as an icon of whiteness and femininity wherever she travels. MacDougall (2003) also looks at Barbie as a commodity in the context of Mexico. She notes that despite efforts by Mattel to blanket diverse markets by adapting Barbie's skin color and clothing, the changes that Barbie has undergone in the hands of non-Western consumers remain striking. Research regarding the reception of transnational products in the Yucatan region of Mexico reveals that Barbie has been reformulated by Mexican consumers to represent local identity rather than emulating the meanings and values she was attributed by Mattel.

More recently, I studied the marketing of Latinx culture in children's toys, including Barbie. As I have noted, Barbie has ventured into diversity efforts in many ways, including the creation of the "Dolls of the World" line. These dolls, as the scholarship I reviewed suggested, present very narrow views of culture and treat any cultural practice as something that can be worn as a costume to be put on or taken off. This collection of "Dolls of the World" takes Barbie's transnationalism to a concrete level, inviting the child to travel to a different country with the doll as the doll also crosses national and geographical boundaries to permeate new places and new markets. Yet, as I have previously examined and as will be visible with the example of Puerto Rican Barbie, the ways Mattel attempts this can be problematic (Aguiló-Pérez 2021). These transnational versions of Barbie serve more as souvenirs and collectible cultures for the child to consume through a tourist gaze. But for better or for worse, Barbie's transnational power cannot be denied. Her presence in childhoods, including those of Puerto Rican girls, is still strong.

Notes

1. I have translated this and subsequent quotes from *Nuestros Niños Cuentan* from Spanish to English.
2. "Possible selves" is "what we might become, hope to become, and fear becoming" (Markus and Niriuus 1986, cited in Lobenstine et al. 2001: 2).
3. For instance, the summer 2012 issue of the *Girlhood Studies* journal was entirely devoted to the study of dolls and their roles in girls' lives. For the most part, dolls have been examined from the perspectives of play studies, girlhood/childhood studies, childhood psychology, and material culture, to name a few. Yet, dolls have progressively become a site of examination, giving way for the establishment of dolls studies as an interdisciplinary field of research of its own (Forman-Brunell and Whitney 2015). While they are closely linked to girlhood and girls' culture, the growing scholarship focused on intersecting dolls with other areas of study has solidified their importance as sites of interrogation. This became one of the main reasons for the compilation of essays that formed *Dolls Studies: The Many Meanings of Girls' Toys and Play*, which was a continuation of the work already established in the "Dolls" issue of *Girlhood Studies*.
4. The Barbie collector cards, *Barbie* and *Barbie Fashion* comic books, *Barbie, the Magazine for Girls*, and the Barbie game *We Girls Can Do Anything*.
5. The authors describe each text and the type of information each one contains. For instance, the collector cards are designed as baseball cards, and they contain information about important women in history (all portrayed by Barbie). In the comic books, fashion is a concurrent topic; however, Barbie also discusses important personal and social issues such as eating disorders. In the game, girls are offered a variety (though not an infinite number) of professions Barbie can be, including an actress, a ballerina, a pilot, a doctor, a musician, and a fashion designer.

❧

CHAPTER 2

The Politics of Barbie in Puerto Rico
A New Icon Emerges

Barbie was a reliable—if frustrating—toy claimed by U.S. *boricuas* to imagine Puerto Ricans as a distinct ethnic group, to make demands on American public culture as a politically disenfranchised minority, and to seek dignified valorization in the marketplace.

—Frances Negrón-Muntaner (2004), *Boricua Pop: Puerto Ricans and the Latinization of American Culture*

Barbie's exact date of arrival to Puerto Rico is difficult to pinpoint. During my research, I gathered document data by examining newspapers from Puerto Rico published between 1959 and 1963 in order to understand the context of when Barbie arrived on the island. Reviewing issues of *El Mundo*, the daily newspaper at the time, I focused on finding articles or advertisements that presented Barbie, who was a new doll during those years. In newspaper issues from 1959 through 1961, Barbie was noticeably absent. There was very little mention of the doll, and she was not present even in Christmas advertisements from various large retail stores such as Gonzalez Padín and Woolworth's, which fervently urged parents to buy toys (including dolls). In the 1 December 1962 issue of the newspaper, Barbie was still absent from

---

Notes for this section can be found on page 69.

any toy ads, including one for Sears (figure 2.1). Yet, *El Mundo* featured a news article titled "Una Curiosa Exposición Internacional," which discussed a large exhibition at the Gallera Museum in Paris that featured three thousand dolls (figure 2.2). Barbie was among the dolls on display, which came from countries around the world, including Japan, Ireland, Ghana, Madagascar, and the United States. The picture included in the article shows three Barbie dolls with a caption that reads: "'Barbie' is a doll born in the United States which incarnates the silhouette and style of the young north American girl of our times" (figure 2.3). The way the caption was written, as if to inform readers of this new and unknown doll, suggests that Barbie had not gained notoriety in Puerto Rico at the time. Moreover, it called attention to the doll's physical characteristics and how they embodied the "American girl." I do not view this as an accidental description. The 1950s and 1960s saw a financial decline in Puerto Rico, which prompted the government to encourage a massive migration to the continental United States, especially to New York City. Selling this new doll as an all-American girl seemed to offer an opportunity for girls to dream of the possibilities (a phrase that decades later became the Barbie brand's motto) beyond their context.

The memories of two of my participants, whom I had interviewed prior to my examination of *El Mundo*, confirmed my supposition of two facts related to Barbie's arrival to the island. The first supposition was that her arrival occurred later than it did in the United States. While products such as toys and movies now arrive at the same time in Puerto Rico, the process was longer in the 1950s–60s, and thus products arrived to the island even a few years later. The second supposition was that Barbie did not immediately become a favorite toy. Perhaps due to economic restraints, a limited quantity of products, or the fact that Barbie invited girls to play differently than they were used to, I found through my review of the newspapers and through the stories of my participants that Barbie did not gain overnight fame in Puerto Rico. When trying to remember the exact year they received their Barbies, the two participants pointed out that they probably became available in 1961 or 1962, and that Barbie "wasn't very known in Puerto Rico either" (Carmen and Lourdes, Group 1 transcript).

The Conditions for Barbie's Arrival

Barbie's first arrival to Puerto Rico coincided with many changes that were brought about by the archipelago's coloniality. During World War II, with military bases around the main island, a federal program of road

Figure 2.1. Sears Christmas ad for *El Mundo* newspaper.

construction was put in place in order to connect these bases. This project led to the establishment of local cement and other manufacturing plants. After the war's culmination, the process of industrialization in Puerto Rico continued with the establishment of "export-oriented, U.S. owned man-ufacturing operations" (Cordero-Guzman 1994: 7). As an incentive to at-tract US companies, products, and capital to Puerto Rico, the government offered tax breaks. The industrial incentives act of 1947 formally initiated what is known today as Operation Bootstrap (or, in Puerto Rico, Manos a la Obra [literally: Let's Do It!]), which was paired with an agricultural reform program aimed at decreasing the island's reliance on the sugar

Figure 2.2. First appearance of Barbie in *El Mundo*.

industry. Santana argues that the purpose of Operation Bootstrap was "to meet the challenge of keeping the strategically vital island loyal to the United States" by "providing a viable livelihood for many, undermining the independence movement, and precluding any attempts to provide alternative

(Foto: A.F.P.)

"Barbie" es una muñeca nacida en los Estados Unidos que encarna la silueta y el estilo de la joven norteamericana de nuestros días.

Tres mil muñecas

Una Curiosa Exposición Internacional

Por Charlotte RIX

[ten subyugados por esos peque- | de tarantela, la elección sería | ravillosa cabellera que le sirve

Figure 2.3. Picture of Barbie dolls from first appearance of Barbie in *El Mundo*.

development models that might increase self-sufficiency" (1998: 88). She adds that the success of this economic development strategy in Puerto Rico was closely tied to the creation of the *estado libre asociado* (free associated state), or the commonwealth political status in 1952, which "offered the appearance of decolonization and self-determination while maintaining U.S. rule in all important respects" (Santana 1998: 88). Unlike the four US states that officially call themselves "commonwealths" (Kentucky, Massachusetts, Pennsylvania, and Virginia) but whose status is no different from other states within the nation, Puerto Rico's commonwealth or free-associated state designation makes it "neither a state of the union nor a foreign country" (Colón 1984: 96). Politically, Puerto Rico is a colony of the United States.

Colonizers will always benefit economically, socially, and politically from their colonies. The system of incentives used to entice US companies to Puerto Rico also included accessing markets without import duties, transferring profits from Puerto Rico to the United States without federal taxation, and providing labor at lower costs than in the continental United States. The latter caused growing unemployment in the 1950s and 1960s, especially as living standards and wages in Puerto Rico escalated,

51

which then resulted in migrations between the island and the continental United States during those decades. All of these elements created the "perfect" conditions for Barbie's arrival (along with other products). Puerto Rico became a tax haven that increased the arrival of US companies and products. While many US military families resided on the island at the time, there was certainly an influx of US populations coming into the archipelago due to its industrialization. Thus, there was a specific market for US products targeted to that population.

Barbie was, then, an import of the United States during a time of economic change that further solidified US colonial hold over Puerto Rico economically and politically. Furthermore, she was a commodity—not everyone had access to her, and she was not initially presented as a product "for the masses." The doll's popularity and availability did, however, increase throughout the years. Progressively, Barbie became and continued to be a highly sought after product among Puerto Rican girls, as well as those elsewhere around the world. Data from the *Pan-Latin American Kids Study 1997* observed that "24 percent of all Latin American girls said that they own a Barbie doll" at the time (Soong 1998: par. 4). The researchers noted that while the rate of Barbie's permeation into Latin America differs by country, the highest penetration at the time of the study occurred in Puerto Rico, with 72 percent of girls owning Barbie dolls (Soong 1998). This proliferation of Barbie in Latin America, and especially in Puerto Rico, was no coincidence. In the late 1980s and early 1990s, US companies saw great consumer potential in various underrepresented groups, including Latinxs (Halter 2000; Schwarz 2005; Valdivia 2016), giving rise to the production of "ethnic" toys and targeted advertisements in media outlets to reach new audiences (Aldama 2013). Mattel, specifically, released a series of "friends" for Barbie: Teresa (Latina) in 1988, Nia (sometimes described as Native American and sometimes as Asian) in 1989, and Kira (Asian) in 1990, among others.

During the decade, Puerto Rico represented an easy market for the United States to access and a potential for great profits, as companies were "so eager to get it right with their promotional appeals to the Hispanic market that some [went] so far as to try out new ideas in Puerto Rico before launching a full-scale campaign at home" (Halter 2000: 143). Thus, the island served as an experimental "lab" for marketing and promoting US-produced goods, including toys. Speaking about market potentials in Puerto Rico, the local president of a US company operating on the island stated, "Puerto Rico is the first step to explore a new market in a stable territory. It is different from the standard U.S. markets but not as exotic or different from them as a Latin American country" (Ryan 1994: 1). The problematic language of "exotic" used to describe Latin American countries—and to measure Puerto Rico against them—serves to otherize certain populations and geographical locations while it centers the US as the "norm." Agreeing with the remarks by the local company's president, the CEO of a restaurant chain in Puerto Rico stated, "Puerto Rico's Latin American heritage enables American franchisers, for almost any type of product or service, to test new and different ideas here to measure market acceptance before a stateside launching. In other words, Puerto Rico serves as a testing ground for products that will be launched in areas with a sizeable Hispanic population" (Ryan 1994: 1). These expressions frame Puerto Rico as separate from the United States but (politically) close enough to it, as well as somewhat Latin American but not as "foreign" as other countries. They rationalized these marketing experiments as groundbreaking and purportedly of mutual benefit. With these marketing tests, the United States was once again exploiting the colonizer/colony relationship by using Puerto Ricans as test subjects, even if the potential risks were not as dangerous as past experiments.[1] The United States saw Puerto Rico as the ideal testing ground because its population was mostly Hispanic (the population companies wanted to reach), and the political relationship between the two made it easy for the United States to permeate. Puerto Ricans were easily accessible US citizens that were "exotic" enough to try new products.

Barbie in Puerto Rico:
A Symbol of Colonization or National Pride?

The colonizer/colony relationship between the United States and Puerto Rico served as the framework for the heated debate about a new Mattel product in 1997: the Puerto Rican Barbie. This new Barbie, which was part of the "Dolls of the World" collection, became "the latest sounding board for Puerto Ricans to examine their political and cultural relationship with the mainland" (Aguilar 1997: par. 1). Speaking of the Puerto Rican Barbie doll, professor Victor Rodríguez observed that the toy "can be seen as something of a pro-statehood move, and certainly a tricky issue when it comes to the question of our identity" (cited in Negrón-Muntaner 2004: 207). This was not a perspective that all Puerto Ricans shared, but it reflected one of the main concerns about the doll. Puerto Rico's governor at the time, Dr. Pedro Rosselló, was investing considerable resources toward legislation on the archipelago's political status in relation to the United States. As a supporter of statehood, he had a vested interest to define Puerto Rico's status. In fact, during his two consecutive terms as governor of Puerto Rico, Rosselló held two referendums on the status, the first in November 1993 and the second in December 1998.

Writing about Barbie's presence in India, Radha S. Hegde notes that "global circulation of products like ethnic Barbie creates a transnational space of contestation over questions of consumption, identity and cultural authenticity" (2001: 130). The production of Puerto Rican Barbie raised opposing views between Puerto Ricans on the island, who met the Puerto Rican Barbie doll with much excitement, and Puerto Ricans in the continental United States, who received the doll with much resistance on accounts of her looks and how she was marketed. They feared, as Negrón-Muntaner describes it, that the doll would be a "Trojan horse of identity destruction" (2004: 207). In other words, Puerto Rican Barbie would physically enter the island and permeate into Puerto Rican popular consciousness to raise debates about national identity. Barbie holds transnational power.

One objection to this new iteration of Barbie came in the form of the history excerpt written on the back of its box, which provided only one aspect of Puerto Rico's "origin story." It read: "My country was discovered in 1493 by Christopher Columbus who claimed it for Spain." This description framed colonization as an act of "discovery," ignoring the inherently violent nature of Spain's colonization of the archipelago (Aguiló-Pérez 2021). Additionally, this depiction of Puerto Rico's history "ignore[d] the [I]ndigenous population" that inhabited the archipelago long before (Rivera-Brooks 1997: par. 10). The description on the box provided only one aspect Puerto Rico's "origin story": *My country was discovered in 1493 by Christopher Columbus who claimed it for Spain.* By providing only this part of the history, "Mattel and its allies connote that all Puerto Ricans are fundamentally Europeans and banish the influence of Natives and Africans to the back of the bus," argued Negrón-Muntaner (2002: 42). Moreover, critics objected to Mattel's description of the island's relationship with the United States, which stated in part that "Puerto Rico was granted permission to write our own constitution in 1952, and since then we have governed ourselves" (Navarro 1997: par. 4). Navarro cites the opinion of Gina Rosario, a forty-six-year-old school art director who was of Puerto Rican descent and lived in the diaspora. Rosario said about the doll, "She looks very, very Anglo, and what was written on the package was very condescending: 'The U.S. Government lets us govern ourselves.'

If you're going to represent a culture, do it properly. Be politically honest" (in Navarro 1997: par. 5). The description on the box suggests a lack of autonomy from Puerto Rico, which had to be "allowed" to govern itself in 1952. The use of the term "allowed" infantilizes Puerto Rico and places the United States as the powerful entity that grants permission or removes it. Yet, in some ways the island in fact had little political autonomy before then. From the time the United States took hold of Puerto Rico after the Spanish-American War in 1898, its governors and political leaders had been appointed by the president of the United States. It was not until 1952, with the election of Luis Muñoz Marín, that Puerto Rico became a self-governing commonwealth of the United States. Even in the present, while Puerto Rico has autonomy in certain political aspects, the archipelago's status as a commonwealth (read: colony) of the United States comes with certain restrictions as well.[2] It is important to also note that at some point, perhaps as a result of the heated debate, parts of the description on the box may have changed. The description on the box of my own Puerto Rican doll (figure 2.4), as well as the one I examined at the doll museum in Quebradillas, does not include the comment about Puerto Ricans being "allowed" to self-govern.

The Puerto Rican Barbie also appeared to be, as suggested by Gina Rosario above and for those who opposed her, too Anglicized. "Some also found Puerto Rican Barbie's skin too white, her features too Caucasian, her hair too straight, and her clothing too suggestive of colonial oppression," Rivera-Brooks pointed out (1997: par. 11). Hair (texture and color) and physical features (nose, eyes, thickness of lips) can be used as racial identifiers in Puerto Rico. As I have argued elsewhere, "there is no one way to be or look Puerto Rican, just as there is no one way of being or looking Latinx, and in isolation, an Anglicized appearance is not necessarily problematic; but P.R. Barbie's Anglicized appearance was part of a broader trend in Mattel's product lines" where white or light skin was the norm (Aguiló-Pérez 2021: 149). In my study of the Latina Barbie dolls in the "Dolls of the World" line, I found that most looked similar to the Puerto Rican Barbie: they have dark eyes, dark hair, and light skin. Out of fifteen Latin American dolls—including those of Indigenous descent—only one, Brazil Barbie (2012), was Black. Thus, "in this context, then, the criticisms of P.R. Barbie's Anglicization point to a problematic whitewashing visible across most Latinx [and other ethnic] Barbie dolls" (Aguiló-Pérez 2021: 149).

In contrast, many Puerto Ricans in the archipelago, "nationalist intellectuals and consumers," embraced the doll (Negrón-Muntaner 2004: 207). Notably missing in the debates and conversations surrounding

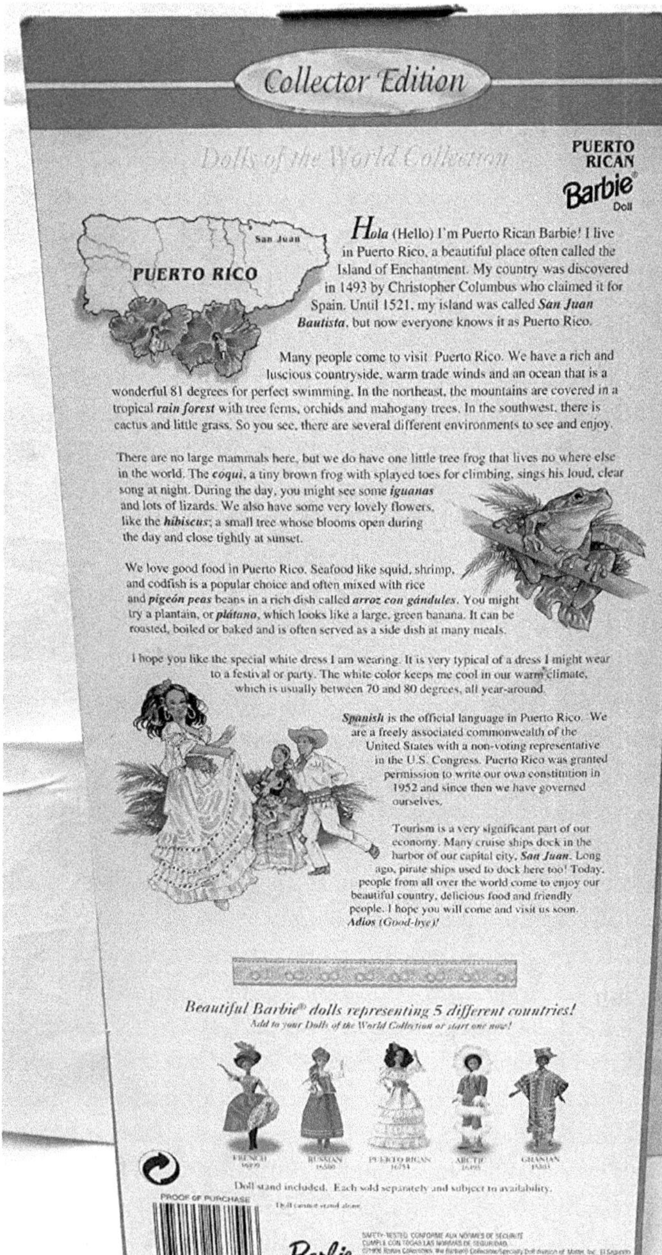

Figure 2.4. Description of Puerto Rico on the box for Puerto Rican Barbie. Photograph by author.

Puerto Rican Barbie, both in the critiques and the embraces, were the perspectives from children who played with the doll at the time and who were the presumed audience for the doll.[3] This was a poignant observation a group of women made during a conversation about Puerto Rican Barbie. In one Facebook conversation, a participant found an article about this debate and stated, "But when we were playing, we never noticed this." This was echoed by other women, even those who as adults are critical of Barbie and who identify as feminists. It is problematic to present criticism of artifacts of girls' culture without attending to girls' voices (Hains 2012). Therefore, it is imperative to revisit this conversation with the addition of the very important perspective of those who interacted with the doll *as girls* at the time it was produced.

Puerto Rican Barbie's name came up in some of the interviews with participants of this study because they had interacted with the doll as children. I, for example, remembered how excited I was when the doll came out and I first saw my country's name and flag decorating its box.[4] Other participants such as Isabel (age thirty) and Gabriela (age twenty-five) also remembered owning a Puerto Rican Barbie and playing with her. Participants Patricia and Marisa, who were already mothers when this Barbie came out, included Puerto Rican Barbie in their (or their daughters') Barbie doll collections. Isabel elaborated on her relationship with the Puerto Rican doll:

> I loved that Barbie. For me she was precious because she was different. When I was in the fourth grade I was dressed as a *jíbara* for a contest of traditional costumes for my school's Noche Puertorriquña [Puerto Rican Night]. They put a flower on my head. My mom made the costume. I won first place and I was very excited. I loved the doll's flower on her hair and her long skirt with lace. I've always admired our culture and perhaps, unconsciously, I admired that about the doll, and I identified with her. Once in a while I'd take her out to play, but most of the time I kept her in her little collection box, decorating my bedroom. (Isabel, personal communication)

One important aspect of this conversation was that it highlighted the contrast between how adults viewed Puerto Rican Barbie and how girls who grew up at the time actually received the doll. Navarro (1997), for example, presented the opinions of two people toward the Puerto Rican Barbie: an adult woman and a girl. As previously discussed, the adult (Gina Rosario) avidly opposed the doll because it looked too American and its box displayed history that was condescending toward Puerto Ricans. The girl's opinion, however, contrasted from that of forty-six-year-old Rosario: "'She's pretty,' Krista, 9, said. 'She's different. She has a Puerto Rican dress.

She's the Puerto Rican Barbie and all the others are not'" (Navarro 1997: par. 2). With the exception of two girls who loved Puerto Rican Barbie's dark hair because it looked like theirs, most girls in this study did not consider these as key traits while relating to the doll. Instead, it was her nationality that resonated with them.

What this example shows is the excitement and sense of pride girls felt by seeing a Barbie doll from their country, which the other Barbie dolls were not. This was an observation that one of the women in the Facebook conversation made: "What I found funny was that the girls, for whom the dolls are made, were very happy" (Woman #2, Facebook conversation). The women in this conversation were about eight to eleven years of age at the time when Puerto Rican Barbie was produced. Their voices and their experiences were not taken into consideration by those who offered criticism about the doll. This small sample could potentially be representative of conversations had by many other girls from the island who interacted with Puerto Rican Barbie during their girlhoods. The interaction between the women, which happened mostly in Spanish and which I have translated, went as follows:

First thread originated by Woman #2 when advertising my call for participants:

> *Woman #1:* I also remember that, even though I didn't play so much with them anymore, I was obsessed with the Barbie from Puerto Rico. I bought her and left her in the box, not for collection but because I was amazed to see a Barbie like that. I handed her down to my little cousins because it wasn't available anymore and they deserved to see themselves there.
>
> *Woman #2:* Hahaha! In the United States people got offended. I posted the link. We didn't even find out at the time.
>
> *Woman #1:* No, man. I'm going to read that because to me it was so special to see a Barbie with the clothes that you only wear during the Semana de la Puertorriqueñidad lol.
>
> *Woman #2:* READ IT. It's good!

Second thread originated by Woman #2 when posting an article about the Puerto Rican Barbie:

> *Woman #1:* I read it and truly I could say sooooooo much about that dilemma. The reality is that for teenagers in a world without Internet like today, seeing such a recognized doll with your same nationality it was more than enough to make us feel patriotic and proud. That's why I handed her down because I wanted my little cousins to feel like I did.
>
> *Woman #3:* What is fascinating for me is the note about how in 1997 there were 4 million inhabitants on the island versus 2.8 million in the U.S. In 20

years the figures have inversed almost exactly. Now there are more Puerto Ricans living in the U.S. than on the island. Everything else is the same shit people complain about Barbie. I had Barbies all my childhood and I didn't develop weight problems, or body image issues. Well, the only thing is that I wanted to be taller than the 5'4" I was given, but whatever we make do.

Woman #2: Nah, nothing like that. What I found funny was that the girls, for whom the dolls are made, were very happy. And I'm also 5'4", but that's what platform shoes are for.

Both Isabel and Woman #1 loved the clothes Puerto Rican Barbie wore. Her *jibarita* dress resembled the type of costume some students were asked to wear for school during the weeklong celebration of Puerto Rican culture (Semana de la Puertorriqueñidad or La Semana Puertorriqueña). During these celebrations, children are assigned roles related to Puerto Rico's history and centered on the island's first colonization. As a result, some students dress as Taínos, others as enslaved people from African countries, others as Spaniards, and others as *jíbaros*, which are the representation of the Puerto Rican—the person whose race was a mixture of the three races. While Barbie's colonial attire was also the focus of criticism (by being a light-skinned *jibarita*, Barbie was stripped of any indications of race and thus became neutral), it was this piece of the doll's accessories that made it clear for girls that she was a Puerto Rican doll. Because many girls usually dressed up in similar attire to the one Barbie was wearing, they further saw themselves reflected in the doll. (This was solidified even further when the representative for Puerto Rico in the Miss Universe pageant, Joyce Giraud, wore a similar dress and looked very similar to Puerto Rican Barbie during the traditional dress portion of the 1998 pageant in Hawaii.)

Parts of the conversations, and Isabel's memory of Puerto Rican Barbie, tapped into girls' identities focused on Puerto Rican national identity. As a commonwealth of the United States Puerto Rico does not have complete political and economic autonomy. As a result, Puerto Ricans have developed a cultural nationalism that renders the population *culturally* distinct from the nation to which it belongs (Negrón-Muntaner 2004). Negrón-Muntaner elaborates on this issue, explaining that "the most patent sign of Puerto Rican specificity is that the high-flying flag of Boricua pride does not represent a sovereign nation" (2004: 1). In fact, in an effort to suppress the independence movement in the island, legislature passed a law that prohibited various acts that demonstrated national pride. From 1948 until 1957, Law 53, better known as Ley de La Mordaza (or Gag Law in English) made it a crime to own or display a Puerto Rican flag, among other acts of pratriotism. While being a US territory and having a population that has American citizenship rather than its own, Puerto Rico gets to show cultural national pride, for example, when it sends representatives to worldwide beauty pageants, such as Miss Universe, and to sporting events, such as the Olympics. What the Puerto Rican Barbie represented then to the girls who accepted her was a symbol of nationality, or being one's own nation with one's own culture, not someone else's. The doll gave girls a feeling of national pride by seeing themselves represented in a famous icon such as Barbie. Furthermore, one of them even passed her doll on to her cousins because she wanted them to have the opportunity to see themselves reflected in a Barbie doll. Puerto Rican Barbie gave her such a sense of pride that she wanted future generations to enjoy her the way she did.

What the conversations reveal is a stark contrast between adults who were looking at Puerto Rican Barbie through a critical lens and the girls who were actually playing with the doll. Girls received the doll with open arms because for the first time in their lives *they* were part of the Barbie doll line. Some of the participants whose experiences I will discuss (e.g., Jessica, Mariela, and Isabel) felt they could not identify with Barbie dolls because they did not look like the dolls. Puerto Rican Barbie presented a space for representation, and even if the girls did not look like this new Barbie, they were still able to identify with her, knowing that the doll was from Puerto Rico. Despite the political issues embedded in the presentation of the doll, girls—who at the time did not have such easy access to images and role models closely related to them (as Woman #1 pointed out)—were happy to finally be able to identify with their dolls. When the women in the Facebook conversation learned about the debate this doll caused, they were surprised about it and also dismissive of it. For them, it was the same as usual: there's always something to criticize about Barbie. Instead, they felt that their case was "nothing like that," that this Barbie was simply a symbol that represented their own nationality and that gave them a deep sense of pride, even if Puerto Rican Barbie, like many Barbies in the "Dolls of the World" collection, was a colonial imagining catering to a white gaze.

Playful Transactions: Negotiating Colonialism through Barbie

During an informal conversation I had with a Puerto Rican academic, she shared with me that Barbie was never allowed in her house because the doll was a product of the United States. Her family, who are actively involved in the movement for Puerto Rico's independence from the United

States, did not allow Barbie in the house because it was a white US icon, not made in Puerto Rico, created for a mostly white audience, and read as a colonizing toy that attempted to impose cultural ideas from the colonizer. Unfortunately, she was not a participant of this study, and I was not able to interview her about this topic. Examples of experiences like hers did not come up during the interviews and conversations with the participants during this study. However, this is not meant to indicate that people have not experienced similar situations.[5] In my analysis of each participant's experience, I paid attention to whether their comments or experiences suggested that they perceived Barbie as a symbol of colonization. Despite having described encounters with Barbie's whiteness and the representation of race in the doll line, none of the participants examined Puerto Ricans' position as colonial subjects and Barbie's position as an American icon. However, some of their experiences of play with Barbie illustrated the various ways in which interactions with the doll could represent or enable connections with the United States and its culture. These experiences also illustrated ways in which colonialism was enacted in the home and how Barbie served as a space to resist it. There was one specific case in which traces of colonialism entered the Barbie play space. Originally, I was examining this aspect through the lens of Barbie as *colonizer*. What I did not realize, however, was that a completely different transaction was presented in one of my participant's encounters, one in which Barbie became an instrument of resistance *against* colonizing practices.

One participant, Carla (age thirty-three), negotiated her experiences with language and US culture through Barbie play. Carla, who in the present is very actively involved in the pro-independence movement, did not grow up in a household that rejected Barbie because it represented the colonizer. During our interview, Carla maintained that she did not buy Barbies for her daughters; however, this had more to do with the messages about the body that her daughters could receive from the doll and less about the doll's status as a symbol of American culture. Moreover, although Carla described her relationship with Barbie during her childhood as that of a "frenemy" (a friend who is an enemy at the same time), the enemy aspect came from the differences in their looks as opposed to Barbie's representation of the United States. Yet, Carla grew up in a house where her mother almost imposed American culture onto the children.

> Mom was . . . she exposed us to American culture a lot. So much that to this day—because I am married to a *gringo* all of my artisan colleagues call me *gringa*, we are the *gringos*—none of them believe that I am a *jíbara* from here. Because they hear me talking to other *gringos* and the accent with which I speak Spanish.

61

And I am not *gringa*. It's simply that my mom is *gringa*,[6] she imposed a *gringo* culture in our house. Not everyone knows this but, in my house, it was English all the time. We couldn't watch *telenovelas*. I had to watch *X-Files*, I had to watch Oprah, I had to watch *Days of Our Lives* because English was fundamental. She paid for cable TV so we could learn to speak English, not for us to be watching Telemundo or Wapa.[7] So in that aspect, [Barbie] was not a cultural shock because I learned about Puerto Rican culture when I was already older. In my house that cultural patriotism, like *I* am teaching my children now, that wasn't there. Because it was all Bon Jovi, it was Thanksgiving Day Parade, and the most culture-related thing I may have had was the Puerto Rican Day Parade in New York and the *fiestas patronales*.[8] So for me it wasn't a cultural shock because in reality I was already inside American culture in my house. (Carla, interview transcript)

Having a Puerto Rican mother who grew up in the United States and whom Carla described at various times as a *gringa* meant that Carla was very familiar with American popular culture. In the excerpt above, Carla begins by describing her contact with US culture as something that happened through exposure: she affirms her mother exposed her and her brother to music, TV shows, and the English language, to name a few examples. However, as Carla continues unfolding her memories, she begins describing this contact more as an imposition. She *could not* watch *telenovelas* but instead *had to* watch American soap operas such as *Days of Our Lives*, she *had to* watch *The X-Files*, she *had to* watch Oprah; she simply *had to*. Carla's obligatory exposure to TV shows and traditions from the United States immersed her in a culture that was somewhat different from her own. According to Carla, because of her immersion in American culture, her interactions with Barbie did not bring up cultural clashes. Although Barbie was part of that culture, Carla did not perceive her as an imposition or as an outsider who was not part of Carla's cultural knowledge. Instead, what brought Carla more difficulties and caused more of a clash in her own identity was the imposition of English as her primary language.

Not only were all the shows Carla *had to* watch and the traditions in which she *had to* participate from the United States, they were, more importantly, also in English. As she stated, her mother paid for cable, which gave them access to American television networks, so the children could learn English. Additionally, the language that Carla was almost required to speak in the house was English. When playing with Barbie, however, Carla used Spanish. In this way Barbie became an outlet to push against the imposition of the language that represents the colonizer. Carla's play with Barbie, or perhaps the language in which she engaged with Barbie, became a decolonizing practice. According to Carla, "My games [with Barbie] were in Spanish because Mom made us speak English, but I was always a little bit of a rebel about that, and so when I was home alone in my room with my dolls, I always spoke Spanish" (interview transcript).

Like that of most of the countries in Latin America and some islands in the Caribbean, the language spoken by the majority of the population in Puerto Rico is Spanish (though it is not the only language spoken). When the United States took control, a military government was established in order to support an Americanization project that would transform the island into a model of democracy in the Caribbean (Grosfoguel 2003). At the time, Puerto Rico was emerging from its colonial status under Spain. As a result, the island found itself in a relationship with a new colonial power whose language and cultural practices were entirely different. In colonial relationships, the colonizer often dismisses the local culture of the colony by silencing its language (Grosfoguel 2003; Memmi 1965; Mohanty 2003). As a result of being dehumanized by the colonizing forces, the colonized tends to accept and adopt the new ways of being in order to become more like the colonizer. What we can witness in the practices Carla's mother exerted in the household is the valorization of American culture over the local. Carla's mother required her children to become familiar with and immersed in US cultural practices so they could become "Americanized," i.e., more like the colonizer. These practices went beyond simply "learning about" US culture through TV shows and traditions. Carla was required to use the new colonizer's language as her main form of communication.

Language is ostensibly the greatest symbol of Puerto Rican identity, despite its rootedness in colonization. While Spanish was the language imposed during the island's first colonial encounter with Spain, and while its imposition eradicated the use of other languages and vernaculars (for example the Taíno language), Puerto Ricans have adopted Spanish as the language that represents their identity. Moreover, constant changes in language laws and policies in schools resulted in English and Spanish being in constant competition. The many attempts to impose English as the language of instruction in the Island solidified the United States, and therefore its language, as a symbol of colonization and imposition.[9] This led Puerto Ricans to value Spanish as the language that represented national identity. At the same time, Spanish became the language of resistance against English, even if it had been the language of the first colonizers. Anzaldúa (1987) writes about how language can be used as a form of oppression: by silencing, limiting, and creating *fronteras* or borders that delineate where a language can be spoken and where it cannot, people become oppressed. This belittles the oppressed or makes them feel belittled, unimportant, useless, and wrong. She describes her experiences with language: not being able to speak Spanish in school, her mother wanting her to sound American (no accent), and even having to take speech classes in college in order to get rid of her accent. By having to do this, pieces of her identity were taken away from her.

> For a people who are neither Spanish nor live in a country in which Spanish is the first language; for a people who live in a country in which English is the reigning tongue but who are not Anglo; for a people who cannot entirely identify with either standard (formal, Castillian) Spanish nor standard English, what recourse is left to them but to create their own language? A language which they can connect their identity to, one capable of communicating the realities and values true to themselves—a language with terms that are neither *español ni inglés*, but both. We speak a patois, a forked tongue, a variation of two languages. (Anzaldúa 1987: 55)

For Anzaldúa, the memories of her experiences with language—English, Spanish, and Spanglish—serve as a vehicle to overcome the oppression and silence and use them as tools in the present. They are not negative experiences anymore but rather memories that empower her in the present, as she can critically think of them and their meaning. In a similar manner, Carla's mother delimited which language should be spoken and where it was appropriate to do so, perhaps imposing the use of English so that her children would become "more American." Carla, then, adopted Spanish as the language of resistance against the imposition of English. Just as a large part of the population in Puerto Rico did, Carla perceived English as an imposition and, thus, a colonizing practice. Notably, in Carla's experience it was the *language* rather than the *doll* itself that was seen as a threat to her own cultural identity. Furthermore, it was through her doll play that Carla fought against this imposition by adopting Spanish as the language for doll play.

Play "offers a key site to begin negotiating certain of the fears and tensions intrinsic to one's cultural and social environment" (Wertheimer 2006: 219). Carla's use of a Barbie doll to subvert the imposition of English in her house illustrated another way in which girls encounter their identities by appropriating objects in order to negotiate those identities, especially related to their cultural and social environments. What becomes even more fascinating in Carla's negotiations is that Barbie—the white, blond "American" Barbie (most of Carla's Barbie dolls were of this kind)—became the vehicle through which she exerted resistance toward the very same culture

THE POLITICS OF BARBIE IN PUERTO RICO

the doll represented. It is important to note that Carla's use of Spanish is not an exception in the play practices of Puerto Rican girls. Just as Spanish was the language in which most of my participants communicated with me during our interviews, most girls in Puerto Rico would play using Spanish, which is the majority of the population's first language. Yet, what is special about Carla's situation, which may be the case for more girls on the island, is that English was the language spoken in her house. Hence, the use of Spanish helped Carla challenge the imposition of the "other" language and construct her own cultural identity through Barbie play.

The experience Carla shared with me was particularly enlightening, especially since I had been approaching encounters with colonialism from a completely different standpoint. My original methodology had positioned Barbie as a representation of the colonizer (the United States), and as such I wanted to find out if girls and women had rejected Barbie because of her position. The example presented through the informal conversation with the professor whose parents did not allow Barbie because she represented the United States serves as an indication that this does indeed happen in Puerto Rican households. However, it was not something that took place in any of my participants' experiences. When my approach shifted, due to a moment of realization about the role of language in Puerto Rican identity, I uncovered a different trace of colonization in Barbie play. In Carla's experience, Barbie was not a symbol of the colonizer, and her presence in the girl's life was not perceived as colonizing. Instead, it was Carla's mother that was bringing traces of colonialism into the house by imposing English as the primary, often exclusive, language. Interestingly, Barbie served as a vehicle of resistance and became a space where Carla could push against colonizing impositions.

Between Two Lands:
Transnational Movements of Doll and Self

Many Puerto Ricans' experience can be described as a *vaivén*, a coming and going, a back and forth between the archipelago and the continental United States. The concept, Duany explains, "implies that some people do not stay put in one place for a long period of time but move incessantly, like the wind or the waves of the sea, in response to shifting tides" (2002: 2). More ominously, he adds, "it connotes unsteadiness, inconsistency, and oscillation" (Duany 2002: 2). The movement, as connoted by the metaphor of waves, is not always permanent but may instead occur as a transient flow where populations are in constant movement.

As seen in the stories of Judith Ortiz Cofer (1990) and Esmeralda Santiago (1993, 1999), many Puerto Rican girlhoods take place in this movement between the island and the United States. This experience was illustrated by some of the participants whose childhoods were spent shifting from one place to another until there was a more permanent, though not necessarily finalized, settlement. Among the participants of this study, five experienced the *vaivén* from Puerto Rico to the United States or vice versa during their childhood years. Sisters Lourdes and Carmen, for instance were born in Puerto Rico and lived there a few years before moving to Key West, Florida. After a couple of years there, they moved back to Puerto Rico. This occurred when they were young, and Carmen had not yet started school. Lisa (age forty-five) was born in New York, but her family moved to Puerto Rico when she was three years of age. Frankie (age thirty) was born in Puerto Rico, but her parents moved the family to the United States when she was young, and she lived there until she was ten years old. Most of the migration movements between the two lands are caused by economic necessities, as populations from the island move to the United States in search of better opportunities. In this sense Puerto Ricans become transnational subjects of two lands. And, for some of them, Barbie became a constant companion, crossing geographical boundaries not only as a product to be sold but also as a friend.

When asked if her experience with Barbie had always been positive and if she had always liked the doll, one participant, Patricia (age fifty-nine), opened up about the ways in which her immersion in Barbie's world during her girlhood was essential. "Yes, all my life," she responded about whether she had always liked Barbie, then added:

> My parents got divorced, and I was left orphaned when I was nine. I came [to Puerto Rico] with my grandmother, and they stayed over there [in New York]. So I came here with my grandma, and all that pain and all that stuff, I would just focus on her [Barbie]. . . . And then, you know, all of that mess from when they were getting divorced and of coming here alone with my grandma and cousins, this helped. For me, Barbie helped. Because I was in her world, not in the world I was living. It helped me a lot. So, I didn't even realize what was happening. I would lock myself in my bedroom, and if my parents fought, I was just playing with her. (Patricia, Group 4 transcript)

Having amassed a collection of 233 Barbie dolls as an adult, Patricia clearly exemplifies passion about Barbie. Yet, she is not just a collector.

Gathering and taking care of Barbie is her way, it seems, of saying "thank you" to the doll that accompanied her through difficult moments in her life, especially her parents' divorce, which forced her to move from New York to Puerto Rico.

In the case of my participants, not all transnational experiences took place by physically moving from one place to another. For some girls, transnationalism transpired in their homes in the form of Barbie. As Negrón-Muntaner notes, "Barbie is one of the most globalized toys in history . . . as well as the most transnational of American icons" (2002: 39). Carla, specifically, remembered how Barbie came into her life as a transnational object. Her mother used to go to the United States and buy the dolls, and she would also ask Carla's aunt from New York to send some or bring some when she visited. Having this movement of the doll from the United States directly into her house provided Carla with a sense of exclusiveness because she had access to dolls that not everyone around her did: "Many Barbies would arrive to my house that weren't available in Puerto Rico because my mom would ask my aunt to get them in New York. And when my mom would go to California for work, she would return with two or three Barbie dolls" (Carla, interview transcript).

Transnationalism with Barbie did not need to take place only through the movement of the doll or by having access to exclusive versions that were only available in the United States. As I previously stated, Mattel markets Barbie dolls and related products as vehicles through which girls can imagine and dream of becoming someone else. This was illustrated through some of the narratives my participants shared about their play with Barbie. By becoming someone else through Barbie play, many girls created an imaginary transnational movement in which they are granted an imagined upward mobility. Morgan (n.d.) argues that the Barbie doll is a medium of communication that instills capitalist American values in those who play with her by placing importance on money, beauty, and upward mobility. Looking at these values from the standpoint of Puerto Rico's sociopolitical relationship with the United States Barbie can be seen as a vehicle through which American cultural values are transmitted and as a medium for Puerto Rican girls to imagine the possibilities they could be afforded through the "American Dream."

It can be said that Barbie's message that "you can be anything" and her ability to have many professions and a luxurious lifestyle represent the American dream, where anyone can be anything as long as they work hard in the "land of opportunities." Times of great economic recession have

led Puerto Ricans to move to the United States in search of better opportunities to thrive economically. The 1950s, when Barbie first came out
and when the first generation of Barbie players were growing up, saw the
largest migration (at the time) of Puerto Ricans to the United States.[10] In
the present, the economic recession that began in 2005 has led to Puerto
Ricans leaving the island for the continental US in numbers not seen since
the 1950s.[11] Barbie serves as a (false) model of how to achieve success and
upward mobility to fully live up to the American Dream. Through her,
girls can envision the life that could supposedly be attained through hard
work in the United States and the possible rewards of their work.

Making Sense of Contradictions

The discussions provided in this chapter began considering the relationship between Puerto Rico and the United States more closely in relation
to Barbie play. While the discussion about Puerto Rico and its status as a
commonwealth of the United States had emerged in 1997 with the arrival
of the Puerto Rican Barbie, not much else had been said about the topic
in the context of Barbie play. This chapter, then, began the conversation
and provided the much-needed but often-forgotten experiences of girls.
The conversations presented here suggest that girls can find ways to use
Barbie against colonizing practices (as showed by the example of Carla)
and that they welcomed any indication of Puerto Rican identity applied
to Barbie. As seen in the example of Carla, Barbie further helps children
construct their identity. Carla's perception of Barbie as a "frenemy," with
whom she could identify in certain respects but from whom she was also
very different, was a recurring theme in our conversations (which I explore
in subsequent chapters).

Yet, with Barbie play, Carla was able to construct part of her identity
in relation to the impositions her mother exerted. Through subversion
with Barbie, Carla "broke" the rules and fashioned her own cultural identity (Puerto Rican). Similarly, the Puerto Rican Barbie provided a space
for Puerto Rican girls to form a national identity. For participant Isabel, as
well as the women in the Facebook conversation, the doll that provoked
such a heated debate about Puerto Ricans in two lands was the very same
doll that ignited a deep sense of pride and love for their culture. No matter
the context, the experiences of girlhood are multiple, complex, and in flux
for each individual that traverses through them.

Notes

1. In the mid-1950s, the makers of the first birth control pill, Enovid, conducted trial testing on poor Puerto Ricans on the island. The women were not asked for consent. In fact, they were never informed that they were taking part of a trial for medication or that there would be risks involved. Three women died from these experiments.

2. For example, Puerto Ricans vote for their own governor, mayors, senators, etc., but even as US citizens, they do not vote for the president of the United States. Moreover, the Jones Act of 1917, which granted US citizenship to Puerto Ricans, also restricts Puerto Rico's trade by requiring the acquisition of goods "from an American-made ship with an American crew" (Bury 2015).

3. Because Puerto Rican Barbie was part of a larger series of collectible dolls, adults were also the targeted audience.

4. I have memories of playing with the doll despite the fact that it was a special edition doll. It was the only time my mother had bought a special edition Barbie doll, and she did not want anyone to play with it. In my memories, there were two of them in my house: one for play and one for collection. While I could not find the one that I supposedly had played with, my mother was able to produce the one for collection, still intact inside its box.

5. I plan to investigate this an aspect of the experiences of Puerto Rican girls with Barbie in more depth in the future.

6. Carla's mother was born and raised in the United States, but she is Puerto Rican (or Nuyorican). While the term "gringo" is typically used to refer to white people, which her mother is not, Carla's usage of it referred to her mother's immersion in US culture.

7. Telemundo and Wapa are two of the Puerto Rican local TV stations/channels.

8. *Fiestas patronales* is the festival each municipality of Puerto Rico holds to celebrate their patron Saint.

9. For example, by 1900 the United States imposed English as the only language in schools as a strategy for assimilation. At the same time, it also prohibited national symbols such as the Puerto Rican flag (Grosfoguel 2003). The imposition of English and Puerto Rican identity has been the subject of study for many researchers on the island, especially in the context of English education (see, for example, Algren de Gutierrez 1987; Barreto 2001; Pousada 1996; and Torres-Gonzalez 2002).

10. According to data from the Center for Puerto Rican Studies, "over 4,200 individuals were estimated to have arrived in the United States each year in the period between 1946 and 1956" (Korrol n.d.: par. 1).

11. According to the Pew Research Center, "U.S. Census Bureau data show that 144,000 more people left the island for the mainland than the other way around from mid-2010 to 2013" (Cohn, Patten, and Lopez 2014: par. 2)

ಲ

Chapter 3

Fashioning a Self
Experiences of Body and
Feminine Identities with Barbie

> Does Barbie foster an unhealthy body image and a superficial ideal of woman-
> hood? Does her essential racial European whiteness (even in ethnic versions)
> marginalize little girls of color? Does she instill an ethic of consumerism? Or
> does Barbie enable imaginative play and provide a safe forum for girls to explore
> femininity and sexuality?
>
> —Wendy Singer Jones (1999), "Barbie's Body Project"

Carmen and Lourdes, two sisters in their sixties, only had one Barbie doll
each when they were growing up. As a result, they resorted to creativity in
order to produce their play. Carmen asserts, "Because it was only one doll,
everything else was . . . What happens is that times come for . . . Emily for
example you didn't have just one Barbie, you had five because you had to
have the doctor, the nurse . . . and for us, you could do everything with just
one Barbie" (Carmen, Group 1 transcript). This creativity extended to their
imaginative play with Barbie when no other doll was involved. When playing "wedding," Carmen enjoyed creating dresses for Barbie and turning objects into something new, like using sewing pins as earrings. Furthermore,

---

Notes for this section can be found on page 97.

her Barbie would marry an imaginary boyfriend because she did not own a Ken doll. Lourdes and Carmen mostly interacted with Barbie through her nature as a fashion doll. They enjoyed changing the doll's clothes and creating more outfits for her. Based on my participants' stories, one of the most notable commonalities among the generation that grew up in the 1960s is that their experiences of Barbie play revolved around playing dress-up with the doll. As described various times by sisters Carmen and Lourdes, and also expressed by avid collector Patricia (age fifty-nine), the point of playing Barbie for them as well as the fun of it was dressing Barbie in her high fashion clothes. In addition, Patricia's play also included some fantasy in that she assigned Barbie different roles. She explained:

> You would dress them up and you would dream that you were a model, a teacher, or a nurse and that was your imagination. I'm sure that many girls became nurses and doctors by dreaming about that. I was a teacher . . . I didn't even study [when I was little]. I would come home and run to play with them. I mean, I would go into that world. That was my world. I would go into my room and there they would get married, have children, go to parties. I would go into my word of fantasy with my dolls. (Patricia, Group 4 transcript)

Part of the appeal of Barbie play is the opportunity it provides girls to become other people, imagine aspects of adult life they have yet to experience—such as having a job—and mold the doll to become exactly what they want her to be. Mattel has adopted this idea in various advertising campaigns for Barbie, as the company presents Barbie as a tool to use for imagining and dreaming. Several of my participants remember playing with Barbie in precisely this way. In addition to playing in scripted ways or living vicariously through Barbie, for many girls interacting with Barbie meant confronting the doll's many complexities and experiencing complicated feelings toward her. The previous chapter illustrated how one doll, Puerto Rican Barbie, elicited contradictory feelings from various groups within Boricuas (Puerto Ricans) and even within the same individual interacting with her. She is a fraught object that can bring joy to the child playing with while also causing that child frustration, especially when the child pays attention to Barbie's body, looks, and lifestyle of opulence.

Barbie Play Allowed Us to Be Ourselves

One of the main motivations for studying different generations of Puerto Rican women and girls who interacted with Barbie was to explore the similarities and differences in the range of interactions. By studying various generations, I wanted to find out what has changed and what has remained the same through the years. This chapter presents narratives my participants shared about how they came in contact with Barbie, how they played with her, what roles they assigned, and other aspects of Barbie play. The stories presented throughout the chapter represent five generations of Puerto Rican women and girls. The interactions with Barbie they narrated often included other products besides the doll, and for some participants the interactions occurred in private, where they could let their imagination run without any outside judgment.

Lisa (age forty-five), for example, used Barbie dolls to engage in conversations when she was alone. She grew up with one brother and no sisters, and so playing was often a solitary activity; when she played by herself, she created dialogues with Barbie dolls. Inspired by her grandmother, a seamstress, Lisa also kept herself entertained by sewing doll clothes. More vividly, Lisa remembered creating stories in her head:

> I would get home from school, and I would play. I would make a lot of stories in my head, like the *telenovelas* (soap operas) because my grandmother watched a lot of *telenovelas*. [*Laughs*] So, I had Barbie. I did like dressing her up and taking her on a stroll. Sometimes I'd even take her on my bicycle. My bicycle had a little basket. I do remember a lot making up things. I would entertain myself with my imagination because we didn't have a lot of distractions at that time. You had to make up your own games. So, because my grandmother watched a lot of *telenovelas*, I would make those stories in my play. I also watched *Wonder Woman* and *Charlie's Angels*, so my Barbies and dolls were them. And so, I made a lot of stories, I took the dolls out, and I made them clothes. . . . But the memories I have were—I don't remember playing Barbie with other girls. Barbies were my friends. (Lisa, Group 3 transcript)

Comparable to Lisa, girls from the generations that followed hers also found inspiration from and created stories akin to those they would see on TV. For instance, Alondra (age thirty-two), who grew up in the 1980s, remembered her episodes of Barbie play being "pretty normal, taken from everyday life and from television" (Alondra, e-mail interview). Her dolls had boyfriends, had jobs, went to the store, and had a family and friends. Jessica (age thirty) and Mariela (age twenty-nine) also used TV shows as inspiration for creating stories, although Jessica noted that her play with Barbie did not incorporate as much storytelling and imagination as Mariela's did.

> Jessica: I liked games that used a lot of imagination, but sitting down with Barbie and imagining things like you two [Mariela and Emily], no. It was like more basic.

Mariela: No, I used to do a lot of soap operas. In fact, I would begin a game on Friday, continue it on Saturday, and if I could, I would keep it going on Sunday. And I could spend the whole weekend inside my bedroom playing with Barbie. I would get out to eat and come back in again. And I would play the *whole* day. It was a routine, and I would imitate an adult's daily life.

Emily: If something happened at school, for example, did you include that in your game?

Mariela: I don't think so.

Emily: I can't remember exactly what my games were about.

Mariela: I never related it like that. The names I used were from *telenovelas*. I never interpreted, I mean, I never took the game to reality. Even if I was mad at something from school, I never related it. (Jessica and Mariela, Group 2 transcript)

In this part of the conversation, Mariela explained how she used Barbie play to imitate and imagine what adults' daily life was like. Most of the references came from watching and creating situations like the ones she would see on Hispanic soap operas. Just as Mariela's example elucidates, part of the scholarship on Barbie discusses how girls play with the doll to both imagine themselves being adults (e.g., having jobs or having children) and incorporate moments of their own lives.

Hains (2012) and Hohmann (1985) examined girls' use of dolls to recreate, negotiate, or even change the outcome of real events from their lives. Some girls used their dolls to reenact moments of racism they had experienced at school (Hains 2012), while in another case a girl used Barbie as a device to imagine having control over her own lived experiences—for example, taking on the role of a mother who disciplines a child (Hohmann 1985). This was one of the ways Carla (age thirty-three) engaged in Barbie play during the early years of her childhood. Carla often used her dolls to recreate scenarios of movies she loved, but more importantly, she also used them to express herself in ways she did not think she could or was allowed to as a child:

When I was little there were two movies that I liked a lot. They were *Pretty Woman* and *Lambada*. So, because I knew the dialogue [*laughs*] of the movies, well I would use the dialogue from the movies and scenes from the movies. Also, a lot of times it was improvised, made up. I also remember that other times it was like including everyday life, like situations that happen, I remember. I remember I used Barbie a lot when I had things that I wanted to say that, you know, sometimes when you're little no one wants to listen to you. So, like, "No one loves me . . ." So, a doll would be Barbie's mom and be like, "Don't worry. Everything will be okay." And she would pat her on the back. You know? (Carla, interview transcript)

73

When children play, they may be imitating what they see others, especially adults, do. In dramatic play, the child may dramatize events in which she is not a direct participator, such as by recreating scenes from a TV show (Hughes 2002). These were the forms of dramatic play many of the girls—Lisa, Mariela, Carla, and even I—were having with Barbie. Yet, there are instances when the doll is used to explore more deeply the events girls experience—Carla used Barbie in this way. When children engage in dramatic play, they are also representing in their own way their understanding of the experiences rather than simply imitating what they see others do. They use objects, actions, and storylines to symbolize the topics that concern them (Leong and Bodrova 2012). For Carla in particular, Barbie became the vehicle through which she could express feelings she would not express otherwise. She gave Barbie the role of a mother when it was needed in order to appease and console another doll—this represented something she wanted in real life but was not receiving. As she stated, playing like this with Barbie was a form "of relief, channeling, in a way that a child could do it" (Carla, interview transcript).

For various reasons, dramatic play with Barbie in my participants' experiences often transpired in private—they played with Barbie by themselves. As some of them pointed out, creating complex narratives that were often dramatic was not something they necessarily wanted to share with others. In studying girlhood, McRobbie and Garber (1991) encouraged researchers to consider the domestic sphere as a primary site for youth recreation. Generally, Barbie play occurs in private—mainly in the child's bedroom. Bedrooms, according to Adams, "were where children nurtured their own individuality by spending time alone-playing, reading, or simply thinking" (1995: 173). During the preteen years bedrooms become, as Mitchell and Reid-Walsh note, "increasingly a private play zone," especially for middle-class children (2002: 124). Mariela and Jessica discussed their own play practices as something that was private, which allowed for their play to manifest without any outside interruptions:

> Mariela: I remember that I made a house, a whole neighborhood in my bedroom. The main house or the house where I participated was behind the door, and no one was allowed to enter my bedroom, it was forbidden.
> Jessica: You know, I liked more playing by myself because I dared to think, to imagine, and there wasn't anyone bothering me. Being by myself, I would let my imagination go. I liked being alone more.
> Mariela: Me too. I would lock myself for some hours. . . . I would really make a soap opera.
> [. . .]

Emily: [*To Jessica*] I don't know if I played Barbie with you. I remember that with Mariela I would go to her house on Saturdays, and I brought my bag full of Barbies. . . . I remember that I liked to play alone in my bedroom, and I would spend hours there. And with my sisters, Camille says we did play a little, but for me it was like that. If I was very creative, I didn't want anyone to make fun of me or for anyone to know what I was saying. (Group 2 transcript)

When I was little, I shared a bedroom with my two sisters. It was not a large room, so it was often crowded. I used the moments of solitude when my sisters were not in the room to play with my dolls. Of the three of us, I was the one who played with Barbie dolls the most. Playing with Barbie dolls (and other toys) was a time for being by myself and creating different scenarios with them. I never wanted to be bothered or for people to see me playing. My interactions with Barbie, as well as Jessica's and Mariela's, were mostly private because we believed the presence of outsiders would hinder our creativity, limit our imagination, or would make us feel judged. The only people with whom I felt comfortable playing were those who created dramatic scenarios like mine, for instance Mariela.

Like that of other participants, Carla's play also took place mostly in her bedroom, although in her case the location was not about maintaining privacy or being afraid of receiving judgment. While she enjoyed play by herself and also with friends, it transpired in the bedroom because that was the area designated by her mother.

Carla: [Barbie play happened] in my room. Yes, I didn't take that out. I didn't dare. My mom didn't let me. It [Barbie] was sacred.

Emily: Was it because you were embarrassed?

Carla: No. When I was little, I was never embarrassed. It was when I was older, when I was about twelve or thirteen. So in school some girls, there were some that at thirteen who were already going out and drinking at pubs. So, I wasn't going to say, "I'm playing with Barbie" when one girl would arrive drunk to the ninth grade. No! I wasn't going to say that! [*Laughs*] But no, it was that my mom was very protective of my toys, and she said it was better in the bedroom. (Carla, interview transcript)

Beyond following her mother's instructions, Carla kept her play private once she entered her teenage years because it was an activity in which very few of her friends participated. According to Mitchell and Reid-Walsh:

There are some tastes that children cannot reveal in public. If a girl still plays with Barbie at age ten and none of her friends do then there is no way she can easily express this in a group. . . . By contrast—behind closed (at least partly closed) doors—bedroom-as-playrooms offer possibilities for exploring popular culture artifacts in ways that are less socially governed. (2002: 118)

Once a teenager, Carla kept Barbie even more private because it was not something she could do freely in front of her peers. In Carla's perspective, her interactions with Barbie served to keep her away from behaviors, such as drinking, in which her peers were engaging. The contrast between her peers' more "adult" activities and her play with dolls, which was viewed as a "child's" activity, became embarrassing for her and thus something she could not share with all of her friends. Many researchers had described girls' bedrooms as "'passive space[s]' . . . associated with minimal physical activity'" (Steele and Brown 1995, as cited in Kearney 2007: 131). Kearney questions these assumptions, arguing that girls have agency even in their bedroom culture. What these examples demonstrate is that girls use Barbie play to negotiate, or push against, and to come to terms with different ideas. Because Barbie play was mostly taking place in the girls' bedrooms, these examples show that the bedroom becomes a place of agency for girls and Barbie becomes a vehicle to achieve it.

Performing a Self through Barbie Artifacts

Girls may also negotiate, resist, or come to terms with lived experiences through other Barbie products and artifacts. Interactions with Barbie occur not only with the doll but also through other products that carry the "Barbie" name. Every year the cornucopia of Barbie products that extend girls' play interactions with the icon—books, magazines, computer games, board games, bicycles, trading cards, movies, and music cassettes, to name a few—continues to grow, providing more spaces for Barbie to be part of girls' lives. Many of my participants identified other Barbie products that they owned during their childhood or with which they interacted in some way. In some cases, the interactions with these products were more common than the interactions with the actual doll, as they were in Camille's case, for instance. For others, these products would sometimes become part of the play with the doll, where girls could continue or expand the exchanges that occurred through doll play onto new forms. The following examples illustrate Barbie's great impact on girlhoods, Puerto Rican girlhoods in this case, by becoming part of girls' lives through other means beyond doll play. Camille (age thirty-two) did not play much with Barbie, but she remembered interacting with other products, such as a Barbie sticker book. During the interview, she was also trying to remember if she owned a Barbie head whose purpose was for girls to practice makeup and hairstyles. Camille recalled having interacted with it and always wanting it because she enjoyed "doing things with the [dolls'] hair" the most (Camille, Group 1 transcript). Carla, who is the same age as Camille, owned some of the same Barbie artifacts as Camille, including a pair of roller skates "that said 'Barbie'" (Carla, interview transcript). Carla also owned Barbie VHS movies and a fashion book with stencils with which the player could create many outfit combinations. Just like Camille, Gabriela (age twenty-five) had Barbie sticker books, and during my visit to her house she showed me one that had survived. She also played Barbie computer games, used Barbie notebooks for school, and owned a copy of the movie *Barbie in the Nutcracker.*

My interactions with Barbie extended to a wide variety of products. I remember having a Barbie Halloween costume, a Barbie exercise video (*Dance! Workout with Barbie*), a Barbie Power Wheels car, miniature Barbie dolls from the McDonald's Happy Meal, a set of binoculars, and a camera, among possibly other products. I remember that the binoculars came with a miniature set for the dolls[1] and that the Barbie camera was possibly my first real picture camera. Isabel (age thirty) was a fan of Barbie as well, and her interactions were not limited to just the doll. During our group interview, she shared pictures of two other Barbie artifacts that were part of her experiences with the doll: a Barbie Power Wheels car, like the one I had, and a certificate of her membership in the official Barbie Fan Club. Her mother subscribed her to the official Barbie Fan Club after seeing it advertised on one of the dolls' packages. Being part of the club provided Isabel an interaction with Barbie that differed from all the other participants. In addition to "authenticating" Isabel as a fan of the doll, it offered more products that expanded her encounters with Barbie:

> They sent me Barbie bracelets, they sent me letters, for my birthday they sent me a card. They gave me the ID. They sent me pictures of Barbie, like this one which they sent me for my birthday. (Isabel, Group 3 transcript; see figure 3.1)

The examples from my participants' interactions with other Barbie products illustrate how Barbie maintains a strong presence in girls' lives and how she becomes part of their identities even through other means. The level of interaction varied among participants, as some of them had more ancillary products than others. In addition, these products differed in purpose—while some were other types of toys, others invited a different form of interaction (e.g., the Barbie Fan Club). Among my participants, Carla had one of the most elaborate play experiences that occurred with other Barbie artifacts; she used the content of the Barbie magazine to develop a play practice different from what she had been doing before:

After about age twelve I didn't play Barbie with anyone else anymore. What happened was that after—when I turned ten, I saw the Barbie magazines for the first time. So when I was ten, that modality of Barbie magazines featured photomontages as if they were comics. So they would put Barbie with her house, and then they took pictures of that, and they added dialogue, and it was like a comic. So that for me completely changed the method, like the game modality. When I saw the magazine, I transformed my play with Barbie to make the comic. . . . I remember that . . . I had my thirty-five-millimeter camera, and I would put my Barbie in the tree or with the car, with Ken and I would take pictures. . . . So that's when the whole dynamic of the game changed when I was a preteenager. It wasn't so much like in the beginning when Barbie and Ken were like [makes kissing sound], and Barbie and Teresa were like talking. . . . But that's also why I changed the whole dynamic [with Barbie] because there came a time when it truly bored me. It bored me to change their clothes so much, it bored me that only she had a boyfriend, it bored me that all her friends were in love with her boyfriend. Like there was a point when reality crashed with the imaginary world of Barbie. And I played with Barbie, but secretly I hated Barbie. Because she was independent, she was a doctor, she was an astronaut, she was a lawyer, she was like seventy years old and looked twenty-five. [Laughs] And she had a younger sister, and she played with her. And so I was little, and my parents didn't play with me. It's like a lot of stuff from when you're little, and so at one point I said, "Let's play but in a different way." (Carla, interview transcript)

Coupling the Barbie magazines with her Barbie dolls elicited for Carla a new negotiation with the doll. Through the images Carla saw in the Barbie magazine, she began changing the way she interacted with Barbie dolls to create her own product. Although the photographs she took of her dolls did not survive to the present, Carla remembered the process of taking pictures of her dolls to create a sort of scrapbook that resembled a comic book and enjoying that aspect of Barbie play more than merely changing the dolls' clothes and creating dramatic scenarios. More importantly, Carla describes in her account all the ways she used Barbie as a girl to create, challenge, and question her identity. Her views on Barbie were continuously shifting—from admiration to jealousy, from love to hate—just as her type of play with Barbie also changed. Once she entered her teenage years, Carla became bored with the way she was expected to play with Barbie, and she grew tired of Barbie being the central figure while the rest of Barbie's friends were supposed to desire what Barbie had. Recreating the magazine spreads, however, offered new opportunities to continue exploring her identities, to grow along with Barbie with more autonomy in terms of how she could create with Barbie objects, and to choose what type of role the doll would play in her life.

Figure 3.1. Barbie birthday gift for Isabel from the official Fan Club. Photograph by author.

Although girls create their own scenarios and assign their own roles to Barbie, as demonstrated by some of the participants previously mentioned, Barbie play in Carla's understanding consisted of making blond Barbie the protagonist, Ken her object of affection, and the other dolls secondary actors. After all, this was how Mattel generally presented the dolls in the Barbie line. All the interactions with Barbie led Carla to develop a love/hate relationship with the doll. As an independent career woman Barbie was everything that Carla admired and had everything Carla wanted, including a sister or someone to play with as well as undying youth. Thus, Carla's interactions with a different Barbie product allowed her to adapt her play practices and engagements with the doll to fit her needs and interrogate her own continuously emerging identities.

In the present, girls continue to experience Barbie not only through the dolls but also (and sometimes more often) through other products. The three girls that participated in this study, who at the time played with

79

Barbie, illustrate Barbie's continuing presence in girls' lives beyond doll play: through books, DVDs, shows on Netflix, and videos on YouTube. Two sisters, K.C. and Annie, eleven and nine years old respectively, talked about the various media they used to interact with Barbie stories. They particularly enjoyed interacting with a book in which Barbie shows different careers that girls can aspire to and explains what each career entails.

> K.C.: This is a book about Barbie about what I want to be when I grow up. There is a cheerleader, a veterinarian, a racecar driver, a ballerina, chef, rocker, and a wedding planner.
> Emily: So, with this book, which has different careers, when Barbie and the others play, do they also have careers?
> Annie: Yes. Like, for example. She has to go to work. Like one is a veterinarian, one is a chef . . .
> Emily: So, they had their jobs.
> Annie: It's like they are real people. (K.C. and Annie, Group 6 transcript)

The sisters' interactions with this book allowed them to explore certain careers that Barbie has had throughout the years. As Annie pointed out, sometimes they incorporated these into their play with the dolls because they use the dolls to imitate what "real people" do. Moreover, this Barbie product and the doll itself inspired K.C. to imagine the possibility of becoming a fashion designer, and she expressed during the interview that she loved to draw. In fact, she had already drawn various designs. Similarly, Sharon, who was eight at the time, also interacted with Barbie through videos and movies, and, like K.C., she was interested in design. Sharon's mother described her as someone who is artistic and who loves fashion. Sharon drew and created her own fashion designs and used her knowledge to repurpose objects and turn them into accessories or outfits for her dolls (for example, turning a hair scrunchie into a shrug). Describing her interest in fashion, Sharon said:

> I have my little diary of fashion things that I do not let anybody look at. . . . Sometimes—I have three dolls and I have two that I like to play and design because this part is like all stuffing. So, I kinda like use them like pincushions and put the clothes on them to like have a place like they're sturdy. And then at the end I sew them. I made them both bathing suits. (Sharon, Group 5 transcript)

K.C.'s and Sharon's experiences resemble those of many girls, including some of the participants in this study—Carmen, Patricia, Camille, Isabel, and Emily—who expressed that at some point during their girlhood they dreamed of becoming a fashion designer. But was this a dream we all had and which we could somewhat fulfill *through* Barbie, or was it a dream we thought we had to achieve *because* of Barbie? Fashion is, after all at the root of Barbie's genesis. She was first and foremost a teenage fashion model. Clothes, accessories, makeup, and luxury are at the forefront of Barbie's life in toys, books, shows, movies, video games, and other media.

Mattel's presentation of Barbie and related products as vehicles through which girls can imagine, create, dream, and become someone/something else was illustrated through the narratives my participants shared about their play with Barbie. Contemporary girls, exemplified through Sharon, K.C., and Annie, continue to use Barbie dolls and products to explore their identities either by following or rejecting Barbie's ideas of femininity or by assigning roles to the dolls through which they can explore them. Their practices support what the scholarship about girls and identity construction suggests: that girls often use dolls to reconfigure meanings and ideas inscribed by society about what it means to be a girl (Weida 2011; Wohlwend 2009, 2015). Some of the aforementioned stories depict moments in which girls used Barbie dolls and products to create their own stories about girlhood and to dream about becoming someone else.

The previous stories of girls' experiences with Barbie begin to showcase Barbie's influence on girls' lives. Through their interactions with Barbie culture, my participants constructed ideas of how they envisioned themselves and who they wanted to be. As previously explained, it is common for girls to use Barbie to construct identities, to question them, to negotiate them, and to encounter issues that are important to them. At the same time, these issues may not be so apparent to them during their girlhood but become critical to their identities once they become adults. For better or for worse, the culture of Barbie centers on femininity, class, and the body. With this in mind, the next section expands on girls' and women's use of Barbie to talk about, explore, create, or question their identities, and it presents my participants' encounters with two important aspects of Barbie culture: femininity and body image.

Teaching to Be a Girl: Barbie as the Epitome of Femininity

Many girls learn that in order to "be a girl" they *must* like Barbie. In the conversation with my family, my aunt made an observation that summarizes Barbie's role as the epitome of femininity and marker of normative girlhood: "It's just that at that time [the 1960s], a *girl* could not be without a Barbie" (Lourdes, Group 1 transcript). Lourdes, however, was not the only participant who identified Barbie as an artifact that girls had to have. Jessica mentioned that she never experienced opposition from her parents to play with Barbie because the doll was held as the "classic" girl object. She perceived how everyone believed that "if you're a girl, you *have* to like Barbie. And it was like automatic. Every Christmas you'd get one" (Jessica, Group 2 transcript). Carla stated that she used Barbie because "all the girls played with Barbie" (Carla, interview transcript). The idea received by these and other participants from those around them was that if you were a girl, you needed to have a Barbie doll. Notably, for most of the participants Barbie was also an artifact they desired and enjoyed, but their assertions elucidate Barbie's status as the epitome of femininity and the quintessential "girl" toy. In response to this idea, some girls preferred not to interact with Barbie. Elsa (age twenty-eight), who participated briefly in a group interview, remembered having received Barbie dolls as birthday presents but never paying much attention to them. As she explained, "My mom knew that I did not like them, so she didn't buy them, but other people would give them to me for my birthday, but I didn't pay much attention. . . . It's just that I saw them so plastic, I don't know. I didn't see myself in Barbie" (Elsa, Group 3 transcript). Her disassociation with Barbie came as a result of not seeing herself reflected in Barbie, not so much in the doll's physical appearance but rather in the ideas of femininity it represented.

Girls also learn to be girls through Barbie when they receive messages about femininity embodied in the image created for Barbie—for example, that femininity is almost exclusively about fashion and beauty. In her description of Barbie, Barbara Coleman notes that, "in all her manifestations, Barbie reveals American cultural ideals of femininity, beauty, and gender roles" (2001: 64). The brand of femininity that Barbie promotes is very specific: affluent white heterosexual femininity. Before discussing how girls experienced Barbie's middle-/upper-middle-class femininity, I present the ways in which the construction of girlhood was presented to them.

Throughout the group interview between colleagues (Group 3), participants Lisa and Frankie constantly identified as "tomboys," especially during their childhoods, while Isabel participated in "tomboy" activities. Lisa remembered playing Barbie for about three years of her childhood and then becoming more interested in playing sports and "playing in the streets." She added, "I was very 'tomboy' too, always climbing up trees and lampposts" (Lisa, Group 3 transcript). Frankie also identified as a "tomboy" and remembered that once she moved to Puerto Rico, she exchanged her Barbie play for mostly outdoor activities. Isabel made clear distinctions between how she would behave according to the type of play at hand: "I could play like a tomboy, very rough with my cousins, and when I played with the Barbies, I could be very delicate, and I took care of them" (Isabel, Group 3 transcript). In some ways Isabel was learning how to "be a girl" through Barbie by adopting the "appropriate" behavior when she was interacting with the doll. While the doll was not envisioned as an educational toy—something creator Ruth Handler made clear—it became one that taught girls how to be girls (Gerber 2009). According to Gerber, Handler once told a reporter that Barbie "is a very educational product: the children learn color coordination, fashion design, good grooming, hair styling, good manners, and people relationships—they interrelate through social situations" (2009: 150). Despite the criticism that Barbie promoted a sexist view of women, mothers were seeing Barbie's value as a tool to educate girls: "'She was such a tomboy before,' one mother wrote. 'Now I've been able to get her to wash her face and comb her hair'" (Gerber 2009: 113). Thus, the doll did serve an "educational" purpose by teaching conduct and how to be a "proper lady"—by teaching girls how to be girls. But this example also brings to light problematic ideas about girlhood: that there is something to "correct" about girls who do not conform to societal gender constructions, that playing rough, not combing their hair, not wearing dresses, etc., are not "correct" ways of being girls. In Isabel's case, she knew that her behavior while interacting with the doll should be different from her behavior while playing with her cousins. For Isabel, it was knowing how and when to behave a certain way: she could be "tomboy-ish" with her cousins but had to switch to "girly-ish" in other contexts. She knew how to code-switch her behavior in order to properly fit gender expectations.

Girls also learn what it means to "be a girl" as soon as they are born, and sometimes even before. Lipkin writes that in American culture, "the pink cap is put on [girls] shortly after birth" (2009: 1). Even before birth, babies are already assigned colors according to their gender—blue for boys and pink for girls. A girl will be brought home from the hospital and her room will be decorated with different shades of pink, she will find that mostly the clothes available to her are pink, and she will know which aisles in the toy store are for her based on the predominant color, pink. These practices are no different in Puerto Rico, where baby showers, children's birthday parties, children's bedrooms, and toy aisles are generally coded either blue or pink. Ostensibly, these practices are a result of the influence of US culture on the island due to its position as a US territory. In Isabel's experience, she was introduced to pink as soon as she was brought home from the hospital: "When I was born, the first thing they did was paint my whole room pink. All the walls were pink! Even the ceiling was pink!" (Isabel, Group 3 transcript). While there is a push toward changing this marked use of colors to immediately impose gender identities on children, the binary still exists. Some of my participants brought up conversations about the color pink and Barbie and how they related to them. Alondra (age thirty-two), for example, noted that she was not a fan of Barbie merchandise other than the toys, mainly due to the predominant use of pink in most of the products:

> I think I didn't even like the clothes, or the coloring books, or the decorations for girls' bedrooms. I didn't like that the predominant color was pink. That's why I fell in love with the motorhome, which was purple and blue. And I played hard with the hospital, which was blue. (Alondra, email interview)

Similarly, the girls in the present recognized the almost exclusive use of pink in the products that feature Barbie, and some of them even expressed a strong dislike of the imposition of this color as *the* color for girls. The following is an exchange with Sharon, who expressed a desire for more color options in the Barbie merchandise:

> Emily: Are there things that you don't like about Barbie?
> Sharon: Yes. She's always dressed in pink!
> Emily: And you don't like pink all the time?
> Sharon: No. I like blue. I love blue! That's why I liked that for a change she wore purple. I made her a blue dress, but it's not that pretty. It was like a set that you could make and put stickers on it.
> Emily: So, you wish there would be more colors for Barbie?
> Sharon: Yes. (Sharon, Group 5 transcript)

Like Sharon, whose favorite color was not (exclusively) pink as is often assumed for all girls, K.C. and Annie also liked other colors and wished to see that variety in items related to Barbie. When K.C. described the Disney princess doll Tiana as her favorite, one of the reasons she provided was the doll's green dress, which was her favorite color.

Historically, Barbie products were not always pink, and pink was not always a "girl" color. In fact, in 1920 pink was considered a masculine color, yet "since World War II, the use of gender-coded décor (especially pink and blue) has been unchanging in children's bedrooms" (Adams 2009;

2010: 60). In the present, cultural associations of girls with the color pink remain strongly ingrained in our ideas of gender identity. Through my research at the Strong National Museum of Play, I had the opportunity to examine a wide array of Barbie products, including the first Barbie dreamhouse, whose façade was painted blue. The colors inside the first Barbie house were varied, bright, and possibly not what would now culturally be considered "girly," or at least they were not overly saturated with pink. The walls were bright yellow with bright red accents, the furniture resembled wood, the pillows and other accessories were dark blue, and the carpets were yellow and red. Her house was mostly decorated with primary colors as opposed to the overpowering pink that is used in the present. While Barbie is a fashion icon, her first house was not entirely about fashion, like modern Barbie houses are. In her living room there was a television, a couple of magazines on the coffee table, and shelves with books that were not about fashion. In my conversation with Isabel and Frankie, I noted that Barbie was not always associated with pink but that there was a time when suddenly "everything that was for girls had to be pink, and it still is that way now" (Emily, Group 3 transcript). Frankie suggested that "it's also a phase because even though I played with Barbies and everything was pink, I didn't want to be a Barbie. I did want a boyfriend like Ken, but the expectations were too high to be a Barbie" (Frankie, Group 3 transcript). Frankie did not adopt pink as a color that defined her identity, but she also did not identify with the doll, which could have served as the entry point into the color pink. Frankie's comment also highlights an important aspect of girls' identities in relation to Barbie: perceiving the doll as the model of what girls should dream of becoming and then learning that this is almost impossible to achieve.

A Plastic Supermodel: Relating to Barbie's Impossible Body

A related aspect of Barbie play that many girls experience is identifying or not identifying with the doll due to her physical characteristics. A number of sources document that the doll's physicality was based on a character from a popular German comic strip (Lord 1994; Rand, 1995). This character's name was Lilli, and her appeal was more for adult men: she is often referred to as a prostitute. Participant Carmen noticed Barbie's sexualized body when she was a girl playing with the doll. When describing Barbie's arrival to Puerto Rico, Carmen and Lourdes remembered her as a novelty because it was a different type of doll from what girls usually owned. It had much to do with her body, which unbeknownst to Carmen and Lourdes—and possibly many girls at the time—had such controversial origins.

> Carmen: She was also a novelty because she was a doll that had a body, breasts, and that was something that . . . also a waist.
>
> Lourdes: It was something that you didn't see in a doll at the time.
>
> Carmen: It was the first doll, at least that I knew about, that was like . . . it was almost like pornographic to have her naked. You couldn't have her naked or anything because imagine that, she had a body and all. (Carmen and Lourdes, Group 1 transcript)

Since Lilli served as the inspiration for Barbie, it is not surprising that her proportions are somewhat exaggerated, which perhaps causes girls to not be able to identify with her or, worse, to go to extremes in order to look like her. The fact that Barbie was produced as a fashion doll contributes to her unusual proportions, which have usually been the center of feminist critique. These "unusual proportions" have been researched and argued to be impossible for real women. For instance, studies made by the Wellness Resource Center at Vanderbilt University in Tennessee confirmed that a human version with Barbie's body proportions would only have room for an esophagus or a trachea in her neck, a tibia or a fibula in her legs, and that she would have to crawl to support her top-heavy frame (Ticona-Vergaray 2009). According to Quindlen (1999) Barbie's life-size measurements would be 40-18-32.

Barbie's body proportions, the message girls receive from Barbie's figure, the effects girls' interactions with the doll may have on their self-esteem, and other issues related to the body have been at the center of Barbie criticism (see, for instance, Dittmar, Halliwell, and Ive 2006; Lipkin 2009; Quindlen 1999; Rand 1995). According to Gerber, in the 1960s "Ruth [Handler] roundly rejected criticism of Barbie as encouraging a sexist view of women or as harmful to young girls' view of themselves" (2009: 113) and "had never understood or agreed with the criticism of Barbie as somehow damaging to girls' image of themselves" (2009: 250). Ruth Handler saw the toy as exactly that, and she had no interest in dictating the fantasies that girls played out through Barbie. As the stories already described in this chapter suggest, one girl can experience Barbie in very different ways compared to another. Interactions with Barbie are not one-dimensional, and the messages that girls receive from the doll and other products can vary according to the specific context and situation where they take place. Not all participants of this study discussed their perceptions of Barbie's body or their own experiences of body image. However, among those who addressed the topic, the responses and perspectives were varied. For some of the participants in this study their interactions with Barbie, and Barbie's body, did not pose any issues about their own body image. In contrast, for some, it was difficult to ignore Barbie's unattainable body and not compare it to their own. These complex interactions with Barbie are explored in this section, beginning with my own.

On a personal note, I never felt that I had to look like Barbie—to have a body like hers, her hair, her eyes—as I was growing up, or at least I do not remember having experienced those thoughts. I do remember dreaming of developing breasts at some point, and I would stuff my bra to imagine how it would look. This is something most of my friends did as well, but I never linked it to my interactions with Barbie. However, as the literature on memories suggests, sometimes we misremember or reconstruct our memories to create an image of our own selves (Mitchell and Reid-Walsh 2002; Muñoz 1999). Perhaps I have forgotten about moments when I wanted to look like Barbie or wanted to have her body.[2] Similarly, other participants did not remember having encountered issues with the doll's proportions. Alondra (age thirty-two), for example, indicated that she did not remember paying attention to Barbie's body. From Alondra's perspective, the criticism about Barbie places too much responsibility on the doll and not so much on the circumstances surrounding the girls who are affected:

> For me, Barbie was pretty, but I never noticed her body was unrealistic. . . . Every time I read the criticism on Barbie I think that the majority of girls recreate life and circumstances similar to theirs in their play, and that she's not the doll responsible of any insecurity or complex. Instead, it's the environment and the education that surround the girl or the boy. (Alondra, email interview)

Commenting on the topic of body image and people who change their appearance because of unrealistic beauty standards, Susan, who is a mother of two girls, believed these issues are a direct result of a lack of education to children. She said:

> I also think there is a lack of education to our children. Because if you teach children values, to love themselves the way they are, the way God made them, then they wouldn't have reason to wish to be like others. And then, if there is a pretty doll, that's good, there's diversity. We can be a little fat or a little thin, and we are pretty and we are loved the same way. But they don't teach those things to children anymore. Now it's like, "You have to be like this. Don't eat because

you'll get fat. Girl, your cheeks are too big! Look at those big legs!" None of that matters! (Susan, Group 6 transcript)

While some scholars have highlighted the influence the child's environment has on the messages they receive from Barbie dolls (McDonough 1999) and others have noted that Barbie's messages are not solely negative (Reid-Walsh and Mitchell 2000), there are some who have found that Barbie dolls have a certain degree of influence on girls' self-esteem. Dittmar et al. (2006), who worked with girls of different ages, argue that while dolls do not have so much influence on older girls (teenagers), they can influence girls who have been exposed early to dolls to desire an unrealistic body, which could contribute to a risk of developing self-esteem issues.

Participants Patricia and Gabriela did not view Barbie as an object that could send distorted ideas of body image to girls who came in contact with her. Both participants claimed that they never desired to look like Barbie and that her figure was not problematic, though their thinking showed more complex negotiations with the doll:

And what people say about the body . . . well, I had four children, and I was always thin. You know, because they say that Barbie dolls don't have a realistic body, and that's not true. It is real. It's real because I was always thin. And I had four children and I stayed thin. . . . But I identified a lot with her [Barbie]. I always tried to dress like her, to stay thin. It's just that you have to take care of yourself. Look, I've seen women whose faces are pretty, but they start eating and eating . . . they lose their beauty. If they only knew how beautiful they are! That beautiful face, they would stop eating, but *no!* (Patricia, Group 4 transcript)

Patricia's recounting of her experience with Barbie suggested that there was no influence from the doll on her own views of beauty. From her standpoint, she wanted to emulate Barbie's elegance by trying to dress like her, taking care of herself, and "staying in shape," but she did not perceive it as a negative influence from the doll. However, in saying that Barbie had no influence and immediately denoting that Barbie's body is real because it was similar to her own, Patricia may serve as an indication that the doll does exert a degree of influence, even if it goes unnoticed by those who play with Barbie. It is interesting to notice Patricia's own notions about Barbie precisely because she appears to have internalized certain beauty ideals without realizing where they may have originated. Similarly, her daughter Gabriela (age twenty-five) attested that she never experienced thinking she had to be perfect like Barbie was: "I liked them. And I never felt like, 'Oh, I have to be perfect like Barbie'" (Gabriela, Group 4 transcript). Patricia agreed to this statement and began describing a specific woman she knew who was pretty but, according to Patricia, had "let herself go" by eating too much and "lost her beauty" (Patricia, Group 4 transcript).

> Look, I knew a woman who was a teacher, a precious woman, blond hair, blue eyes. But she was overweight. And I guess everyone told her, "You're so beautiful," and she lost weight. I don't know what she did, but she lost weight. And she got pretty again. Well, even her husband left her because he had married a beautiful woman. (Patricia, Group 4 transcript)

Problematically, Patricia blamed her friend for her husband's leaving since he had originally married a "beautiful woman" and in Patricia's opinion, her friend's weight gain had taken away her beauty. Patricia's unexamined ideological assumptions that emerged through her opposing statements specifically illustrate one of the ideals about beauty that critics argue Barbie promotes: that in order to be beautiful you must have the "perfect looks." These looks, based on Barbie and based on Patricia's description, involve being thin yet busty, having the right curves in the right places, and having a pretty face. (Note that a pretty face consists of blue or green eyes, like Barbie's eyes. I examine this particular characteristic further in the next chapter). Her comments about the body and ideal beauty are not exclusive to her individually; rather, they are a product of our culture. In Puerto Rico women are constantly told that they have "una cara bonita, pero . . ." (a pretty face, but. . .). It is interesting that this notion is propagated so much in a culture that exhibits such pride in its curvy and voluptuous women, including Jennifer Lopez and Iris Chacón.[3] As Negrón-Muntaner proposes, "for *boricuas* the big rear end acts as an identification site for Latinas to reclaim their beauty" especially in the United States (2004: 240). This is an intriguing aspect of the values of beauty woven into the cultural fabric of Latinx populations, and Puerto Ricans in this case. In her study of beauty standards, Hilda Lloréns (2013) describes the ideal Latina as being thin with a flat stomach, wide hips, and a big butt. Patricia's comment pointed to this ideal of beauty, where there are strategic or "right" places in the body where fatness or curves are "appropriate." It is an ideal that holds curvy women in high regard but also asks them to watch their figure. It is a culture that reveres the voluptuous body while simultaneously valuing the more American ideal of beauty promoted in various media, including Barbie dolls.

It is no surprise then that the names "Barbie" along with the doll's male counterpart "Ken" have become synonymous to beauty. Lipkin notes that the mention of either name evokes the images of "women and men who emulate or resemble the dolls' physical presentations and, correspondingly, a kind of vapid look that both dolls share" (2009: 55). A short conversation between Lisa (age forty-five) and Frankie (age thirty) reveals the meaning of the name Barbie in relation to beauty ideals in addition to more negative connotations:

> Frankie: There's still that concept of looking like Barbie or being like a Barbie.
> Lisa: And in movies they make reference a lot to looking like Barbie. Also, when they're a bimbo. I just remembered the movie *Legally Blonde* in the second part when they call her a "Malibu Barbie."
> Frankie: It's also used in a derogatory manner. They use it to call someone dumb or clueless. (Frankie and Lisa, Group 3 transcript)

Being called "a Barbie," according to both participants, can be in reference to a person's looks, mainly taken to mean that the person is beautiful (and possibly white and blond) and that they have a "perfect" body. However, it can also refer to the person's intellect, suggesting that they are dumb, an airhead, and not intellectual at all. At the same time, people have taken the moniker Barbie as a term of empowerment, as is the case of rapper Nicki Minaj. In her analysis of Nicki Minaj's use of the Barbie image, Jennifer Dawn Whitney argues that "Minaj's relationship with, and co-option of, the Barbie brand of femininity complicates the traditional feminist perspective of the doll" (2012: 147) by adopting a hyperfeminized persona. Minaj satirizes white Barbie and challenges whiteness and the doll's version of femininity as the standard.

The notions about the "perfect person" that the dolls' names raise are further propelled through the lessons about heteronormativity girls learn through them. Frankie, for example, shared that she "always wanted a boyfriend like Ken" (Frankie, Group 3 transcript). When Jessica (age thirty) encountered Barbie and Ken's bodies, she learned that she needed to look like Barbie if she wanted to find someone who looked like Ken. After all, he was the male version of Barbie.

> I thought I had to look like her. Yes, because it was like that's how you'd find the perfect boyfriend, which was Ken. Which is also an ideology about how a man should look. If I see a man like that, I'd be like, "There's nothing down there!" [*Laughs*] (Jessica, Group 2 transcript)[4]

What Jessica's observation suggests is that some girls feel pressured to look like Barbie in order to fulfill the heteronormative expectations of finding a suitable man. Carla's experience with Barbie saw her identifying the doll as "frenemy," mainly because Barbie embodied everything that Carla was not.

> You have known me since I was little. You know that I was always a little fat. So, for me Barbie was a "frenemy." Barbie for me was a friend because I played with Barbie, but Barbie also represented everything I was not. And sometimes what we would like to be, a little bit, like very deep inside. But when you're a child, you don't know how to channel that. Everything for you is anger and ire and sometimes even a little bit of jealousy, when you're a child. You know? And you channel that the way a child does. (Carla, interview transcript).

Carla viewed and still views Barbie as a "frenemy," a term she used during the interview various times. Her experience serves as an example of the complexity of girls' interactions with Barbie are and the conflicting perceptions they have of the doll. Carla considered Barbie a friend because it was one of her favorite toys and one with which she played regularly. However, that was not Barbie's only role in Carla's life. The doll represented an ideal that Carla did not think she could achieve. When Carla looked at a Barbie doll, she did not see herself reflected in it. This provoked anger, jealousy, and frustration toward the doll. Interestingly, as described earlier in this chapter, it was through the doll that Carla often channeled her emotions. Thus, the very artifact that sometimes caused her pain was the artifact that helped her work through it. Moreover, in this description of Carla's perception of Barbie I noticed a sense of shame, similar to that demonstrated by many women who have played with Barbie, as noted by Reid-Walsh and Mitchell (2000). When Carla was telling me that "Barbie also represented everything I was not . . . *and sometimes what we would like to be, a little bit, like very deep inside,*" the tone of her voice changed. Despite being the only two people in a room of a library, Carla said the last part in a quieter voice, as if she had been somewhat embarrassed for ever wanting to be like Barbie, even if it had been "a little bit."

Mariela (age twenty-nine), in contrast, did not remember encountering many issues with Barbie's body when she was playing with the doll. She did, however, identify one particular concern that made her envy Barbie's body.

> Well, what frustrated me . . . My main thing with the body was that I always wanted to have big and perky breasts, just like she had. They were like very spectacular, but that never happened. But that was, about Barbie's body, the only thing. The rest, well—because Barbies had flat butts and their small waist didn't cause me stress because I was thin at that time. Not in the beginning. In the beginning when I was little, I probably didn't have that malice. At the end,

> when I was twelve or thirteen, that's when you start to imitate her, wanting to look like her. (Mariela, Group 2 transcript)

The interest Mariela showed in having breasts like Barbie's once she became a teenager was similar to my own experience, and possibly that of many teenagers who are entering puberty and already want to have the body of an adult. Author Pamela Brant writes precisely about the attention teenagers pay to Barbie's breasts: "We weren't interested in any other part of the anatomy but Barbie's breasts. . . . Their stability and solidity were impressive" (1999: 53–54). Mattel understood girls' and teens' potential fascination with the doll's breasts. In 1975, the company introduced Growing Up Skipper,[5] whose breasts would "develop" and whose height would grow two inches taller when the player rotated her arm. In contrast to the experiences documented in some of the research about Barbie, Mariela's only issue growing up was about wanting to have breasts like Barbie rather than everything else in her body. This was because Mariela viewed her thin body as similar to Barbie's but also because there was nothing else about Barbie's body that she considered worthy of envy (notably the fact that Barbie's butt was too "flat" in Mariela's opinion). Mariela's comment about Barbie's butt speaks to the veneration of the rear that became a way to challenge the "shame of Boricua identity in the United States" (Negrón-Muntaner 2004: 234). As Negrón-Muntaner explains of Jennifer Lopez's body, her much admired butt served to diversify the concept of beauty and, further, to popularize an "'attitude' in relation to hegemonic culture" that defied certain beauty standards (2004: 234). Lopez's "popularization" of the big butt awakened a new sentiment of pride in body types that defied what US media constantly presented as "ideally beautiful." As a child, Mariela may not have perceived her comment about Barbie's "flat" butt as a challenge to beauty standards, but she understood that Barbie's body was not an ideal she needed to achieve.

Despite not having encountered many issues with Barbie's body during her girlhood, Mariela feels differently in the present as an adult and a mother:

> Look, after all the polemic, scandals, and everything that's happened with Barbie, which they've looked for ways of making different models, I keep seeing the same reality. I don't notice much difference, but they have come out with versions that are more flat-chested, with a less defined waist, and I think that's good. But their publicity should be based upon not giving much importance to looks, something that educates. If Barbie is already an educational tool, the tool for entertainment for girls, they should make a campaign based on how to

educate for good self-esteem, and that person can grow up appreciating what she has. I don't see that happening much in reality. And so, from my part, it's not something I would deny my daughter, but it's also something that I won't force, that she has to play with Barbie. (Mariela, Group 2 transcript)

Mariela sees Barbie as an educational tool, whether the inherent purpose of the doll is to educate or not. She understands Barbie as a toy that sends a message to girls, and girls receive that message according to their own lived experiences. Barbie is also, in Mariela's opinion, a tool to entertain girls, so girls are often in contact with the doll. As a result, she stresses the importance of Mattel shifting the focus of the message and marketing toward girls' self-esteem and away from the doll's looks. This is something that Mattel has done through various campaigns that attempt to highlight Barbie's careers and the possibilities that girls create through Barbie, such as the "We Girls Can Do Anything" campaign in the 1980s and 1990s and the "Imagine the Possibilities" ad in 2015. Nevertheless, critics point to the continuous focus on the physical, and that "the majority of Barbies and her female friends have activities and accouterments that emphasize the body" (Jones 1999: 94).

The girls that played with Barbie at the time of my study did not indicate that Barbie's body had negatively affected the views about their own body image. In fact, neither Sharon (age eight) nor K.C. (age eleven) discussed Barbie's body proportions, nor did they mention their own perspectives about body image. Of the three girls I interviewed, Annie (age nine) was the most vocal about Barbie's body. Yet, girls made observations about the differences in the bodies of their various dolls. During part of the conversation with sisters K.C. and Annie, the discussion turned to a doll called Nancy. The girls talked about the differences between this doll and Barbie, and according to them, the Nancy doll is a more adult Barbie, but her body proportions are nothing like Barbie's. This one, they said, has a rounder figure, has chubbier legs, and wears tennis shoes. "She's like us!" added Annie. When I followed up on her comment by asking, "Do you think Barbie is not so much like you? When you look at Barbie you don't think she is like you?" Annie responded, "No, because not all women are that thin" (Annie, Group 6 transcript). Annie's comments about how the Nancy doll is more "like us"[6] and Barbie in contrast does not look like her are important aspects of her own identity. Annie did not express any discomfort with her own body, but she understood that her body was very different from Barbie's. In her observations of both dolls, there was a clear identification with the doll that has a rounder figure and looks more like her and a disassociation from the doll that looks like a model. Annie was also the one who brought up an important issue about Barbie's potential influence on girls' and adults' identities. For some scholars and critics, not only is the doll's image problematic for girls' self-esteem and views on body image as they are growing up, but these views may also transfer into adulthood. Women wanting to resemble Barbie dolls have gone to the extent of undergoing surgery in order to look like a life-size version of the doll. Such are the cases of Cindy Jackson, who by 1993 had undergone nineteen operations (Lord 1994), and more recently Valeriya Lukyanova (also known as "human Barbie"), who claims her striking resemblance to Barbie comes from genetics and make-up tricks, denying that she has undergone surgery (Beck 2012). Yet, her Barbie-like figure does provoke the opinion that there has been some surgery involved. A brief conversation between mother Susan (age forty) and daughter Annie (age nine) highlighted precisely the extremes to which people go in order to look like Barbie and even Ken.

> Annie: Now I'm going to tell you something that happened with a woman and a man. First, the woman had so many operations done, this was a long time ago. She had so many surgeries done that she turned herself into a Barbie. And she was the same, blue eyes and blond.
> Susan: That is not normal because if we look at Barbie on a real scale, you are not going to find a woman who looks like that. Unless it has been done through surgery, like that woman. But in terms of the size of her breasts, which is what Annie was saying, it's exaggerated. The woman's. It's that she did not do it like Barbie's. She made it bigger than Barbie's. A friend of ours was telling us about the Puerto Rican Barbie and Ken—no, the Barbie and Ken is the Puerto Rican one, she isn't.
> Annie: The Ken is Puerto Rican, but he did not look like Ken at all, only when he cut his hair.
> Susan: By the way, he died.[7]
> Annie: When he was twenty because he had so much plastic in his body, and he wanted to have plastic wings and . . .
> Susan: There were complications during his operation and—apparently there were other health issues, but he had many surgeries done. On his lips, his eyes, his nose, all over his body. He exercised a lot. And in reality, he didn't look like Ken. But he said he was the Ken. (Susan and Annie, Group 6 transcript)

In this conversation we see the perspectives of both an adult and a girl who think Barbie's body is an exaggeration. Furthermore, they think it is dangerous that people may want to look like Barbie or Ken so much that they undergo dangerous surgeries. Annie, along with her mother Susan, was well aware of the dangers posed by overvaluing Barbie's and Ken's bodies to the point of altering one's own. Thus, while Annie may not receive negative messages from Barbie, nor would she internalize those messages if she did, she brought up how other people have been influenced by the dolls to the point of changing their physical appearance. In a precarious developmental phase such as girlhood, internalizing messages that prompt girls to view themselves negatively can be dangerous.

Challenging the Status Quo of Barbie's Physicality

Girls in my study who played with Barbie encountered Barbie's infamous body in both positive and negative ways. Their experiences, which were varied and complex, depict the wide range of interactions girls may have with the doll and how the experiences are closely tied to girls' lived experiences and their worldviews. Some of the participants attested to having never received any damaging messages from the doll, while others experienced difficult and sometimes conflicting interactions with Barbie. The opportunity to identify with the doll either physically or through her lifestyle can serve as a venue for girls to see themselves reflected in their toys. Yet at times the combination of Barbie's body shape and other aspects of her physical appearance may deny girls the opportunity to relate to the doll. Girls may look at Barbie's body and feel that it's impossible to achieve it. They may see her standards of femininity as unattainable.

The range of comments about the body—both Barbie's and those of real-life women or girls—that the participants made offers insight into differing views about beauty and femininity that coexist in the same context. For the generation that grew up in the 1960s, Barbie was an ideal of beauty, poise, and grace. While they did not see Barbie's body as problematic and felt that the doll did not send negative messages about beauty standard, these women followed a discourse to discuss women's looks that pointed to an internalization of beauty standards that favor certain body types. Participants who grew up with Barbie in the 1990s, for the most part, did not feel like Barbie's body influenced their own views about the body growing up—with the exception of Carla, whose relationship with Barbie was complicated precisely because of the doll's looks. For some of the women, Barbie did serve as a reminder that they did not fit within specific ideas about femininity. Yet, as adults, most of them demonstrated concern over Barbie's body and paid attention to aspects they did not remember noticing as children. Insightfully, the girls in the present observed Barbie's body and commented on how her unrealistic proportions can be damaging for people (not just girls and women). These intergenerational experiences illustrate shifts in societal beauty norms and discourses around the body through the years.

Months after most of the interviews with my participants took place, Mattel released the "Barbie Fashionistas" line, which included "Curvy" Barbie. I received dozens of emails, Facebook messages, Facebook posts, and texts sharing news articles announcing the new line. A variation of "Did you hear there's a new curvy Barbie?" accompanied each link shared. The 2016 "Barbies Fashionistas" collection included four different body types (along with a variety of physical characteristics): regular, tall, petite, and curvy. Interestingly, despite there being various body types, curvy Barbie was the object of attention, not only from those sharing the news but also from Mattel's official announcements. Media and girlhood scholar Rebecca Hains observes that Mattel's public relations team "cued the media to focus on Barbie's body type changes. In major headlines that followed, the body types took center stage, and curvy Barbie commanded special attention" (2021: 272). This was Mattel's way of responding "unapologetically," Hains (2021) adds, to decades of criticism about Barbie's impossibly thin and tall body. Mattel gave the appearance of challenging the status quo, but this was only on the surface. Mattel's response was to focus on Barbie's new curves, as if to imply that this eliminated any potential issues that critics, especially feminists, could find with the doll. More problematically, their message remained focused on Barbie's body. While Mattel was protesting how much attention Barbie's body continuously received (the caption for an exclusive article published in the *Los Angeles Times* read, "Now can we stop talking about my body?"),[8] the company was using Barbie's (new curvy) body to sell the line. Even when the new dolls also offered diversity of skin tones (much more than ever before), hairstyles/colors, and even facial details, their marketing continued the problem that participant Mariela (age twenty-nine) had identified as an adult: that their publicity focused too much on giving importance to looks, and the body in particular—both the dolls' and girls'.

Notes

1. My memories of them include using them to play "Baywatch" (both in my pretend play and my Barbie play) since the lifeguards used binoculars to watch the waters. Sometime after this, I actually got the Baywatch Barbie, which included binoculars, a Frisbee, visors, the red bathing suit, a dolphin, and, of course—the one item I really wanted—the red life saver.

2. As someone who played so much with Barbie, even when I was confronted with the research regarding Barbie's damaging messages of body image, it was difficult to understand how a doll, a toy, could have so much influence on a person's identity. Yet, it does in many ways, as I have discussed thus far and as I continue to explore in this project. By reading the extensive research about Barbie and as I conducted my own, I was able to see how some girls experience Barbie in these ways and how important it is to acknowledge those experiences of identity construction that take place because of/despite Barbie.

3. Iris Chacón is a singer, dancer, and "showgirl" from Puerto Rico who was famous for her voluptuous bottom.

4. During Ken's creation, Ruth Handler was aware of the fact that he was missing a critical part of his body. Gerber writes: "Ruth felt the design team lacked 'the guts' to give the Ken doll even the suggestion of male sex organs. She saw herself as ahead of her time, arguing that there should at least be a bulge that would suggest realism. . . . Despite ordering prototypes with varying degrees of bulge in the crotch the male designers resisted all but the barest hint of a penis" (2009: 142).

5. Skipper is one of Barbie's younger sisters, who was introduced in 1964.

6. It is in fact more like the girls. After learning about this doll, I looked it up and found that the doll is almost a mix between a Barbie doll (tall and fashionable) and the American Girl doll (which is supposed to be a girl, not an adult).

7. This real-life Ken they were discussing was from Brazil, and he died of Leukemia, which had been discovered five months prior while being treated for infections caused by a product called "hydrogel."

8. For a deep analysis of Mattel's PR approach and control over media stories about the 2016 "Barbie Fashionistas" collection, see Hains (2021).

꧁

Chapter 4

Accessing Barbie
Conversations about Class and Race

I was seven and had never had a doll. I wanted a baby doll like my cousin Jenny's, with pink skin and blue eyes that shut when she lay her down.

—Esmeralda Santiago (1996), *A Doll for Navidades*

Race and social class play a chief role in delimiting who has access to Barbie or who plays with her. Compared to other lines, such as American Girl, whose dolls sell for over sixty dollars each, Barbie is considerably less expensive and more accessible.[1] The dolls are sold in stores such as Walmart, whereas American Girl dolls are sold exclusively in their own store. Still, much of the appeal of Barbie comes from the seemingly endless panoply of accessories that serve to enhance play with her. This is where accessibility becomes more limited since many low-income families cannot afford to buy numerous amounts of Barbie clothes, Barbie's car, or especially her Dreamhouse.

As Hohmann (1985) notes in his play interaction with a girl named Jennifer, it is difficult for a middle-class girl to have a great number of pieces of clothing and other accessories such as furniture for her doll(s). However, in this case, Jennifer was able to make up for this lack through her imaginative play. Jennifer was inventive in how she created furniture for her dollhouse; for instance, she used pieces of cardboard to create the closet and also the refrigerator, while an ashtray served as a bathtub. But girls are not always open to dressing up their dolls with clothes made by their mothers or grandmothers, as these items indicate a low social status. Rand (1995) points out that in the child's world, custom-made originals usually have less value than the clothes Mattel produce. Clothes not manufactured by Mattel signal a class status and often remind girls that they cannot afford "real" Barbie clothes. She elucidates this through the example of Georgia, whose mother used to make her Barbie clothes and who remembered how enraged she was that she could not have store-bought Barbie clothes: "I didn't want to take Barbie in her homemade clothes around kids who had the store-bought stuff. I tried to compensate quality with quantity . . . but it didn't really work" (Rand 1995: 97). The Mattel brand confers value, but not everyone can afford it, thus not everyone has access to playing with Barbie, and if they do, there may be limitations to how they play with her. Barbie, some have argued, is a representation of capitalism because the American ideology places value on money, successful careers, material objects, and physical beauty—all things that the Barbie doll and the Barbie brand embody (see Morgan n.d.).

The Material Girl

Barbie's model of femininity may prove difficult for girls to attain because it involves very specific characteristics. The doll's life centers on being a consumer—of fashion, of cars, of houses, and of a luxurious lifestyle (Forman-Brunell 2002; Hade 2001; Morgan n.d.; Rand 1995). Scholars have argued that Barbie presents femininity as something to be consumed, and as a result, girls have to become avid consumers of everything that Barbie offers. Barbie invites its player to become a consumer in various ways. The doll is known for her extensive and expensive wardrobe, which grows larger every year as Mattel continues to produce new designs. Clothes are an essential part of Barbie's life and the image she promotes, as she is after all a fashion doll. Hence, the doll is perceived as a "fashion leader" (Morgan n.d.) because Barbie is always up to date with and even sets the current fashion trends. Some of the participants, especially those who were among the first generation of Barbie players, talked about loving Barbie precisely because of her fashion. The first generations of Barbie dolls were about depicting sophistication, or as Lourdes and Carmen described it, "She was never a doctor or a nurse . . . she was always high fashion, a model" (Lourdes, Group 1 transcript). Patricia (age fifty-nine), who owns a collection of more than two hundred dolls, remembered vividly why she began collecting. As other participants expressed, Barbie's clothes were fascinating to her, and they were the objects of her desire. Yet, because they were so expensive, even more expensive than the doll, her mother could not afford them and would not spend money of them.

> Yes, sometimes I would make the clothes, but I wanted her clothes. And that's what I have been collecting, her clothes, which I could not have when I was little. And so as an adult, whenever I saw a little dress, I'd buy it. And I have been putting money together to complete them. I see the books with the dresses. That one came with the book.[2] That little book is what would sell the doll because one would look at the book and begin to dream. (Patricia, Group 4 transcript)

Forman-Brunell notes that in the postwar years, when the doll was created, "though dressed in her foundational bathing suit, Barbie's extensive wardrobe exemplified the ethos of an expanding consumer culture where spending replaced saving. While thrift and frugality had prevailed among Depression and war-time generations these were no longer valued; Americans were encouraged to find fulfillment in goods and gadgets" (Forman-Brunell 2002: par. 4). Patricia's case highlights the value that Mattel invites girls to place on Barbie's accessories and on consuming products. The company established the doll as a fashion icon and specifically marketed her clothes as the item(s) to desire. For many girls, including Patricia, Carmen, and Lourdes, the desire was to own the clothes for themselves, but since they were not made for girls, the doll served as their fashion proxy—one that was not affordable.

Barbie's clothes are not the sole example of Barbie's luxurious life. With so many houses (beach houses, Dreamhouse, and mansions) and vehicles (Corvettes, campers, motorcycles, and airplanes), a real person would have to be a millionaire to afford them (Morgan n.d.). Currently, it is not the doll and play sets alone that invite those who play with Barbie to be consumers; Barbie electronic games, fashion plates, and even books constantly remind the audience—the consumer—that it is important to buy. In his examination of how children's books have become venues for corporations to produce profit and to capitalize from children's culture, Hade argues that "children today are viewed by the large corporations who make children's books not as readers of books, but as consumers of ideas" (2001: 164). The same can be said for toys, as big corporations and producers of toys view children as the main group of consumers of the ideas their toys promote. Rather than allowing children to play with toys for the sake of playing, corporations see in children an opportunity to promote certain ideas; with Barbie, those who play with her are presented with ideas that value beauty and luxury, an extensive wardrobe, cars, and a life of leisure.

Beyond the values and ideas of femininity that the doll promotes through her products, Barbie's embodiment of affluent femininity was something that many of my participants encountered in the limited access they had to some of these products. Carmen and Lourdes, who racially identify as white/mixed, emphasized many times how expensive Barbie's clothes were at the time they played with the doll during the early 1960s. Without being prompted to talk about class or the prices of Barbie arti-facts, the sisters talked about the accessibility to Barbie accoutrements nu-merous times in our conversation. As they described their love for Barbie because of her fashion and their own love for high fashion, they stressed this point:

> Carmen: We arrived at Puerto Rico in 1960. Barbie came out in 1959. And it was like a novelty. And so, our parents would give us a little bit of money and, like Lourdes said, we would go buy them clothes, which were really expensive. At that time Barbie clothes were like six or seven dollars.
> Lourdes: The money Carmen and I saved was for Barbie clothes. But they were expensive clothes.
> Carmen: They were expensive, but fashion.
> Lourdes: It wasn't like today's clothes.
> Carmen: And it was satin.
> Lourdes: And what was made of leather, it was real leather.
> Carmen: And we didn't buy more because it was really expensive. (Carmen and Lourdes, Group 1 transcript)

Patricia, who also grew up during the 1960s, discussed how the prices of Barbie clothes posed a limitation in her access to the doll's accessories:

> My mother would buy me, well these. Those that are over here. Every time new outfits came out, I asked for them for my birthday, for Christmas. And she didn't like them because they were really small clothes and really expensive. So she saw them as little. But I, I wanted Barbie, and the clothes cost more than the doll. (Patricia, Group 4 transcript)

This is not new in the study of Barbie culture, and it is not exclusive to Puerto Rican girls. Many low-income and even middle-class families cannot afford the plethora of products that are supposed to accompany the doll, especially if they have to be the "real thing." As Rand points out,

"Barbie's status often depended on the brand name as well as the product. Early Barbie commercials direct viewers to look for the Mattel tag to make sure of getting authentic Barbie products" (1995: 96). While many of the Puerto Rican women in my research did not mind having homemade clothes or creating their own objects of play to use with Barbie (like using shoeboxes as beds), they were well aware of the significance the presence of the Mattel name had in determining the quality of the product. The Mattel brand bestows a certain value to the product that identifies it as "authentic," but those who cannot afford the "real" product may feel like their play cannot be complete without it. Jessica (age thirty), for instance, always longed for one particular play set that she never received because it was not affordable for her family.

> And if I can tell you something that they never gave me, and that made me mad because that was something I *did* want, it was when the Barbie store came out. It was like a clothing store set, like a fashionista. It was like a platform with fitting rooms, but my parents never bought it. It was too expensive. (Jessica, Group 2 transcript)

Consider Jessica's memory. While the doll itself was accessible (she even had more than one), there were accessories, which Mattel marketed as almost essential for doll play, that were too expensive to have. Moreover, the clothing store set to which Jessica refers serves as an example of a broader trend in Barbie merchandise: centering fashion in order to spark girls' interest in shopping and acquiring clothes and accessories for their dolls and themselves. In so doing, girls become consumers-in-the-making.

Scholar Daniel Hade observed the kind of consumerist messaging that many Barbie products were depicting. He offers the example of his younger daughter, who enjoyed playing with Barbie dolls when she was around seven years old:

> One day she brought home from school a Barbie chapter book she had purchased through the book club. I don't remember the title or much of the plot, but it had something to do with Barbie saving the prom. What I do remember is that the most detailed parts of the book were when Barbie was picking out her clothes and accessories and when she went shopping at the mall. Then the book described in great detail what Barbie was wearing and what she was purchasing, whether the items had much to do with the plot or not. This kind of commercialized text is increasing. (Hade 2002: 164)

Much of Barbie media has focused on audiences interacting with her material belongings. For instance, not only can children own Barbie's

Dreamhouse for their dolls, they can also watch the online web series *Barbie: Life in the Dreamhouse* (2012–15), stream the newer Netflix series *Barbie Dreamhouse Adventures* (2018–present), and play with the Barbie Dreamhouse Adventures app (2018–present). A cursory internet search for "Barbie fashion games" or "Barbie shopping games" yields a number of results, such as recent apps *Barbie Fashion Closet* and *Barbie's Magical Fashion*; computer games like *Barbie Fashion Designer* (1996), *Barbie Fashion Show: An Eye for Style* (2008), and video games like *Barbie Jet, Set, & Style* (2011). Just this sample of Barbie games illustrates how much focus the Barbie "ideal" places on consumerism.

Even if, compared to other contemporaneous dolls and toys, Barbie's price seems accessible, the reality is that not everyone can afford the doll—and much less so much of the Barbie merchandise that girls are invited to consume. For Susan (age forty), who identified as a Black Latina, not having a Barbie at a specific point of her girlhood created a feeling of shame because she could not become part of what was assumed was part of every girl's experience.

> Susan: . . . But Barbie for me, I mean if I can say something. There's something I don't like about Barbie. Well, two things that are really important for me. First, that, at least during the time I grew up, because now mothers make any sacrifice possible to buy their children what they want. But they were really expensive, and not every girl had access. On one occasion, I was in the fifth grade, a teacher told all the girls, "Bring your Barbies to class," assuming that everyone had a Barbie. I didn't have a Barbie. So, I was really "happy" [said sarcastically], you could imagine. Those are things that . . . I am a teacher, and I am very careful about that because of the experiences I have gone through.
>
> Emily: Yes, because one cannot think that all students have access to everything. So, what did you do?
>
> Susan: Nothing. I don't remember because I always remember that after that happened my mother bought me a Barbie. With a lot of sacrifice. And she gave it to me, and I always remember that doll was one that a girl brought to class when the teacher asked for them. It had a nightgown and a teddy bear. (Susan, Group 6 transcript)

As Susan shared her experience with me, I could see the pain it still caused decades later. Not only did she feel left out of a classroom event, but worse, she felt singled out because she could not afford and therefore did not have the one item she was expected to bring to class. She appreciated that her mother was able to provide a Barbie doll for her, and she recognized the sacrifices her parents made in order to afford it. But she should have never been made to feel like she needed to have the doll in order to be included.

Jessica's, Susan's, and other participants' experiences show how capital and socioeconomic class create certain affordances—physical and social—that affect the kinds of play opportunities that are available to children when they interact with Barbie. Furthermore, Susan's childhood experience illustrates the way that Barbie can become a signifier of class and of affluence. Susan's teacher's assumptions that every girl had a Barbie doll speak to the doll's status as the epitome of femininity, as an object that *all girls* must have (as perceived by many participants), and to the limited interactions some girls may actually have with her.

"Diversifying" Barbie: Whiteness at the Center of the Brand

Of equal importance in accessibility to Barbie is the lack of ethnic and racial variety that existed back when Barbie was created and when most of the women and girls whose experiences I describe in this book interacted with the doll. Jessica (age thirty) and Mariela (age twenty-nine), for example, complained about the lack of diversity in Barbie dolls and how they were not able to completely identify with Barbie as a result.

> Emily: Jessica, you were saying that you were tired of the blond ones.
> Jessica: Yes.
> Emily: Did you want her to look more like you?
> Jessica: Yes. I mean, I say that I was never a typical girl who played with Barbie. But I used to say, "Why do they have to be blond?" Because I was not blond, I didn't have blue eyes. You know? I never had a body like Barbie's. And I think that's why there came a time that—I stopped playing when I was thirteen, but since a little before I had lost interest. Because I couldn't find any similarities with me.
> Mariela: You couldn't identify. The same happened to me. That's why I liked Teresa more because she looked more natural than the typical blond Barbie.
> (Jessica and Mariela, Group 2 transcript)

There were two notable issues with Mattel's "diversification" of the Barbie brand as the company attempted to address the lack of racial and ethnic variety: nonwhite dolls were essentially "carbon copies" of white Barbie (duCille 1999), and even with the addition of dolls, white Barbie remained the central figure of the brand. Barbie's whiteness and her position as central as *the* brand's main image was a point of observation many participants made.

Sarasohn-Kahn (1996) maps Mattel's attempts at addressing diversity among the Barbie products so they reflect the growing diversity in the population of the United States.

Growing ethnic diversity in the U.S. has played a role in the design of Barbie dolls since the mid-1960s. In 1967, "Colored Francie" (#1100) was presented as the first Black doll in the Barbie product line. Francie was the first so-called "colored" friend of Barbie (which is the way her ethnicity is treated on the doll's packaging). In 1968, Mattel introduced two additional Black dolls to Barbie's world: Talking Julia (#1128) and Talking Christie (#1126). . . . In 1977, Mattel presented Hawaiian Barbie (#7470), a new ethnic variation . . . (1996: 143)

It was not until 1980 that Black and Hispanic dolls named "Barbie" were introduced into the Barbie line. As Carla observed of her experience playing with the doll, carrying the actual name "Barbie" as opposed to Christie, Francie, or Teresa, among others, legitimizes the dolls as *the* Barbie. While the other names represent Barbie's friends or family members, being *Barbie* means being the central figure. Participant Carla (age thirty-three), who described herself as Black, raised the question about Barbie being defined by the white, blue-eyed, blond doll: "Why is it that *Barbie* has to be white, blond, and with green eyes?" (Carla, interview transcript). In other words, Carla questioned why dolls of color were not called Barbie and why they were considered friends of the white, blond Barbie.

Despite Mattel's half-hearted efforts to bring ethnic and racial variety to the Barbie brand through the creation of Hispanic, Native American, and Black dolls, among others, the central figure in everything dolls, the central figure of any other product within the Barbie brand (e.g., dolls, video games, notebooks, the official Barbie website, and girls' clothes, among others) continues to be the white, blue-eyed, blond doll (duCille 1994, 1999; Rand 1995). Barbie's ethnically and racially "diverse" friends are generally assigned a secondary role in the Barbie line of dolls and other products, including TV shows, which critics see as a potential harm for girls of color who may perceive themselves as second-class citizens (duCille 1999). Take, for instance, Barbie's Latina friend Teresa, whom many participants in this study described as one of their favorite dolls. In the 1995 commercial for Twirling Ballerina Barbie and Teresa, Teresa appears backstage while Barbie performs her spotlight solo throughout most of the commercial. It is only at the end of the ad that Teresa joins Barbie onstage. Additionally, Teresa is only mentioned in the voiceover at the commercial's end and never referenced in the song that plays throughout. This was similar to other commercials in the Barbie ad campaign at the time, which also focused on Barbie and only mentioned her friends at the end, if at all. In more recent Barbie media, Mattel features Barbie's friends more prominently, though they remain supporting characters for

Barbie rather than protagonists of their own accord. In the animated show *Barbie Dreamhouse Adventures*, produced by Mattel Television, Barbie's best friends Teresa Rivera (described as Latina), Nikki Watkins (described as African American), and Renee Chow (described as Chinese American) join her in many of her adventures. Through the show audiences get to know their interests and personalities more than they could through commercials for the toys. Yet, because they are Barbie's friends, these characters are not present all the time.

Another approach in Mattel's diversification of their toy lines was through the production of dolls celebrating cultures through the "Dolls of the World" Barbie line, of which Puerto Rican Barbie (discussed in chapter 2) was a part. In my examination of specific dolls in this line I have noted that the doll line and especially "ethnic" dolls "sold an easily accessible version of culture" (Aguiló-Pérez 2021: 148). The "Dolls of the World" line was an easy way to provide consumers with information about countries and cultures around the world and to offer superficial accounts of diversity via "dye-dipped versions" of white Barbie (duCille 1994: 49) that required minimal changes to the mass-produced dolls' construction. Moreover, these dolls were not advertised as playthings. Instead, they were collectible items; therefore, child players' interactions with Barbie dolls still centered on white Barbie, "leaving dolls of color in the margins or as items to collect and exhibit, much like 'exotic' specimens collected and preserved in a colonial era for a white gaze" (Aguiló-Pérez 2021: 148). Barbie's "diverse" friends, then—both in the "main" line for play and the collectible line—continue to serve as accessories to the white, blond doll.

Decentering Barbie's Whiteness: Girls Take Matters into Their Own Play

When working with girls' construction of identity through dolls, one of the most important aspects is being able to see themselves reflected in the doll (Chin 1999; Hains 2012; Rand 1995). Decisions regarding girls' and women's interactions with Barbie can often be informed by the brand's racial representation. Parents may dissuade their daughters from playing Barbie because of the brand's lack of racial and ethnic diversity (in addition to lack of representation regarding disability). For instance, during an informal conversation about Barbie play, a woman told me that her mother did not want her to play with Barbie or other dolls (except for one specific doll) because they were white, and her mother wanted to find dolls that better represented her daughter. At the same time, there are situations in which girls decide not to play with Barbie because of race issues, and there are other instances when a specific doll appeals to them because of her color. Rand (1995), for instance, discusses the problem a participant named Rebecca faced: she was half Native American and half white, and when she used to play Barbie with her friends (most of whom were Latinx and Black), none of them wanted to be "that blonde Barbie" and she did not want to be the blond Barbie either. However, Rand (1995) notes, Rebecca liked her Barbie better than her Cher doll, which was Native American just like her. Rand (1995) also presents the case of Lisa Jones, a Black journalist, who remembered that, before Black Barbie or Barbie's Black friends came out, she wanted Barbie enough to buy two blond ones, cut their hair, dress them in African fabric, and send them off to live with Black G.I. Joe. However, after an incident at school, where all the girls looked like Barbie and none of them looked like her, she severed her ties with her dolls. If a child who wants to play with a doll with which they can identify has difficulty finding one, it might drive the child to reject the doll and end up not playing with it. Therefore, ethnic diversity plays an important role in providing accessibility to the doll and, in turn, offering a site where girls can see themselves represented well and valued.

Despite Mattel's efforts, my participants shared experiences describing the limited availability of Barbies of color and the continuous placement of white Barbie as *the* true Barbie doll, which many girls find troubling. Mariela and Jessica, who grew up in the 1990s when Mattel's diversification efforts were on the rise, talked about why their favorite Barbie dolls were not the white version, including how they saw themselves in Brown dolls.

> Mariela: I only have three surviving Barbies. Three survivors because they had an emotional meaning. . . . I have one from 1987, the girl from *The Hunchback of Notre Dame* that has black hair, and Teresa who had brown hair and skin and was my favorite. That was me.
>
> Emily: I liked that one too. Why did you like her?
>
> Mariela: Maybe because she was not blond like all the others and her skin was brown. More tanned. She looked like me.
>
> Jessica: I remember that I asked for one—I didn't want blond Barbies because I was tired of them. And I still keep this one, it is the one that is in the best condition. It was Teacher Barbie, which came with two children. She was black,

> Black Barbie, and that one is in its original state because for me she was . . . I
> kept her well. But it was so stupid, why did Barbie have to be blond?
>
> Jessica: Mine were the Black one, a blond one, and one with brown hair,
> nothing else. (Group 2 transcript)

As illustrated above, both Mariela and Jessica favored Barbies of color
over white Barbie. Mariela, who identified as a Brown Latina, saw herself
in Teresa, the Latina doll with brown skin. Furthermore, out of all the
dolls Mariela had in her childhood, only three survived into her adulthood because they were the dolls that held an emotional meaning for her,
while she gave away the rest. These "surviving" dolls were her favorite
dolls because they were not white and blond. Jessica, who describe her
race as "other" because she does not see herself as fully white or fully
Black, grew tired of Barbies with blond hair and thus, Barbies with dark
hair or dark skin colors became her favorite ones. There's an interesting
predicament in Mariela's and Jessica's preferences for a Brown doll, like
Teresa, as well as Black dolls. Beyond seeing themselves more reflected
in some of the dolls of color, both women preferred them because they
grew tired of seeing white Barbie everywhere. The dolls' *difference* and
otherness from the white doll, and the fact that there were not as many of
them, made them more desirable, to the point that they preserved some
of these dolls into adulthood. Their examples showcase Mattel's commodification of difference and otherness. The small numbers of dolls of
color in the Barbie lines cause an erasure of racial and ethnic diversity. At
the same time, the dolls' "otherness" paired with their low availability create items that are much desired and, therefore, more commercially valuable. The *Collector's Encyclopedia of Barbie Dolls* lists the Colored Francie
doll, which was produced in 1967, as one of the most highly sought after
Mattel dolls. Reportedly, a new-in-box doll is worth between $700 and
$900 (duCille 1999).

Alondra's favorite Barbie dolls were the ones with dark hair. Moreover,
Alondra (age thirty-two) was the only participant who described (or remembered) changing her dolls' ethnicity to transform them into Puerto
Rican characters, using household items to create Puerto Rican food their
dolls could eat, and constructing play scenarios that took place in or were
about Puerto Rico.

> The Barbie, Ken, and other dolls I used had to have brown hair, or in its defect,
> red. The blond ones, although they were the majority of the dolls, were sec-
> ondary characters, or I would lend them to other girls. My Barbies were Puerto

Rican, and the scenarios of play were about/in Puerto Rico. It is possible that at some moment I created a foreign character, but I don't remember it with exactness. I do know that they ate rice and beans. I would put out a little plate (from the Picnic set) with dry grains of rice and achiote[3] seeds, which became the beans for the rice. (Alondra, email interview)

Alondra's play with Barbie pushed against Mattel's lineup that highlighted blond Barbie as the main character. By mostly playing with dolls that did not have blond hair, she provided them with protagonist roles in her play and in her life. Blond Barbies, as a result, were moved to secondary roles, if any, or they were simply given to other people for play. This interchange in the roles the dolls were assigned subverted Mattel's continuous promotion of white, blond Barbie as the central figure. Moreover, even when Alondra assigned white, blond Barbie a protagonist role, she often changed the doll's nationality or her ethnicity (creating her own Puerto Rican doll) to better fit her own reality and experiences. Alondra's case serves as an example of how girls may challenge established narratives in order to provide for themselves the play experiences that they want, need, and deserve. By deciding that white, blond Barbie would become a background character in her play, and by assigning protagonist roles to the other dolls, Alondra was playing against the dominant narrative created by Mattel that positioned white Barbie as central.

Even though the introduction of the first Black Barbie doll and the first Hispanic Barbie doll in 1979 and 1980 was a step toward racial and ethnic diversity in the Barbie collection, their "sameness" was also very problematic. Scholars have pointed out that these and other ethnic dolls are simply a copy of white Barbie colored in various shades (duCille 1994, 1999, 2003; Rand 1995). There are, for the most part, no other changes to, for instance, her hair texture, her facial features, and her body type, to name a few. Mattel's efforts to diversify Barbie and address the concerns about race also materialized in the creation of the "ethnically correct" fashion doll Shani and her friends Asha and Nichelle in 1991 (Chin 1999). The company saw these dolls as the answer to major criticism about their Barbies of color. These new dolls were not like other dolls Mattel had produced, as they came in light, medium, and dark skin tones and their faces were sculpted differently from Barbie dolls, "purportedly based on real African American faces" (Chin 1999: 305). This line was discontinued in 1999, although the head and body molds kept being used for other dolls in the Barbie line. While Mattel has continued working on these issues, girls who interact(ed) with Barbie are aware of these problems with the doll:

That [Barbie's race], during the first years, was not relevant. That became relevant when I was more an adolescent. That was something that *did* go through my mind, but it was during the last years when I played with Barbie. Because she was always Barbie, she was unique. I became confused when Teresa entered the picture and the *morenita*,[4] whose name I can't remember. I know that it wasn't until someone gave me Teresa and the *morenita* that I said, "Oh shoot! Barbie also comes in Black and comes as a Latina!" But then when I see the name, I realize that it's not Barbie. It's Barbie's *friend*. It's a completely different person with the same body, same eyes, same dimensions. The only thing that changes is the skin color and hair color, but nothing else. Because they were the same. So then, why aren't they Barbie as well? That was my inquiry. Why do they have other names if they are the same? Why don't they want Barbie to be Black? Why does Barbie have to be white? And the Latina [has to be] Teresa? If you can clearly see that they are the same doll? So yes, that to me—but it was when I had more mentality to understand that it was the same doll with a different color and a different name. (Carla, interview transcript)

Carla (age thirty-three) describes precisely what Ann duCille has argued about Barbie dolls of color: that they are mere carbon copies of white Barbie, clad in blackface, different yet the "same" (1994, 1999). Carla's account positions her as a girl who suddenly encountered two aspects of Barbie's race. On the one hand, she realized after a long time of Barbie play that there were other dolls that were not white and blond like the Barbie with which she had mostly interacted. On the other hand, this encounter came with the realization that the dolls looked very similar to each other, yet those that were not white were not supposed to be called "Barbie." Thus, she questioned, "Why does Barbie have to be white . . . if you can clearly see that they are the same doll?" These are questions that girls today have about Barbie and her friends. They certainly notice the difference in the dolls' positions within the Barbie line: *the* Barbie is white and blond. Anyone else is Barbie's friend, but not *the* Barbie. Such was the case during a short exchange between Annie (age nine) and her mother Susan, when I asked about two dolls she brought to the interview:

Emily: Oh! You have the same one in different colors. Are they ballerinas?
Annie: Yes. But in reality, they're not the same, because if you see, she is white and she is *negrita*. One has blond hair. That's Barbie, pure Barbie.
Emily: And what is this one?
Susan: That one is also Barbie.
Annie: Yes, I know. But this one is *the same* as Barbie. She's blond, white, pink. [*Laughs*]

Annie acknowledged the differences in her two dolls' skin color and hair. Moreover, she identified white, blond, pink-wearing Barbie as *the* Barbie. No matter what other dolls come out, the only "true" Barbie continues to be the white blond one. This is something that Carla questioned when she was a teenager still playing with Barbie and is something that girls notice in the present, despite Mattel's efforts to diversify. Yet, if their attempts are only about creating more dolls but not about placing other dolls at the center, some girls may continue to see white Barbie as the "true" Barbie doll. Girls have found ways to negotiate white Barbie's place as the central figure (and the mold for all other dolls) by changing the doll's looks (Chin 1999). As a play object, Barbie is bound to be transformed, but certain transformations of the doll have illustrated that Mattel's diversity efforts are inadequate and insufficiently authentic for the audiences it claims to reach. For example, in the Yucatan region of Mexico, Mac-Dougall (2003) observed how local Maya people redesigned Barbie by producing culturally appropriate clothing for dolls, making her a more culturally meaningful icon. Mexican consumers indigenized an American product to represent their local cultures (MacDougall 2003). Chin notes that Black girls in her study "tended to have white dolls that they tended to bring into their own worlds, often through styling their hair" (1999: 306). Such was the case of Sharon (age eight), another participant in this study, who also noted that white, blond Barbie was the central figure of the doll line, a fact that caused her much frustration.

To appease her dislike of certain Barbie dolls with blond hair, Sharon took coloring markers and painted one of her dolls' hair. She said, "I painted her hair with markers because she looked pretty with them, but then my mom said my dad was gonna be angry so, she's at the bottom of my toy box. . . . She has pink, blue, green, yellow, red [hair]" (Sharon, Group 5 transcript). When I asked why she came up with the idea of painting her hair, Sharon explained: "I just thought that blond wasn't really the color that I liked for hair." She also painted another doll's hair half blue and half pink and added that, while she likes experimenting with Barbie's hair, she never experimented with one particular doll because she thought "she was beautiful the way she was" (Sharon, Group 5 transcript). When it comes to racial identity and encountering Barbie's race, the doll's hair plays a central role (Negrón-Muntaner 2004). After all, playing with Barbie's hair is one of the favorite activities (if not *the* favorite activity) girls engage in while playing with the doll. By coloring her doll's hair, Sharon took matters into her own hands and transformed her doll into what she thought Barbie should be, and in doing so she challenged Mattel's centering of white, blond Barbie. Sharon's doll transformation was not explicitly about Barbie's race, but it was about her whiteness. Just like how Alondra (age thirty-two) had changed her dolls' nationality and ethnicity in her play, Sharon was attempting to mitigate what she saw as one of the most salient characteristics of Barbie's whiteness—her blond hair.

Racial Identity in Puerto Rico

My participants' encounters with race were not only about racially identifying with Barbie or noticing the lack of diversity among the dolls from the Barbie line; they were also about the way that race is talked about in Puerto Rico, often constructing *negritud* or Blackness as something ugly and shameful. When the conversation with participant Group 3 turned to diversity and race within the Barbie line, Frankie (age thirty) remembered that she never had a Black Barbie doll but that her niece had one, and she learned to see the doll as ugly because of the discourse used around it. Frankie said, "I never had a *negrita* Barbie, but someone gave one to my niece, and my great-grandmother was a little racist. She would tell my niece that the doll was ugly. So, then my niece began saying that that Barbie was ugly" (Frankie, Group 3 transcript). The case of Frankie's niece reveals an important part of how girls (and children) learn what to love and what to hate about themselves. Just as some participants observed that girls receive messages about their bodies not only through Barbie but also through what the people around them say, Frankie's niece learned that Blackness equaled ugliness.

Discussing her experience being the first Black Puerto Rican to win the Miss Universe Puerto Rico beauty pageant, Alba G. Reyes remembers how she experienced racism as her claim to the crown was followed by a barrage of criticism for not fitting into "beauty standards." In other words, she was not white. A little over a decade after Reyes became Miss Universe Puerto Rico, the franchise selected Madison Anderson as the 2019 Miss Universe Puerto Rico, to represent the island at the international pageant. Her selection was initially controversial because she was not born or raised in Puerto Rico, but her mother is Puerto Rican. Because Madison also did not speak Spanish, many Puerto Ricans did not feel that she represented them. Yet, they eventually embraced her, calling her a Puerto Rican Barbie because her blond her, blue eyes, and white skin resembled the doll's features. At the international pageant, when the choice for the crown was between Anderson (a white, blond woman representing Puerto Rico) and Zozibini Tunzi (a Black woman with short hair, representing South Africa), Boricuas were notably excited at the possibility of winning. However, when Tunzi was crowned Miss Universe, it was not long before racist comments made their way through social media. In dubbing Tunzi "ugly," or "monstrous" even, while calling Anderson a beautiful Barbie, some of the discourses about race on the island became evident. Also telling were the knee-jerk responses whenever these comments were called out as racist. There was some variation of "Puerto Ricans can't be racist because we have African roots," or "I am a mix of three races, so I'm not being racist." Negrón-Muntaner (2004) and Ferrer (2016) point out how the population's history of *mestizaje* (mixture) has led to discourses of racism. *Mestizaje*, which is the blending of the three races—*blanca, india, y negra*[5]—is what "causes Puerto Ricans to believe that we all are racially mixed the exact same way therefore there can be no 'true' difference" (Ferrer 2016: par. 3), and, thus, no racism. Lloréns (2020) explains that in Puerto Rico, as in most of Latin America, anti-Black racism is embedded precisely in the state's and society's denial that it exists. Moreover, the belief that "we are all mixed" is weaponized against Black people who demand racial justice, often invisibilizing them and minimizing their plight.

Kinsbruner (1996) notes that in Puerto Rico there was a historic disassociation from African and Afro-American roots since the Spanish colonization until the island's occupation by the United States in 1898. Having been taught in school that the Puerto Rican race was born through the combination[6] of three races—Spanish, African, and Taíno (our Indigenous peoples)—many Puerto Ricans choose to self-identify as white (according to the 2010 Census published by the U.S. Census Bureau 2012). Loveman and Muñiz (2007) provide insight into the "whitening" of Puerto Ricans' racial identification, explaining that,

> in a census taken by the U.S. Department of War in 1899, a year after the island came under U.S. dominion, 61.8 percent of Puerto Ricans were classified as white. By 1950, census enumerators classified 79.7 percent of the Puerto Rican population as white—just shy of the 80.5 percent of Puerto Ricans on the island who self-identified as white in the 2000 U.S. Census. (2007: 915–16)

There are sometimes overlapping systems at work that produce this "whitening" in Puerto Rican racial identification. First, there are "gaps and silences, produced through vacillation, ambivalence, and avoidance" regarding racial identification (Rodríguez-Silva 2012: 2). In his ethnographic work, anthropologist Jorge Duany captures some of this ambivalence when he recounts, "I asked our informants, 'What race do you consider yourself to belong to?' Responses to this seemingly innocuous question ranged from embarrassment and amazement to ambivalence and silence" (2002: 236). I was met with similar responses from some participants. Because the question about how they racially identified was open-ended, participants often provided an explanation to their answers that reflected some of their ambivalence and confusion, brought about in part due to the ways that census questions frame race. The most recent census report offers the following categories under "Race and Hispanic Origin":

- White alone
- Black or African American alone
- Asian alone
- Native Hawaiian and Other Pacific Islander alone
- Two or More Races
- Hispanic or Latino
- White alone, not Hispanic or Latino

My question did not offer any categories because I did not want to delineate how participants could identify. As a result, there was a range of responses that illustrates some of this confusion: at least three participants answered with just "Latina," while another one added more descriptors: "Hispana, Latina, Puertorriqueña." Others were more specific and even asked questions about what the possible categories were. For example, Isabel asked, "What are the indicators? If they are from the census, then I am Black Hispanic or Multiracial." Because their skin color is very light, Carmen, Frances, and Camille explained their choice based on what the census offers as choices: "If there is an option for Hispanic/Latina, I choose that, otherwise I put 'white' unless there is an option for 'more than one' or 'other.'" Jessica explained that she does not know if it's correct or not, but that she usually identifies as "other" because despite being *jincha* or very light-skinned, she does not feel that she is white. Because there are more than a dozen racial terms used in Puerto Rico (like *moreno, trigueño, blanco,* and *de color*), the Black/white dichotomy used in the United States does not fit neatly in the island's context: "In American racial terminology, most of our subjects would probably classify themselves as 'other,' that is neither white nor black" (Duany 2002: 237). Moreover, because ancestry is not as much of an indicator as are phenotypical characteristics such as facial features and skin color, some of these participants who answered "white" or "other" made reference to their light skin, especially because some of them felt that answering "Black" when their skin is light (even if there is Black ancestry in their family) would be appropriating or falsely claiming Blackness, a prevalent and damaging "trend" among white people.[7]

To further complicate whiteness in Puerto Rico, the white blood that heads the list of *mestizaje* is given a greater value and "allows for a larger number of 'mixed-race' people to qualify as *blancos*" (Negrón-Muntaner 2004: 212). Rodríguez-Silva notes that Puerto Ricans who are challenging the prevalent notions that racial hierarchies and racism on the island do not exist have explained that Puerto Ricans have associated Blackness with "diminished intellectual abilities and negative aesthetic images persistent since slavery" (2012: 2). Consequently, Puerto Ricans have resorted to identifying as white as a vehicle for socioeconomic advancement. At the same time, Negrón-Muntaner (2004) explains, Puerto Ricans of African descent are socially encouraged to seek upward mobility by tuning out their Black blood furthermore in each subsequent generation. They are encouraged to *mejorar la raza* or improve the race by further mixing their Black attributes—skin tone, thick lips, nose, wideness, and hair texture—with whiter ones.

Currently, there is a growing movement within the Puerto Rican population of the island to highlight and celebrate AfroBoricuas.[8] In many instances Puerto Ricans use skin color and other physical characteristics to identify themselves in terms of race (Peña-Pérez 2016). At the same time, other aspects considered for racial identification are color, class, facial features, and texture of hair (often referred to as *pelo malo* [bad hair] in a racist manner), thus resulting in a variety of racial classifications that are not recognized in North American society. Yolanda Arroyo Pizarro, renowned AfroBoricua writer and director of the Department of AfroPuerto-Rican Studies,[9] for instance, challenges "normative" ideas about beauty and especially the descriptor *pelo malo* for Black natural hair. Through her children's book *Pelo Bueno* (2018), Arroyo Pizarro reframes natural hair—which has historically also been deemed unprofessional—as a symbol of self-love, identity, respect, and care.

While AfroBoricuas have highlighted these characteristics to empower and demonstrate pride in their African roots, the majority population has historically used them with negative connotations. Moreover, in the discourse about Blackness, the word "Black" is often followed by a modifier that seems to serve the purpose of "making it better." In recounting some of the comments he has received as a Black Puerto Rican, sociologist Eduardo Bonilla-Silva offers the example of being "elevated" to "'negro pero bueno' (Black but decent)" (2010: 445). Reyes (2015) illustrates this through an example from another contestant in the beauty pageant who was told by a member of the judge panel, "You are a beautiful Black [woman]."[10] The author comments that this remark expresses something beyond just telling the participant she is beautiful; it is "as if that was something exceptional, out of the norm, that is it suggests in a subtle way that she is beautiful, for a Black woman" (Reyes 2015: par. 8). When it comes to dolls, this internalization of what is pretty and what is not can take shape in the person's preference for features like white skin, blue or green eyes, and blond hair—features that Barbie embodies and that make her undoubtedly "her."

Examining Discourses of Race through Barbie

Barbie's white (and blond) image constantly entering girls' play spaces, especially girls of color who do not look like her, creates a space of contention and tensions where girls may not identify with the doll. At the same time, there is a tendency for some participants to view themselves as white and identify mostly with white Barbie. Because the characteristics of race in Puerto Rico are not limited solely to skin color, it is critical to take into consideration both the doll's and the girls' physical characteristics that go deeper than skin, if they pay or paid attention to overt differences, and how they negotiated them. Descriptors such as hair color and texture, facial features, and skin color came up in my discussion of the participants' encounters with race within Barbie.

Racial identification in Puerto Rico, Negrón-Muntaner (2004) explains, "is partly determined by a combination of phenotypical factors," one of which is hair texture, and I add, in relation to Barbie, hair color as well. Barbie's hair came up in many of the interviews as an important characteristic for girls who wanted to identify with the doll. Patricia (age fifty-nine), who identified as white, shared that she always wanted the doll with darker hair color. Despite having a vast collection of Barbie dolls with a variety of hair colors, she reminisced as she held one of her dolls about liking the one with dark hair the most when she was growing.

Mine was always brunette. Since I had black hair, I identified with her. . . .
I didn't like the blond one, you know why? Because it was blond, but her skin
was like *trigueña* [light brown] and it looked bad. When I chose my Barbie, I
had the blond one in my hand. It's just that it didn't match because the skin was
trigueña and the hair was blond, and it didn't look good. I chose the one with
black hair. (Patricia, Group 4 transcript)

Contextualized in the experiences of Puerto Rican girls and women, race
and the body have much in common. Patricia noted that she saw herself
in the brunette doll because her own hair was black, therefore she could
identify with Barbie. Moreover, she did not like blond Barbie, not necessarily because the doll's hair color was different from hers or as a rejection
of her whiteness (like others did), but because Patricia could not conceive
a person with darker skin color being blond. In her opinion, a person
could not possess those two physical traits and look good.

Citing the famous study conducted by Kenneth and Mamie Clark in
the 1940s and replicated by Darlene Powell-Hopson and Derek Hopson in
1990, duCille (1999) notes that girls may see Black dolls as "bad" or ugly
and reject them. It was this association of Blackness with ugliness, perpet-
uated by her grandmother, that made Frankie's niece reject Black Barbie
dolls. This seemed to also be the case with Gabriela (age twenty-five), who
identified as white and was the only participant who openly stated her dislike of Black Barbie dolls specifically rather than all Barbie dolls.

Gabriela: I didn't like the Black ones, I hated them. One time someone gave
me a Black one and I started to cry, right Mom? But I always wanted one that
was Latina. One that was like me, white with curly hair. All of them were white
and blond.
Emily: And the Latinas were more *trigueñitas*.
Gabriela: Always, there's never one that looks like me.
[. . .]
Gabriela: So, I don't know why I hated the Black one. I don't know why.
Emily: But what about other colors, like brown?
Gabriela: For me, they had to be white. It's not that I'm racist! But I don't
know, when I was little I liked the blond, white ones. To me those were prettier. . . .
If they asked me to choose between a *trigueña* or a white one, I chose the white
one. Unless it was from a movie or if they came in sets. For example, this one
had the same doll in different colors, so I wanted all of them, except the "ne-
grita." [See figure 4.1]
Emily: I never had the Black one or the Asian one. I always wanted one. And
I liked Teresa a lot for her skin color because I saw her so different from the others. I liked the dolls with dark hair, I think because most of mine were blond, so
I wanted ones that were different. (Gabriela, Group 4 transcript)

117

In this moment of our conversation, Gabriela expressed not just dislike but also *hatred* toward Black Barbie dolls. Moreover, if she had the options of choosing either white Barbie or Black Barbie, she would choose the white one. This response from children was recorded in both the study by the Clarks in the 1940s and its replication in 1990. One notable difference is that Gabriela's skin color is not Black, as opposed to the children in the studies. More notably, Gabriela repeatedly stated that her dislike of Black Barbies was not caused by racism. While this might be true, there are ways in which people internalize what is "beautiful," not only in what a girl's body shape should be but also in what bodies are valued (i.e., white bodies). As duCille (1999) notes, these responses do not always represent how one feels about race, but they convey the knowledge one has about societal attitudes toward the racially marked. In Gabriela's interactions with Barbie, we mostly saw a rejection of Black Barbie dolls and, in turn, perhaps a rejection of Blackness and a valorization of white features. What Gabriela's response to Black Barbie may illustrate is the valorization of whiteness in Puerto Rican cultural ideologies.

Gabriela's mother, Patricia, demonstrated a similar valorization of phenotypically white features. In the previous chapter, I examined Patricia's comments about a friend who gained weight in relation to internalized beauty standards. Yet, her comment also points to internalized beauty ideals that seem to favor whiteness. In her statement, she described her friend as precious *because* she had blond hair and blue eyes. Her friend's "downfall" was that she was not skinny.

Patricia's contradiction illustrated the very ideals about beauty that Barbie promotes: that in order to be beautiful you must be thin yet busty, white, blond, and have blue or green eyes. Yet, this is a complex anecdote that also raises issues about race. Patricia's comments about her friend's eyes give light to the discourse around race that is often propagated in Puerto Rican culture. She described a lady who was beautiful, as she was blond and blue-eyed. Patricia had so internalized this particular ideal of beauty that she did not examine why she specifically used her friend's blue eyes and blond hair as markers of beauty. This description of beauty is not exclusive to her. As Negrón-Muntaner (2004) pointed out, Puerto Ricans, especially dark-skinned ones, are consistently told to marry someone with a lighter skin tone, perhaps with light eye color too, so that they can improve the race—"para mejorar la raza." Lloréns (2013) describes this ideal as the *Maja*, the Latina who is light-skinned, has straight, blond, or brown hair, has fine facial features, and is curvy but thin.

Figure 4.1. A sample of Gabriela's dolls (*top*). Close-up to one of her dolls from a set (*bottom*). Photographs by author.

Historically the majority population has used color, class, facial features, and texture of hair (often referred to as *pelo malo* [bad hair]) with
negative connotations. Reyes elucidates the array of characteristics and
descriptors negatively given to her as she became the first Black Puerto
Rican beauty queen: "I was described as ugly, my nose as a bicycle seat,
among others, I remember receiving recommendations about how to
whiten my elbows and knees because they were too dark" (2015: par. 1).
Reyes (2015) uses the term *sillín de bicicleta* (bicycle seat) because it is a
common descriptor used in Puerto Rico to refer to a nose that is wide
(with the connotation that it is ugly). For one participant, thirty-year-old
Isabel, these characteristics of Blackness were valued not only by her but
also her parents, so much so that she remembered vividly why none of her
dolls were white: "My dad would buy me the Black Barbie and he'd tell
me that, to him, she looked more like me than the blond one. And I liked
the Black one more as well" (Isabel, Group 3 transcript). For Isabel's dad,
it was crucial to show her that beauty was not limited to whiteness, and
by principally providing access to Black Barbie, he gave Isabel the opportunity to see herself reflected in her artifacts of play.

Reflections on Race

From my exchange between Gabriela and me, it is important to also examine my own discourse on race. DuCille (1999) discusses the exoticization of Barbie when she is seen as an "Other," a Barbie of color. In my
own experience I was always attracted to Barbies with dark hair, darker
skin, different facial traits (from the "standard" Barbie), red hair, and dark
eyes—basically any doll that was not the white, blond Barbie. Primarily
my attraction was due to their rarity, their "Otherness." They were not
the common and typical blond style of Barbie, and I liked that. Thinking
more critically about this, I realize that I was exoticizing these dolls, and
while I may belong to these "Other" bodies, the exoticization stems from
my own perceptions that my skin tone is not brown, as Latinx bodies are
typically depicted in media. While I lived on a tropical island surrounded
by the beach, my status as a *jincha* (a term to refer to people with pale skin
in Puerto Rico) made me see dolls of darker skin color as "Others" and
exotic. When I said, "And the Latinas were more *trigueñitas*," Gabriela
replied that it was always like that, that "there's never one that looks like
me." Yet this also highlights Puerto Ricans' practice of whitening their

race. As Negrón-Muntaner notes, "Whereas one drop of 'black blood' makes you African American in the United States, one of 'white' can have the opposite effect in the Island, where a person does not need to claim exclusively European lineage to access the benefits of whiteness" (2004: 43). As a result, this allows more mixed-race people on the island to qualify as "white." But while Gabriela did not see herself in Latina Barbie dolls, the reality is that many of the Latina dolls in the Barbie line are light-skinned. Meanwhile, Black Puerto Ricans or Black Latinxs have been excluded from Barbie lines and even the "Dolls of the World" collection, which purportedly celebrates cultural, national, and racial diversity.

In the conversations about race that transpired with my participants, it is also important to note not only *what* they talked about in relation to their experiences with race but also *how* they talked about them. As I transcribed the audio recordings, I encountered the different terms my participants were using to talk about Blackness. Furthermore, I realized I was using those same terms when I commented on something participants said, perhaps as to not change the meaning of their words or to describe my own experiences in my comments. Frankie said, "I never had a *negrita* Barbie." The terms used—*morena/morenita, quemadita, trigueña/trigueñita*, and *negrita*—assign a different degree of Blackness than what the word *negra* or Black would. In transcribing and translating, I had to think about how I would present these terms in English and how/why the participants and I were using it. I asked myself, *How do I translate all the different words Puerto Ricans (and other Spanish-speaking peoples) use to talk about race and Blackness?* Addressing how Latinos talk about race, Godreau (2008) explains:

> It is a well-known fact among scholars of race relations in Latin America that racial terminology is highly situational and intimately linked to context of usage. Negro, for example, often carries pejorative connotations because of its association with slave status. Yet, . . . it can also be used to mark racial solidarity or "sameness" among those who openly identify themselves as [B]lack. Nonetheless, in other instances, the use of negro or its diminutive form negrito (or negra, negrita) may communicate affection and intimacy regardless of the skin color of the person to which it refers, but not regardless of the relationship between the speakers. Which meaning is to be ascribed depends on who says it, when, and how. (2008: 6)

We have these various words that refer to Blackness, but they are different shades of Blackness, and they are also sometimes used as terms of endearment. Beauty queen Alba Reyes delineates how various terms are used to almost erase Blackness. She explains, "It is very common to use terms like *mulato, trigueños, moreno* for people who, due to a lighter skin tone, are not considered Black, but they are also not white" (Reyes 2015: par. 3). Duany lists these and other terms as "Major Folk Racial Terms Used in Puerto Rico," defining them as follows: *morena/morenita*—"dark skinned; usually dark mulatto"; *trigueña/trigueñita*—"literally, wheat colored or brunette; usually light mulatto"; and *negrita*—"literally, little black; often used as a term of endearment" and separate from *negra*, which he defines as "Black; rarely used as a direct term of reference" (2002: 238). To address my question about how I could translate the different shades of Blackness in the various terms used, I decided to leave all terms in their Spanish form instead of attempting to translate them. By leaving them as the participants said them, I aimed to remain true to their expressions and descriptions about Barbie's race and to maintain the nuances embedded in the range of descriptors used. The only word I changed into English was *negra*, which directly translates to and carries the meanings of the word "Black."

Racial encounters with Barbie and the discourses used to discuss experiences with the doll offer a small window into the larger discussions about race in Puerto Rico. Just as Barbie embodies so many contradictions, views on race in Puerto Rico are in constant conflict. There is a denial of anti-Blackness racism, which in itself is one of the most deceptive forms of racism, as it not only dismisses Black Puerto Ricans' own experiences but it also allows those enacting racism to deny any wrongdoing. The stories presented here illustrated the different views about race that participants had in relation to Barbie and to their own identities. Some of the participants lamented the lack of diversity in the line of Barbie dolls and pointed out how, even in its attempt to diversify, Mattel continued depicting white Barbie as the signature Barbie. While some of the participants expressed an aversion toward white, blond Barbie, one participant loved this particular model of the doll. Her preference for the white doll and her hatred toward the Black one exemplified the cultural notions about race, which often classify racialized bodies as "bad."

Notes

1. With the exception of collectible or limited-edition dolls.
2. Barbie dolls used to include a small manual that contained instructions and information about the doll.
3. Achiote is a spice made from the red seed of the annatto tree (*Merriam-Webster Dictionary*). The seeds are red, which can make them look like miniature beans.
4. While the English translation of *morena* is brunette, brunette often refers only to the hair color. In Puerto Rico, *morena* is used to talk about a skin color that is dark but not quite Black. The closest translation would be olive-colored skin. As explained in the discussion at the end of the section, there is always an apprehension to use the word *negra*, which means Black, to talk about skin color.
5. White (from Spain), Indigenous (from the Taínos), and Black (from Africa). In Puerto Rican schools, students learn that these are the races that make up our Puerto Rican "race," and they generally learn them and list them in that same order.
6. In most cases, history is sanitized to appear as if the mixture of these races occurred willingly and peacefully.
7. For example, the recent case of Jessica Krug who pretended to be North African, then Black American, and then Black Caribbean and navigated academic, social, and cultural spaces disguising her whiteness (see Figueroa-Vásquez and Bonilla, 2020).
8. The term "Boricua" stems from the island's original Taíno name: Borikén.
9. A performative project of creative writing based at the Casa Museo Ashford in San Juan, Puerto Rico.
10. I have translated this and subsequent quotes from Reyes's "Ser negra en Puerto Rico" from Spanish to English.

CS

Chapter 5

All in the Family
Barbie's Place in Familial Dynamics

> Lana: Do you know that I didn't want to buy you a Barbie ever? Do you know how you got your first Barbie? . . .
>
> Caitlin: Dad. It was when we were moving. There was nothing left at home to play with so we went to Toys R Us, and I wanted to buy a Barbie because I never had one before.
>
> –Lana F. Rakow and Caitlin S. Rakow (1999), "Educating Barbie"

The official lore about Barbie's creation narrates how in 1959 Ruth Handler, wanting a toy with which her daughter could play, and which did not require girls to assume the role of a mother, produced an adult fashion doll through which girls could live and become their dreamed selves. Barbie is a cultural icon that has been present since 1959 and has been a popular toy among girls since then. While the Barbie doll's creation purportedly emerged from a mother's desire to provide more options for her daughter, the relationship between mothers and Barbie has often been tumultuous and complicated, with some mothers rejecting the doll (Quindlen 1999; Rakow and Rakow 1999) and others embracing it (McDonough 1999).

Author Meg Wolitzer, for instance, talks about her own experiences, both as a child and as a mother, with parental involvement in Barbie play. She explains that her mother did not allow her or her sister to have a Barbie, but she did allow Skipper. Similar to my friend's views on Barbie, Wolitzer (1999) affirms that if she had been a mother of girls, she would be scared that Barbie's presence in the girls' lives would send them wrong messages. Yet, she did allow her sons to play with Barbie. I questioned why she thought Barbie, as an object, was okay for boys but not for girls. Her rationale was as follows:

> But as far as my two boys go, I don't need to worry unduly about the political "message" aspect of Barbie, because, for the most part, neither of my sons dwells on her anatomy or wardrobe or vacuous, made-up face. . . . No, for them Barbie is merely another *thing* to be played with, manipulated, occasionally talked to . . . (Wolitzer 1999: 208, emphasis in original)

These are just some examples of the many ways Barbie contributes to women's identities and how women continue to view the doll, either in relation to their own childhood experiences or as adults who do not want to promote Barbie play among their own offspring. In my encounters with some preliminary participants—before I made the decision to focus on Puerto Rican women and girls—I learned about various ways in which parents intervened in girls' play, even before the object of play was acquired. This motivated me to inquire further about parental influence on Barbie play and how the doll affected familial relationships, chiefly between mothers and daughters. Since much had been written about mothers' perceptions about Barbie in contexts such as the United States and Canada, my aim was to investigate if the same perceptions occurred in Puerto Rico.

The thematic findings discussed in the previous chapters pertained, for the most part, to the individual experiences my participants had with Barbie play. This chapter continues to address Barbie's impact on Puerto Rican girlhoods and her influence on girls' identities seeded in collective experiences. Drawing from the interviews with women and girls between the ages of eight and sixty-two conducted throughout this study, this chapter examines familial female relationships in the context of Puerto Rican girlhoods. It describes Barbie's place in the dynamics between family members, especially between mothers, daughters, and sisters, and presents a discussion of their conversations about their decisions to play or not play with Barbie. In some particular cases, brothers and fathers were involved. While the men were not interviewed, these brief stories are offered through the voices of girls and women to account for their own experiences of girlhood.

The Mother and Daughter Relationship

"What mother doesn't love sharing with her daughter, enjoying when we wear the same size and like the same things?" asks Amy Newmark (2012: xi). There is a strong bond that often (though not always) grows between mothers and daughters. As Newmark observes, little girls emulate their mothers by dressing like them and wanting to be like them. Similarly, she says, "over time, we mothers find ourselves emulating our daughters too. I always tell mine, employing a technology-world term, that she is 'Version 2.0'—me, but much improved. I learn so much from her—not only about how to dress, but about fitness and nutrition, current events . . ." (2012: xii). While the little girl often emulates the mother, there are moments, especially during specific life stages, where the girl longs for separation. In a moving piece about her transition from being a daughter to being a mother, Therese Guy illustrates these shifting stages:

> I'm five and my mom is everything. . . . I'm twelve and now she is embarrassing. . . . I'm seventeen and all I can manage is an eyeball roll at her antiquated lectures. . . . I'm twenty-one and she seems a little smarter now. . . . I'm thirty-seven and my fourteen-year-old daughter yells at me for emerging from the car when I pick her up at the dance. . . . I'm fifty and my daughter is expecting. It is a girl. As I hold my hand against her protruding belly the baby kicks. My daughter smiles and says, 'I think I understand you better now, Mom.' . . . (2012: 109–10)

By virtue of being female (at least in the biological sense but oftentimes in terms of gender) mothers and daughters share important life experiences. These can foster essential understandings about what it means to be girl and lead to collaboration between mothers and daughters to further explore these meanings and experiences.

Working with mothers and daughters, Lobenstine et al. "saw mothers as important cultural messengers, and . . . wanted to examine the mother's role in shaping her daughter's possible selves" (2001: 2). They found many similarities between mothers' and daughters' answers. A testimony written by one of the mothers participating in the project, in which mothers and daughters collaborated to examine their experiences of possible selves (as discussed in chapter 2), reveals that she thought the age difference between her daughter and her and their different upbringings would result in different likes and dislikes. However, she was surprised to find they had much in common: "Here are two women who grew up in different environments (culture) but yet want so much of the same things" (Lobenstine et al. 2001: 7). Comparably, my examination of mothers' and daughters' (as well as sisters) experiences with Barbie revealed similarities within each family group. At the same time, as a testament to each person's individuality, the distinctions between each member were clearly marked. Moreover, in Puerto Rican culture, the relationship between mothers and daughters involves the transmission from older generations to new generations of stories that teach girls how to be women. Santiago (1993, 1999) and Ortiz Cofer (1990) offer examples of learning through their mothers and grandmothers about how a girl should behave, the values she should seek, and the dreams she should have for the future. Based on this important dynamic between matriarchal figures and girls in Puerto Rico, the dynamics between mothers and daughters—as well as between sisters—become an important part of Barbie play to examine.

What follow are accounts selected from those of my participants that provide insight to the types of relationships fostered through and the different dynamics that emerged from play with Barbie. Specifically, they bring light to how different yet similar the experiences among women within a family group can be. Moreover, they serve as examples of the varying levels of parental involvement in girls' Barbie play and the rationale behind the allowance or disproval of play with such a contested doll.

"I Hated Her, She Loved Her!"
Similar and Different Experiences of Barbie Play

One of the most interesting parts of interviewing women and girls from a range of generations was being able to learn about so many different experiences with Barbie, some similar to my own, but others very contrasting. It was especially illuminating to learn about how girls related to Barbie in the past, when she had just been "born." The journey into the multiple generations of girls that played with Barbie began with a conversation with my own family—a conversation with which I begin this section. Within this specific group interview there were two family generations—two sisters and the daughters of one of the sisters—who were born in various decades: two were born in the 1950s, two were born in the 1980s, and one was born in the beginning of the 1990s. Their own experiences and views about Barbie provided a preview of what the rest of my participants may have experienced and what their thoughts on Barbie may have been.

The lived experiences within a family can be very similar, not only between mothers and daughters but also between sisters. Sharing a space and oftentimes the same toys may lead to disagreements and fights between siblings, but they can also lead to collaboration. As illustrated by Lourdes and Carmen, two sisters in their sixties, who belong to the first generation of Barbie players, Barbie can serve as an object and a play space that creates bonds in female relationships:

> Lourdes: The fun was . . . how we played with them, or at least how *I* played with her wasn't so much that she was a doll . . . it was the fashion, what we bought for her, which cost a *lot* of money at that time. We would stop buying other things so we could buy clothes for Barbie, but it was like *designer clothes* [*Carmen, her sister, says this at the same time*], upscale, like, if they were hats, they had leather.
>
> Carmen: I mean, they were like the clothes that we would see . . . let's say, artists [wearing].
>
> Lourdes: They were fashion . . . that we would have liked to have, but obviously didn't have the money to have them.
>
> [. . .]
>
> Lourdes: And we spent money. Our dad would scold us for spending so much money—four, five, six dollars in that era in dresses for . . . some dolls, but really what we enjoyed, at least I did, what we enjoyed more than the doll itself was changing her clothes. [*Carmen agrees*] Those clothes like high fashion, the style of Audrey Hepburn. You know, changing them, those blouses . . .
>
> Carmen: And the little heels and the purses. Almost everything came . . . in a big carton. And then, additionally I liked, I tried to sew, and I would make her the same design that I would make with all the scraps of fabric I'd find. And I would make her little necklaces and little chains and whatever I found. That was the fun, I mean it wasn't having a *lot* of dolls, it was having one and *dressing her* [*Lourdes says this at the same time*]. It wasn't having her and playing with her. The fun for us was having that doll that we could dress the way we would have wanted to dress and for me, because I liked to sew, making her things, you know, and be entertained with that. (Lourdes and Carmen, Group 1 transcript)

It is interesting how the memories are so shared and the experiences of these sisters so similar that, at many points during their parts of the conversation, they would say the same words at the same time. Despite the fact that their play with Barbie did not always take place together, they enjoyed the doll for the very same reasons.

As the sisters' conversation suggests, they avidly interacted with Barbie. Their play, though, differs from the experiences of many of the participants who created complex narratives through the doll (most of the time using more than one doll). Lourdes and Carmen experienced Barbie as a fashion doll, the very same role she had been assigned by her creator Ruth Handler. Their play with Barbie consisted of having only one doll each with a variety of outfits so they could change the doll in and out of them. My mother was always fascinated by Barbie's wardrobe, especially the high fashion of the earlier iterations of Barbie in the 1960s, when my mother played with her. For her, the pleasure of Barbie play stemmed from the creation of clothes and accessories for her doll and Barbie's space for fantasy, as my mother could live a more fashionable life through her doll.

Within the same family there were different levels of interaction as well. Carmen's three daughters—Camille (age thirty-two), me (age twenty-nine), and Frances (age twenty-five)—were never discouraged from playing or obligated to play with Barbie. We all had access to Barbie dolls, accessories, and other play materials such as sticker books and Halloween costumes. Nevertheless, each sister experienced Barbie very differently from the others. The oldest, Camille, experienced Barbie in ways that mirrored how our mother and aunt experienced her, specifically in the confection of Barbie clothes and the admiration for Barbie's astounding wardrobe.

> Well I do remember having played with Barbie, but I think I played more when I was with someone. I never played alone, I don't think so. But I do remember having tried to sew some clothes for her. I always remember that I made at least one skirt. [Laughs] And it was by hand because what I saw was by hand. Well I made a skirt, but also what I liked the most were her clothes because whenever we went to Toys R Us, I wasn't interested in the dolls . . . unless they were the collectors Barbies. What I liked was looking at the clothes because I wanted all those clothes for me. I always said I was going to buy them so I could make the pattern for myself and sew them in my size. (Camille, Group 1 transcript)

While Barbie play was not a main activity in Camille's life, she imagined herself through the doll. In similar ways as our mother saw in Barbie a model of feminine beauty, Camille admired the doll's sophisticated sense of fashion and dreamed of wearing her elegant clothes, albeit she did not necessarily want to physically look like the doll. For a while, Camille also took up the practice of sewing simple outfits for the dolls. It was through this small practice that she also exercised her desire to become a designer. More than anything, Camille longed to dress the way Barbie dressed.

Camille's play was very different from mine. As I introduced earlier in this book, my play was mostly private and occurred by myself, and I only had a few specific friends with whom I liked to play. Moreover, the delight in playing with Barbie came from more than simply changing her clothes. My play, as that of many of my participants, was performative; it was deep play with Barbie where we created many scenarios of lived experiences using the dolls. As I have expressed before, Barbie was an important part of my girlhood. My overall experiences with dolls were very similar to my mother's. We both loved baby dolls and paper dolls to the point that I realized we both had created dresses for our own paper dolls. We both liked to use objects from around the house or our environment to include in our play. One difference was that my mother's interactions included sewing clothes for Barbie, something that I was never able to do because I was not good at sewing. The number of Barbies we each owned marked another difference between us. Since my mother only had one doll, her play was significantly different from mine. That single doll provided hours of stimulation and imaginative play for her. I, on the other hand, had more than one doll, including Ken, which allowed me to create a variety of scenarios with multiple characters.

My younger sister's experience did not resemble anyone else's. Frances's interactions with Barbie are a stark contrast to her mother's, Carmen, who loved the doll. Her experiences also differed from our aunt's, our older sister's, and certainly mine. We could say that her experiences and mine were the most divergent. I was at one extreme, obsessed with Barbie and playing with the doll almost every day. At the other extreme, Frances hated Barbie and barely ever played with her. I found Frances's experiences the most fascinating within our family because of her overt rejection of the doll. She remembered a birthday when she almost cried because *all* of the presents were Barbie dolls:

> I remember my birthday that, I think, was when I was in kinder or first grade and it was in McDonald's, that basically *all* the presents were Barbie. I was almost crying because I didn't like her. . . . But the only one I remember playing with at least one or two times was the SeaWorld Barbie. Because it was water . . . like it changed colors in the water. But it is the *only* one that I remember playing with, and I didn't change her clothes. No . . . I didn't play. (Frances, Group 1 transcript)

When I asked if she remembered why she did not like Barbie dolls and why she virtually never played with them, only once or twice with her Sea-World Barbie, she recalled that perhaps the fact that doll play required creativity steered her away. She concluded: "Because . . . No, I don't remember why I didn't like them. What I can think now is that it required too much creativity . . . And I didn't like that. I preferred a Nintendo game . . . Mr. Brainy, something that didn't require imagining and creating conversations with myself" (Frances, Group 1 transcript). Frances's memory of rejection draws from her observations of *my own* play, where I created complex scenarios and conversations that almost resembled *telenovelas*.

Girlhood in Puerto Rico is often learned through *telenovelas*, or through the binaries that commonly frame *telenovela* plots: the good girl versus the bad girl. A *telenovela* is a Latin American soap opera. It was through *telenovelas*, as writers Ortiz Cofer (1990) and Santiago (1993, 1999) wrote in their memoirs, that Puerto Rican girls learned the opposite binaries of being woman: you were either a good girl or you were bad. They learned there was no middle ground or continuum; you were either or. While I did not watch many *telenovelas* because they were not encouraged at home, I was familiar with this duality of womanhood they often depicted. Moreover, although I cannot remember specific episodes of my own play, I do remember having included at certain points of my play the plot of good girl Barbie versus bad girl Barbie. Perhaps Frances's rejection of Barbie was also a rejection of this binary that she witnessed in my performative Barbie play.

Having more background knowledge about her helped me further interpret certain aspects of her relationship with Barbie. In contextualizing, I am not attempting to overpower Frances's or anyone else's voice but rather inquire further into her rejection. As Frances's sister, I remember her preference for Nintendo games and brain games, such as puzzles and Sudoku. Growing up she was also never into fashion, makeup, shopping—all of which are often termed "girl" activities. In her discussion of her relationship with Barbie, Frances does not link Barbie's embodiment of a homogenous femininity with her own rejection of the very same idea. However, I think there is a relationship between her rejection of Barbie as an object of play and her rejection of "feminine" activities. If what Barbie was selling was the idea that girls thrive in activities related to fashion—such as shopping, playing dress-up, and wearing makeup and heels—Frances wasn't buying it. She preferred the physical and often coded "unladylike" activities of playing basketball, riding a scooter, wearing tennis shoes, etc.

As the conversation between us siblings progressed, we also realized the different dynamics of play that existed in each of our individual and collective experiences. Lourdes and Carmen played together, mostly undressing and dressing Barbie, but they could spend hours doing so. They never played with their older sister, who did not have a Barbie doll, perhaps because she had already surpassed the age of doll play. My experience with my sisters was different. We knew for certain that neither Camille nor I had played with our youngest sister Frances because she never enjoyed Barbie. Yet, we went back and forth trying to figure out if we had played together. Camille, who is the oldest sister, noted that the few times she and I played, the interactions consisted mainly of changing Barbie's clothes and brushing her hair, since she did not enjoy creating dramatic scenarios or conversations with the dolls. Moreover, she pointed out that because she did not do dramatic play might have been the reason why I would play so much with our neighbor—from whom we inherited a great number of Barbie dolls and accessories. My older sister's memories of *her* play include very few episodes where she played with a neighbor and me: "But when I played it was with you, Emily, and our neighbor, but not by myself" (Camille, Group 1 transcript). Yet, in my own memories of Barbie play I never saw myself having played with my older sister. During this part of the conversation, I was trying to remember instances when she and I had played. Although I could not remember specific episodes, I did realize after the conversation that we had played together at least one time with our neighbor. My sister added: "Yes, we did play, but you know . . . but usually I played for only a little bit and then I stayed by myself because the two of you got too involved [in the play] and I just stayed there in a corner playing" (Camille, Group 1 transcript).

As a participant in this group interview at this moment of the conversation, I engaged in our attempt to find out what had happened back then and what had not. As a researcher listening to and reading the conversation, I shifted my focus toward the actual dynamic that was taking place among all sisters. Together we were engaging in collective memory-work (Haug et al. 1987) by trying to reconstruct each other's memories and to remember how we interacted not only with Barbie but also with each other through Barbie play. Despite the three of us not having played Barbie together, that night we helped each other remember details about our girlhoods that we had forgotten. The dynamic displayed during this interview where both groups of sisters either shared memories or helped one another remember elucidated Morgan and Krueger's (1993) argument in favor of using group interviews in order to learn in greater depth about participants' experiences. Furthermore, what I found fascinating in the conversation among the women in my family (particularly my sisters and I) was the very distinct way in which each one of us, despite having grown up in the same household with the same opportunities for play with Barbie, interacted with the doll. While my mother and her sister experienced Barbie in such parallel ways, my sisters and I did not: one liked the doll, one was obsessed with the doll, and one completely rejected the doll.

In a different group interview, one participant, Frankie (age thirty), briefly talked about her own play experiences with her sisters. Though her sisters were not part of the interview, Frankie's description of their overall dynamics serves as a point of contrast to my own experiences with my sisters. Firstly, all sisters liked Barbie and interacted with the doll in one way or another. Secondly, their play always occurred together, despite the differences in their age. Thirdly, Frankie recalled the play spaces they would use around their house and the dynamics that surfaced during Barbie play:

> We had a closet when we lived in the United States, a large closet, and there we put everything that was for Barbie, and the four of us played. We spent hours playing there. My sister [the oldest] was always the one that gave commands, she would tell us what we had to do. . . . We always had to play together because my older sister took hold of the Barbies and wouldn't give them to us unless she was playing. We had to play together. (Frankie, Group 3 transcript)

As briefly illustrated by the range of experiences among the women in my family, interactions with Barbie may also differ between mothers and daughters. The generational differences and the objects of play available to girls during each era contributed to the diverse experiences with Barbie among my participants. Within my family, the generational divide was marked by the amount of Barbie dolls used for play: the older generation engaged in play using only one Barbie doll and no Ken dolls, while the younger generation used many Barbie dolls and at least one Ken. As Carmen expressed, the fun of it was having only one doll and many outfits. Susan, who played with Barbie during the 1980s, remembers how important it was to have not only a Barbie doll but also a Ken:

> During our times there were other dolls like Ever After or Monster High. And [Barbie] was the main one. I mean, if you didn't have Barbie, you were out. And you could have ten Barbies, but if you did not have a Ken, you didn't have Barbie. And we didn't have Barbie, much less Ken. And Ken sometimes was even more expensive than Barbie. But we did play. (Susan, Group 6 transcript)

This is a generational difference from the girls who grew up with the first iterations of Barbie. In those previous generations, Ken was not a necessary of Barbie play, and his presence was not essential. Yet for Susan's generation, in her experience, having a Ken was not only necessary, it was required.

Creating and Collecting: Mothers Pass Down Barbie Traditions

The similarities and differences in the play practices and the types of inter-actions encountered with Barbie can also manifest when mothers become collectors and curators of Barbie for their daughters. The access to Barbie fostered by mothers often reveals the ways in which they live their child-hood dreams vicariously through their daughters. For some who as girls never owned or played with Barbie, the acquisition and collection of the doll presents a space to look at the dolls and dream of the possibilities.

There are various means through which mothers pass down the tra-ditions of Barbie play or owning Barbie artifacts, one of which is creative productions. Though the most common form of creation is when mothers design and sew dresses for their daughters' dolls, it is not the only one. The stories I gathered through my interviews extended my ideas of how mothers create and pass down traditions to their children. I present here creative production through the confection of artifacts (such as clothes and accessories), through the collection of Barbie dolls and artifacts, and through the curation of these artifacts (mothers choosing how to display dolls and why).

In my own experiences with Barbie, before I started buying clothes for my dolls, my mother would make some for them. As she told me, this is how she used to play with her Barbie doll; she would take different scraps of fabric and make different outfits for her, and that is what she did for my dolls. I most vividly remember two pieces my mother made using scraps of fabric from our old school uniforms. One of the pieces was a maroon tube maxi dress for Barbie and the other one a maroon pair of shorts for Ken. I remember incorporating those outfits into my play as if they were outfits produced by Mattel, and I especially liked having more options for Ken since I did not buy a lot of clothes for the Ken dolls.

Some of my participants also remembered having clothes made by their mothers, or sometimes their aunts or grandmothers. For instance, K.C. and Annie (eleven and nine respectively) showed me a doll that was dressed in clothes their aunt had made for them. Annie said she loved the dress, but she did not like that her aunt glued the dress to the doll because she could not change the doll's outfit. Autumn (forty) also talked about the outfits her mother made for her Barbie dolls:

> When I was thinking of you coming over today, I was remembering that my
> mom when I was the age of Sharon [her daughter] made Barbie doll clothes,

like by hand. Well, with sewing machines and everything. And she, and so my Barbies had this amazing wardrobe of clothes, and she would sell them at flea markets. And I wish, of course now, that I had one of everything and I wish I had all my old stuff, but you know, it's all gone and lost along the way. (Autumn, Group 5 transcript)

When I asked her if having mostly homemade doll clothes embarrassed her, she said it never happened. In fact, she explained that for her, the clothes her mother made were the "most awesome looking clothes." She added:

I had some real clothes, I remember specifically I had a Pretty in Pink Barbie, which was, she had like a beautiful cape with like pink fur around the edges and stuff. But all my other clothes were homemade, but they were spectacular. Like my mom, I still remember like, velvet capes and very detailed bridal dresses. (Autumn, Group 5 transcript)

Her mother also made underwear for all of her Barbie dolls, so this was an additional detail that made Autumn feel like her dolls were special since Barbie dolls usually do not include underwear. In the present, Autumn likes to sew, and from time to time she tries to make outfits for her daughter Sharon's dolls. Experiencing this made Autumn appreciate her mother's work sewing Barbie outfits even more: "When I think about, 'cause I sew, but when I think about how tiny Barbie clothes are, I think, 'Wow, these are hard to sew in a sewing machine!' But yeah, she had everything" (Autumn, Group 5 transcript).

Unlike the experiences of some women for whom "custom-made originals frequently had less value than clothes off the Mattel rack" (Rand 1995: 96), some of my participants had clothes and accessories made by their mothers, meaning they had one-of-a-kind pieces. At the same time, several of these homemade pieces were created by the girls themselves, as were the cases of Camille, Carla, Carmen, and Lourdes. Yet some participants, including those who loved their homemade outfits and those who created outfits as well, expressed preference for the Mattel-made accessories because they fit the doll better and were the "real deal." In addition to the economic factors that contribute to the need for homemade materials, the significance of mothers designing and sewing outfits for their daughters' dolls underlines a labor of love. It creates a connection between the past and the present—between the ways the past generations may have interacted with Barbie and the new ways the younger generations relate to the doll. Within the context of my participants, this labor of love also manifested through the collection of Barbie dolls, especially from two mothers.

In the 1990s Mattel shifted its marketing strategy to specifically target adult collectors. According to John Amerman, Mattel's CEO at the time, "The doll was previously 'undermarketed'" (Sarasohn-Kahn 1996: 54), yet "the average American girl has an estimated eight-plus Barbie dolls in her collection. . . . Mattel recognizes that both children and adults are consumers of Barbie dolls and related products" (Sarasohn-Kahn 1996: 1). This shift in marketing acknowledged an important consumer of Barbie—adults driven by nostalgia who were beginning to collect the doll. Nostalgia produced by memories of their childhood play with Barbie is what drove thousands of women to the (Barbie) Doll Museum in Quebradillas, Puerto Rico, where owner Luis Felipe Orama exhibits about 850 Barbie dolls. During my visit to this museum, he explained that many of the visitors were women who wanted to either take a look at some of the dolls they used to have as girls or buy dolls to add to their collections. Nostalgia certainly emerged during my visit as I walked through each aisle and recognized the dolls from my childhood.

This sense of nostalgia and longing for her childhood was influential in one mother's creation of her collection of Barbie dolls. To the date of our interview in May 2015, Patricia had collected an assortment of 233 Barbie dolls. Her collection grows every day and is composed of Barbie and friends, old and new, some of which were like the ones she owned in her childhood. Some of the dolls in her personal collection on display in her home include Barbies from the 1960s to the present, along with her friends Ken, Allan, Mitch, Midge, and Skipper, to name a few. It also includes dolls for play and dolls from collector's and designer editions, such as the Holidays edition, Bob Mackie dolls, and Christian Dior designer dolls (see figure 5.1 for a sample of Patricia's collection). Patricia began collecting as a result of the joy brought by the memories of Barbie play and the sadness of not having her dolls anymore because she gave some away and because her husband threw out the rest when they moved.

> Patricia: So I was four years old. I saw that doll and I became fascinated with her. So my mother, these are mine, bought me a Barbie but I gave her away [later on]. And I missed her so much. So I began collecting. Since I was four I began . . . I fell in love with her. And then I began. I had my little group in a suitcase, and couldn't throw them out, but then my niece came around, and I gave her my Barbie.
>   [. . .]

Figure 5.1. A sample of Patricia's collection of 233 Barbie dolls. *Top*: Holidays Barbie and Twilight movie dolls. *Bottom*: Classic Skipper dolls. Photographs by author.

> Gabriela: That was the [book] she used to have, and my dad threw it out.
> Patricia: In fact, when we bought this house, he threw all of it out. . . . And I have been buying everything he threw out. I had the house, clothes. I had this little book that came with the doll, and there I would spend time dreaming that I wanted that dress. I would spend much time looking at that book. So then, little by little, I have bought almost everything on eBay. [See figure 5.2] (Patricia and Gabriela, Group 4 transcript)

Yet collecting was not only about Paticia's own childhood memories. She continues to search for dresses and dolls that she would like to add. For her, buying a Barbie doll or a dress is more enjoyable than buying a dress for herself, and she even admitted that she'd rather buy a Barbie than buy herself a dress. As she did when she was little, she still asks for

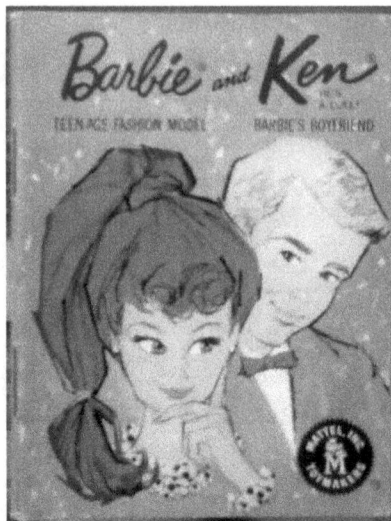

Figure 5.2. A booklet that was included with Barbie dolls during Barbie's early years. This one is similar to the one Patricia's husband had thrown away. Photograph by author.

Barbie dolls and outfits as presents. She stated that her goal in collecting Barbie dolls and outfits was not so much about acquiring a certain number of dolls or about the size of the collection but rather, she said, "My goal was to buy what I desired when I was little" (Patricia, Group 4 transcript). What is interesting in this case is how the mother/daughter dynamic shifts from the norm. While her daughter asked for Barbie dolls during her childhood, it is currently Patricia who asks for Barbie dolls whenever there is opportunity to give her a present. Her daughter Gabriela admits that she does not like getting her mother any Barbie artifacts as gifts:

> Gabriela: She asks for Barbies as gifts. I don't give her [Barbies], only my brother does.
> Patricia: Yes, my boy gives them to me.
> Gabriela: And at night she goes onto eBay and she continues looking. (Gabriela and Patricia, Group 4 transcript)

While her collection of 233 dolls—which are displayed in glass shelves as if they were part of an exhibition—belongs to her, Patricia also acquired dolls for Gabriela when she was growing up. At the present, these 131 dolls are still well kept, looking almost exactly as they did when Gabriela was a child. These dolls are kept in a box, just as they had been during Gabriela's girlhood.

In similar ways Marisa, a woman in her fifties, created a collection of Barbie dolls. Marisa is a long-time family friend, and her daughter is a few years younger than I am. Though our conversation was not long because she never played with Barbie when she was young and her daughter does not live in Puerto Rico anymore, I wanted to talk to her about the doll collection she still has in her house. I have many memories of visiting her house when I was younger and admiring the vast collection of Barbie dolls she had. The collection was composed of collector's edition Barbie dolls, limited editions, and dolls from the Barbie "Dolls of the World" line with a total of thirty-eight dolls. Her daughter had a different set of Barbie dolls she used exclusively for play. The collection, just like Patricia's, was also kept on shelves, displayed as if in a museum. I asked Marisa if any of the dolls were hers or if she had acquired some of them for her own pleasure. She explained: "No, all of the dolls are hers. I never had any. But she had a lot because everyone knew she liked dolls, and she had all kinds of dolls" (Marisa, interview transcript). Marisa never played with Barbie, so while the dolls in the collection belonged to her daughter, it seemed this collection was as much for her as it was for her daughter. The collection that survives is there because both mother and daughter like to admire the dolls. I think for Marisa especially it is a way of having what she did not have growing up. As her daughter grew up and grew out of her doll play phase, they both began getting rid of what Marisa called the "normal Barbie dolls." These were the ones with which her daughter had played, and these were not special editions of Barbie, nor were they expensive.

Looking at Marisa and her daughter's experience through the lens of the mother and daughter dynamic, we can see how the collection of Barbie dolls brought them together. Moreover, Marisa enabled her daughter's contact with Barbie by providing a prominent space in the house for her daughter's doll collection. She carefully arranged the dolls in order to be viewed and admired by anyone who walked through their home. Additionally, mother and daughter decided together which dolls would become part of the collection and which dolls were objects for play.

What is seen in these two cases of mothers creating collections, either or both for themselves and their daughters, is an interest in passing along Barbie traditions. In Marisa's case, while she did not play with Barbie as a child, she wanted her daughter to be able to interact with the doll. In allowing this interaction, which often came thanks to friends and family members gifting her daughter with Barbie dolls, she was able to live vicariously through her daughter. As a mother, Patricia felt a genuine love for Barbie that she wanted to share with her daughter as much as she could. She saw herself in her daughter and wanted to give her the opportunity to play with Barbie, to immerse herself in her world just like she had done. However, it is not always the case that parents will provide opportunities for children to play with Barbie, or if they do, they might exert control over how the child interacts with the doll.

"Don't Play with This One": Parental Control of Barbie Play

Erica Jong advocates for Barbie as something that children need just as they need books of fantasy, to let their imagination be creative. Yet, in order to achieve this, she says, adults should not be involved in their child's play. Jong uses literary adventure stories as examples in which "magic happens when the adults aren't looking" and reiterates that "adults *have* to be banished for the childhood magic to occur" (1999: 202). While I concur that children should be allowed their space for play, the stories of my participants' experiences also suggest that parents and children can work in tandem to create fruitful and meaningful play. At the same time, too much involvement or control could become restrictive and hindering for the child. In this sense, Jong's advocacy for an adult-free play space is highly valid.

One type of restrictive practice that could obstruct the adventures and the magic of play is parental involvement to keep Barbie dolls intact. This may represent the parent's own childhood desire to collect Barbie dolls. Patricia, who began collecting as an adult and whose passion for Barbie shows in her continuous acquisition of dolls for her daughter Gabriela, restricted her daughter's interactions with Barbie at times by guiding how she could play with the doll.

> Gabriela: I could not cut their hair or anything.
> Emily: Oh, I was going to ask you that, if you did something different to them.
> Gabriela: She didn't let me. Well, behind her back. She didn't let me cut their hair. I messed up one doll's hair. I flat ironed her hair. And then my mom was trying to make the hair better, but she didn't let me. I couldn't break them, no. They're still identical [to when I got them].

Patricia: They all even have their shoes and everything, well kept. I would take their shoes off. Gabriela would ask me, "Mom, can I cut their hair?" and then I would put them away. I would take their shoes off.

Emily: Because shoes are the first things to get lost?

Patricia: I took the shoes off so she wouldn't eat them either. I have all of the shoes with all the outfits and all of her stuff. Everything is there. (Gabriela and Patricia, Group 4 transcript)

My older sister, who was pregnant at the time, talked about how she would handle having a child who wanted to play with Barbie. Her views on how she envisioned interactions with Barbie could become restrictive in practice, but not in the same ways that the literature about Barbie has documented. She expressed no qualms against the doll, and she would not object to buying Barbie dolls for a daughter or son if the child asked for them. Yet, she wanted to delineate what the child could do with the doll and how the child could play with it. It sparked a constructive conversation between all the women in the family, from different generations, about the usefulness of delineating how a child can play with a doll.

Camille: If I have a child and they ask me for Barbie, I will get them. Now I think about whether I would let them play with the dolls or if I should keep them in their boxes for her to look at them [*Laughs*].

Carmen: No!

Lourdes: If you're going to buy them for the box, don't buy them. Don't waste money.

Frances: If I had a daughter who asked for a Barbie just to keep her safe and look at it, I would only buy one and that's it. I don't know, when I asked for all those Barbies and I never used them—

Carmen: I just gave them away.

Frances: Exactly. That's the same thing I would do. If she asks for a Barbie, okay. She doesn't want to play with it? Then no more Barbie for you.

Camille: But they look so pretty in their boxes.

Frances: No! They look pretty taking up space?

Carmen: Toys are for playing.

Camille: Anyway, I'm going to let my child play as long as they do not damage the dolls.

Emily: And what is "damaging" for you?

Camille: Writing on them. I know all children do this because I did it too.

Emily: I was going to say, what if the child cuts her hair?

Camille: Then I have to teach them how to style it. [*Laughs*]

Carmen: Not writing on it. I had my Thumbelina [a baby doll] and I played with her, and a cousin of mine wrote on her. She wrote on her forehead. I never wrote on her, never mistreated her. (Group 1 transcript)

141

By the time this book was in production, Camille's first child was five years old. He played with cars, LEGO, dinosaurs, blocks, and electronic games; he enjoyed painting, reading, and creating with cardboard boxes. In addition, he also wanted a princess doll just like his mother had. While Camille's princess doll remained in its box, she did not restrict her child's interactions with his own doll. What Camille's hypothetical scenario shows is her desire to keep dolls in pristine condition because this was the kind of interaction that she had with some of her own dolls growing up. Carmen responding "Not writing on it" when asked what she considers "damaging" reflects her own childhood experiences when another child "destroyed" her treasured doll in that way. She did not initiate the "destructive" interaction and therefore felt that someone else was taking control of her doll and her play.

Regardless of whether the parental control is enacted (as in the case of Patricia) or presented as hypothetical (as in the case of Camille), these views about dolls' place in the household are common, especially with a doll such as Barbie. The plethora of versions of Barbie dolls, some of which are actually collector's items, invite girls to desire play with her and adults to collect them. The previous section described the ways that mothers collect Barbie for their daughters but also for themselves. This in itself is not restrictive, but if girls are not allowed to touch their dolls or if their interactions are being policed, their agency with the dolls is taken away. Carla offered an example of her childhood friend who owned about twenty-five to thirty Barbie dolls, though she was never allowed to play with them:

> And my friend, her mom would buy her [Barbie dolls] and then put them up in her dresser. And then she had all her Barbies, about twenty-five to thirty in their boxes. And that girl was so miserable. So, then she would go to my house, she played with my Barbies, my shoes, she would take then, borrowed them, she played with them because I had bins full of Barbies and all their stuff. (Carla, interview transcript)

In cases such as this, the parental control is about conserving Barbie in pristine condition, perhaps as a result of rectifying the ways the parent interacted with dolls during childhood. Yet, this presents restrictions to how the child may interact with a toy. It is a way in which parental involvement results in the loss of the magic to which Jong (1999) referred.

Parental involvement and control over Barbie play mostly occurs in response to the issues they find in the doll. These issues, which I discussed in chapter 4 from the individual perspectives of my participants, are related to Barbie's controversial body and her race. The conversations outlined in this part reveal the often conflicting views, including ambivalence, that parents have toward Barbie and examine their children's ways of negotiating the issues parents fear will negatively affect them. Parents' perceptions of Barbie and their involvement in their children's play is a recurring theme in the conversations about the doll. Anna Quindlen (1999) and Jane Smiley (1999) claim the doll has a big influence on girls, while Yona Zeldis McDonough (1999) attributes that role to the real women who surround girls. While McDonough argues that "girls learn how to be women not from their dolls but from the women around them. Most often this means Mom" (1999: 112), Smiley asserts that she did not believe she had an influence on her own daughters. She states, "If my daughters were to learn certain Hollywood-inspired essentials of American womanhood, it wasn't going to be from me, it was going to be from Barbie" (Smiley 1999: 190). The comments from two of my participants, who are mothers of girls, concur with McDonough's views that the real influence comes from the women around girls, not from Barbie herself.

For example, Susan's views about Barbie's influence on girls, which I presented in the previous chapter, point to the responsibility parents have of educating children about values and self-love. During the conversation about a young woman and a young man who changed their appearances to look like Barbie and Ken, Susan, a mother of two girls I interviewed, argued that those actions are a result of "a lack of education to our children" and that if we teach children to love themselves, then having a pretty doll should not have an effect on them. Carla (age thirty-three), a mother of two girls—whom I was unable to interview due to conflicting schedules—spoke about how children depict through their play what they have learned. She highlights that it is what they learn from their homes, *not* what they learn from their toys. As she explained to me, she remembers her Barbie days fondly because she experienced "beautiful moments, opportunities of play that maybe children today don't have" (Carla, interview transcript). She added:

> Everything today is so sexualized. . . . Believe me, girls today play with Barbie in ways that are different from how you and I played. And I have babysat girls who play with Barbie and Barbie rapes Ken! And that is not about the game. It is a reflection of what is happening inside the child's head. So then you could argue that the game of Barbie and Ken—it is *not* the game of Barbie and Ken. It is, first of all, what you teach your children, what you let them be exposed to, and

then based on that it's how your child will react to the rest of her environment. I am very aware of that. (Carla, interview transcript)

At the same time, some of the participants debated whether giving their daughters Barbie dolls would be the best idea. Barbie has often been labeled as a projection of a sexualized body: she is an object that portrays "perfect" looks, leading to unrealistic body expectations and causing body image issues in young girls. This was a concern for Moore-Henecke who admitted that, "like most feminists, I have been less than enthusiastic about Barbie. When asked to purchase Barbies for my nieces, I have wondered if this was really the best gift to give them. Would I be contributing to their eventual battles with bulimia?" (1997: 1). Many mothers share similar feelings; they do not want their daughters to play with Barbie because of potential body image issues. For instance, Riddick (2001) explains that many mothers see Barbie as a negative influence because they believe the doll teaches girls that they have to be blond and beautiful to get a boyfriend or a career. As a result, some women do not allow Barbies into their homes to prevent their daughters from learning this. These negative views on Barbie have an effect on women who used to play with the doll when they were younger but have now grown up to consider themselves feminists. It creates an internal debate of whether Barbie is a good toy for little girls, and it even makes women feel ashamed to admit they played with the doll; even more, they feel ashamed to admit they still like the doll, as documented by Reid-Walsh and Mitchell (2000). An example of this internal debate came from Carla who, as a child and teenager, played with Barbie. Responding to my question asking if she would prefer her daughters to play with something more realistic, she suggested that the influence of the doll is dependent upon the education girls receive about certain topics. Carla examined her own prejudices against Barbie as someone who used to play with the doll but does not want her daughters to play with her.

Because . . . you know, when I think about it, I don't even know why. Like, I don't know, I don't know. Like, I prefer they played with a toy that resembles reality more. I don't know. I think I'm frustrating them big time because children need to be children and they should use their imagination, and now I'm realizing my stupidity. Thank you. [*Laughs*] But I don't know. It seems like it might be because of my own prejudice or discrimination, maybe because *I* felt in some ways inferior to Barbie or to any girl who could look like Barbie, maybe I think that my girls could feel the same. It could be that. I think I'll run to the mall to buy them a Barbie. (Carla, interview transcript)

Carla's love/hate relationship with Barbie gave her certain prejudices toward the doll and colored her opinion of how good it really is. However, she also admitted how much she enjoyed the doll during her childhood, despite Barbie's position as her "frenemy," and she questioned why, if she had educated her daughters well, she still thought they should not have contact with the doll. Carla's moment of deliberation and debate is interesting because it provides insight to the contesting views that many women, including those of us who loved Barbie as children, have about the doll. In this case, the deliberation occurred in the moment, as the questions that came up during the interview invited Carla to really engage with her own memories, experiences as a child, and perceptions as an adult. She realized that, perhaps, if she believed that it is not about the game and the toy but about what children learn from their environment, then she should not prohibit her daughters from playing with Barbie.

In contrast, for one daughter and mother pair, Barbie was never out of the question. The mother, Patricia, who had played with Barbie and remembered those times with fondness, wanted her daughter to have the positive memories she had of Barbie play. For Patricia and her daughter Gabriela, Barbie was simply a doll through which they could act out their fantasies, mainly about being someone different every day. In their opinion, Barbie did not promote unrealistic ideals about body image, therefore Patricia never forbade Gabriela from playing with the doll.

Barbie is a symbol of US culture, whiteness, and (heterosexual) femininity. These different levels of identity are in tension in the experiences of some Puerto Rican girls, who may not fit Barbie's mold in one or more of these categories. While some may look like Barbie, they see that she is not a representation of a majority of Puerto Rican girls, yet they are held to beauty standards posed by Barbie's white, blond, tall, and thin figure—the American ideal of beauty. The idea that beauty is only represented in whiteness, blondness, and blue eyes is exactly what motivated Autumn, a forty-year-old white woman (my only non–Puerto Rican participant), and her Puerto Rican husband to keep their eight-year-old daughter away from Barbie. Since Autumn had played with Barbie as a child, I was interested in finding out if that was something she wanted to pass onto her daughter. She said, "You know, truthfully, not really. I really didn't want the whole princess thing, I didn't want the overly pink Barbie, especially 'cause she's blond and blue-eyed" (Autumn, Group 5 transcript). Her daughter Sharon responded by complaining about the lack of Barbie variety and the saturation of white, blond Barbie: "I know! All the Barbies are blond, well almost all. I saw in the store like a Barbie that was the friend of her in the movie of the ballerina slipper thing, and I saw the reddish hair one and the brown hair one, but they wouldn't get them for me!" (Sharon, Group 5 transcript). Autumn explained that they had wanted to keep princesses and Barbies away for a long time, but when they were trying to wean Sharon off her pacifier, they told her she could have whatever she wanted. "She picked a Barbie. And so that's when she got her first Barbie," Autumn explained, "but when I think back about *my* experience with Barbie, I have a lot of great memories playing with my sister and other friends with our Barbies. I especially . . . the white blue-eyed thing, that was my whole problem with most of the princesses, you know with all that. So that's what we were trying to kind of avoid" (Autumn, Group 5 transcript).

Even though this mother, and the father as well, wanted to keep the girl away from Barbie and princesses because of the messages about femininity they promoted, they also did not control their daughter's choices and honored her wish to have a Barbie only when she had expressed interest in her. To Sharon's credit, her interactions with Barbie did not ignore the problems the doll presents that have been so vastly identified by scholars. Instead, Sharon was critically engaging with a product that she understood was problematic. She identified the need for diversity in the Barbie products, and she expressed her frustration with blond, white Barbie being the central figure in the doll line. This is something she also manifested by coloring her Barbie's hair with red, blue, green, and orange highlighters. Although there are many tutorials on YouTube where girls use markers and highlighters to color Barbie's hair, they do so more as fashion statements. In contrast, Sharon's alteration of Barbie's hair was an act of subversion and protest against the doll's ideals of beauty. Objects become what their subject wants them to be: "the subject reconstitutes the object"; as a result, the object can tell us about the person who interacted with it (Brown 1998). In many cases, such as the examples Brown provides, the object is used in subversive ways that are not intended. This is a common practice described in the literature about Barbie play, where the owners often make modifications to the dolls to adjust them to their play practices (see, for example, Chin 1999; McDonough 1999; Rand 1995). Pike suggests that "media narratives are best understood when the pleasures and possibilities they offer to girls are considered alongside criticisms of their textual limitations" (2015: 154). Sharon serves as an important critic of an object made for girls, made for her. And while she enjoys the pleasures of Barbie play, she maintains a critical perspective of Barbie's limitations and what they mean for girls. More importantly, in the exploration of familial relationships, Sharon's critical view of Barbie would not have occurred if her parents had completely controlled her interactions with dolls and Barbie culture. By allowing her to interact with the object of their derision, her parents opened the space for Sharon's practice of critical thinking, able to draw her own conclusions about Barbie, and to explore the various issues inherent in the doll.

Similar to Autumn, Susan (K.C. and Annie's mother) admitted she did not feel comfortable with her daughters playing with Barbie, despite having played with the doll during her childhood. As an adult, she recognized that certain aspects of Barbie were problematic, especially in relation to class as discussed in the previous chapter. As a mother, she considered at times not letting her daughters play with Barbie: "Of course. Of course, I thought about it. And I've never given Barbie to these girls. All those Barbies you see there have been gifts from my sister, my friends, their grandmothers" (Susan, Group 6 transcript). She continued:

> To answer your question, no. I never bought them because there were like, the white one was the refined one. . . . And God made us the way we are and all of us need to respect each other, and each person has value, and each person is useful, and each person is. But that was something I did not like a lot, that they were so like cutesy. (Susan, Group 6 transcript)

Despite her views on Barbie and the fact that she was not the one providing access to the doll, Susan, like Autumn, also did not restrict the girls' interactions with her. She understood that her daughters could play with the doll and enjoy her the same way they enjoyed other dolls (for example, Monster High dolls, Ever After High dolls, and even Bratz) while simultaneously remaining critical of the issues that were present. Moreover, she understood that her daughters could use the dolls as play objects that enabled them to live vicariously and to assume the roles *they* decided to assign.

To Barbie or Not to Barbie?

In this chapter, I have presented various roles Barbie has in the familial dynamics between mothers and daughters, but also between sisters in Puerto Rico: the differences and similarities in play practices with Barbie that take place within a family group, the ways in which mothers and daughters may also have similar yet very distinct experiences with Barbie, the means through which mothers continue or pass down Barbie traditions onto their daughters, and mothers' interventions in their daughters' play with Barbie. Mothers (and fathers) may want to control how their children play or with which toys they can play, and sometimes the control stems from a desire to keep toys undamaged and in good condition. Namely, though, parents might question how much their girls should interact with Barbie because of the problematic issues Barbie presents, such as her body shape and her whiteness.

The differences and similarities in the experiences between mothers and daughters attest Barbie's versatility to produce a range of experiences that depend mostly, though not exclusively, on who interacts with her. The similar interactions illustrated in some participants' dynamics denote Barbie's power to create bonds between mothers and daughters (and other types of relationships) who share certain ideas about femininity or who remember the doll differently according to their own individual interests. Yet, the differences open the space for a more critical look at the doll to understand that femininity is not a singular, homogenous experience. In addition, seeing Barbie's offerings and limitations bring up specific issues about the messages she embodies can motivate mothers and parental figures to limit or eradicate girls' interactions with Barbie culture.

A number of adult participants noted that Barbie still appealed to them and that they would share Barbie with future generations, although they qualified this by explaining that they are also now more critical of Barbie products and overall Barbie culture because they are older and understand the various problematic layers of what the doll represents. It is hard to pinpoint exactly how much of the influence on girls comes from Barbie and how much comes from mothers. Perhaps it is a combination of both; perhaps there *needs* to be a combination of both in equal parts so that play with Barbie can become fruitful. By taking away or denying Barbie to girls because they might "dwell in her anatomy," as Wolitzer (1999) suggests, we are giving little credit to girls' abilities to be critical thinkers and to engage with Barbie in meaningful ways. Listening to my participants' very diverse experiences gave me insight into the fascinating range of interactions that are afforded through Barbie, and the ways in which each family approached Barbie. There were mothers who held Barbie so dearly in their hearts that they wanted their daughters to experience Barbie in positive ways. Conversely, there were mothers who were apprehensive about allowing their daughters to be in constant contact with the doll. Then there are the many different interactions within the same family nucleus. In my house, our mother enjoyed Barbie in her childhood, but she neither made us play nor restricted our play with Barbie. What resulted were three very distinct interactions with Barbie within the same household: one daughter who somewhat played with, one who obsessively played with, and one who completely rejected Barbie.

Moreover, I was able to witness how two sisters who are now growing up with Barbie and other dolls interacted not only with each other but also with their mother. In this case, they both enjoyed playing with Barbie and other dolls, and at the same time they were keenly aware of the issues Barbie presents. Their mother played an important role in this awareness. While she did not discourage her daughters from playing with Barbie, she complemented their play with conversations about body image, race, and gender. This edification helped her daughters understand that, while they can take pleasure from the dolls with which they play, these dolls should not be seen as role models for them. The conversations happening alongside Barbie play resulted in the doll becoming an instrument through which important topics could be discussed.

Growing Up with Barbie
Impacts on Puerto Rican Girlhoods

I began this book by describing Barbie as a transnational object (Hegde 2001; MacDougall 2003; Negrón-Muntaner 2002) that has crossed national and cultural borders. She embodies a definition of transnationalism that expands beyond physical borders; thus, Barbie can be transnational not just in the ways she travels across the world and is adopted into local cultures but also in the ways she affords imagined transnationalisms. The study presented in this book has explored the role that Barbie dolls have played in Puerto Rican girlhoods by examining Puerto Rican women and girls' experiences with the doll within the contexts of their childhood play. The inclusion of five generations of women and girls provided a broad, intergenerational perspective about Barbie's impact on Puerto Rican girlhoods and her role as a transnational object.

"All the girls played with Barbie," Carla expressed. "At the time a *girl* could not be without a Barbie," Lourdes remembered. A similar sentiment was expressed by a number of my participants: every girl had/needed to have a Barbie. While some of them actually believed every girl had or needed to have a Barbie because they loved the doll (e.g., Lourdes), others felt like this was the expectation when they were growing up either from adults or from peers. For one participant, the experience left a negative memory of Barbie. Susan's memory of a teacher that presumed every girl had a Barbie was an example of how the idea is so embedded in the popular consciousness, yet in her experience this statement was not true because she did not have a Barbie. Moreover, she felt at the time and believes now as an adult that it is a damaging assumption.

Perhaps the chief indication of the degree to which Barbie made an impact in the lived experiences of multiple generations of Puerto Rican girls is in their avid consumption and enjoyment of various Barbie products. The infiltration into girls' lives took shape not only through the doll and the accessories that are "necessary" to play with her but also through other media, such as notebooks, magazines, sticker books, child-size cars to be driven by girls, movies, storybooks, and her "exclusive" fan club. While a small number of participants only owned Barbie products related to doll play (dolls, clothes and accessories, house, car), the majority owned many of the other products, allowing for further interactions with Barbie. Thus, Barbie affected Puerto Rican girlhoods in ways that mirror what the Barbie scholarship has suggested. For girls in the present, these same artifacts in tandem with new media such as YouTube and Netflix provide even more options for Barbie's constant presence in girls' lives.

A notable fact about girls' play with dolls in the present came to light in my conversations with both the three girls I interviewed and with adults who are mothers of girls. In the past, Barbie was the "it" girl, she was the doll to have—this is evident in the childhoods of the women I interviewed, and it is evident in my childhood as well. This was mostly because there was no other fashion doll like her, as most other dolls were baby dolls, which invited girls to *care* for them rather than *become* them. Present generations, however, have more options from which to choose, and girls are making choices beyond Barbie. These choices include Bratz dolls, Monster High dolls, and Ever After High dolls. What this could mean is that Barbie's influence in Puerto Rican girlhoods, while once at a high level, may be beginning to decline for the current generation (and possibly future ones).

Barbie has been given to girls as a gift from family and friends, has passed through generations as a hand-me-down, has passed from mothers to their children as a tradition of doll play, has been given as a reward through hard work in school, and has made inroads to different cultures through transnational movements of the doll, just to name a few examples of how Barbie has entered girls' lives. I have highlighted the various ways that girls have come into contact with Barbie. Interactions with Barbie are varied; there is no one single way to experience Barbie. The interactions occur through the doll as well as other artifacts, and they happen individually and also collectively, with friends, with family. The interactions may embrace Barbie as a favorite toy, but interactions with her may also serve to negotiate certain aspects of the doll that girls find problematic. In these ways Barbie becomes part of girls' and women's identities.

Barbie has been a site of ideals. Girls may see the doll as someone to emulate—not necessarily her "perfect" unattainable body but often her essence of femininity. This occurred especially for the first generation of girls who played with Barbie, who described Barbie play as centered on high fashion. For them, Barbie was a symbol of elegance, and as a result they wanted to emulate this characteristic of the doll. For a number of participants in this book, their passion for Barbie was about more than collecting her or being like her. As we saw in Patricia's case, for example, Barbie played a significant role in her girlhood. With the divorce of her parents and having to move to Puerto Rico with her grandmother, Patricia turned to Barbie as the only constant presence in her life. So great was Barbie's significance for Patricia that the act of giving her first doll to her cousin as a hand-me-down still elicits painful memories. Moreover, once her husband threw out her Barbie dolls during a move, she committed to collecting Barbie. She wanted to share Barbie with her daughter and give her the opportunity to live vicariously through the doll, the same opportunity that she had.

Barbie was also a site of contention. For some participants, the relationship with Barbie was tense and fraught. Carla, for example, saw Barbie as a friend and an enemy, a doll with whom she could identify in some respects but not in those where she could not see herself reflected. Carla's complicated relationship with Barbie elucidates why Barbie is such a fraught object. As a girl, Carla did not see herself reflected physically in the doll; they were complete opposites, and that resulted in Carla perceiving Barbie as an enemy. At the same time, Barbie was independent, confident, sociable, and fashionable, all characteristics with which Carla identified, and as such Barbie was her friend. Furthermore, Barbie served as the vehicle through which Carla fought back against impositions, channeled her emotions, and recreated aspects of her life that she wanted to change.

This book has also showed how the Puerto Rican Barbie specifically was important for girls' identities. Despite the inclusion of a Latina doll (Teresa) in the main Barbie line, this was not enough to allow some girls to identify with Barbie. The introduction of Puerto Rican Barbie in 1997 offered Puerto Rican girls the opportunity to be part of the Barbie family for the first time. This doll was from *Puerto Rico*, and no matter what her looks were, this was, for some girls, someone with whom they could identify because they came from the same place and wore clothes similar to those she was wearing, clothes that girls would wear when celebrating their Puertorriqueñidad. Moreover, the doll helped establish a strong feeling of Puerto Rican pride among girls who interacted with it, to the point where they wanted to pass it on to future generations of Puerto Rican girls.

Identity was also established with the rejection of the doll. For example, Frances, whose story I described in chapter 5, did not see Barbie play as something interesting or fun. She preferred brain games and outdoor activities. As a result, Frances overtly rejected Barbie, even if it was supposed to be the doll that *all girls* had to have. As another example, Frankie did play with Barbie dolls during her childhood, although Barbie play could only take place with her sisters. Although she participated in Barbie play, Frankie usually played Ken because none of her sisters wanted to be him. Furthermore, she firmly stated that she did not want to be Barbie because the "expectations were too high."

Other products that carry Barbie's name also become instruments girls can use to construct their identities. Many of the women in this study recounted how their use of other Barbie products allowed them to continue the narratives they created through doll play (e.g., Emily), how they explored their own dreams through other products (e.g., Isabel, who wanted to become a fashion designer), or how they negotiated aspects of their identities (notably Carla, who used Barbie magazines to produce her own artifact of play). In the present, girls continue to use Barbie dolls and other products to explore their identities. We saw in the examples of Sharon, K.C., and Annie how they use these products to negotiate ideas of femininity and to assign roles through which they can explore how they perceive themselves.

For the most part, the women and girls in this study perceived their interactions with Barbie as positive in relation to their lived experiences. Even mothers of young girls who have reservations about Barbie still view Barbie play in general as a positive part of girlhood. Susan, whose initial access to Barbie was limited and who pointed out certain problematic characteristics of Barbie, still viewed her experiences with Barbie as good ones. Susan, who had felt excluded as a child for not having a Barbie doll, even bought herself a Barbie doll to celebrate her college graduation in 2003. Other participants, such as Isabel, who wished she could have identified more with Barbie, talked about her Barbie years as happy because she was able to create different play scenarios. Participant Autumn shared that she loved Barbie when she was little and that she remembers those years as positive. Yet when she became a mother, Autumn did not want her daughter Sharon to play with Barbie dolls or to become too invested in the princess and pink culture of dolls. Thus, despite her own positive experiences, she was apprehensive about introducing her daughter to the culture of Barbie and other dolls. Nevertheless, when Sharon showed interest in Barbie, Autumn and her husband acquiesced and allowed Barbie dolls in the house.

Participants Jessica and Carla looked back on their experiences with Barbie and recognized the doll's contributions to shaping who they became as adults. Jessica, for instance, acknowledged that the ideologies of beauty Barbie embodies can be problematic, but at the same time, she found that having a doll that represented these ideologies was positive for her. As she stated, her interactions with Barbie served as learning experiences about the expectations for women and girls. For Carla, despite a complicated relationship with Barbie, no negative aspects carried over into adulthood, and, thus, she viewed Barbie play as a positive experience.

For others, Barbie was a friend and a loyal companion, especially for girls who felt lonely because they did not have many friends or they were the only girl in their families. As Alondra and Patricia shared, they went through difficult situations during their girlhood years. Whether they experienced health-related issues or painful family dynamics, they both needed a friend to help them live through difficult times. Barbie was that friend, and for that reason they viewed their experiences with Barbie as very positive. These meaningful interactions illustrate how important Barbie can become in girls' lives and how they transcend into adulthood.

While other participants, such as Carmen, did not have many Barbie dolls during their girlhoods, their experiences and memories of play were joyful. In Carmen's case, she remembered the doll as beautiful, whose elegance she wanted to emulate. Moreover, when Carmen had daughters, she did not present any restrictions on their interactions with Barbie precisely because her memories were so positive. This provided me, one of her daughters, with the opportunity to play extensively with Barbie and create my own memories with the doll. My own memories, as I have presented, are happy. I never saw Barbie as a negative figure, and I do not remember receiving any negative messages from her.

Yet, this was not the case for everyone. We saw how Susan felt humiliated as a child when her teacher asked all the girls in the classroom to bring a Barbie doll, but Susan did not have one. In addition to these experiences of inaccessibility to Barbie or her products, Barbie embodies affluent femininity by inviting girls to consume through the lifestyle she leads, which not all girls can attain. Barbie's world centers on fashion and luxury. Her extensive wardrobe, the variety of homes she owns, the numerous vehicles she drives, and her overall lifestyle gives girls the idea that this is the type of lifestyle they should desire and work hard to attain. This is the kind of socioeconomic minefield that girls like Susan must navigate in relation to Barbie.

This issue of affluent femininity was one that a number of participants raised because they experienced how Barbie can be a marker of class and how it can be difficult to access the doll and her products. Her lifestyle invites one to consume, to spend, and to live luxuriously. For many girls, especially those from the first generation of Barbie, access to the doll was limited, and Barbie represented a fantasy of luxury and high fashion that they desired. The clothes themselves were expensive, as elucidated in Carmen's, Lourdes's, and Patricia's testimonies.

In terms of gender, many participants pointed out that Barbie is the quintessential girl toy. "Every girl should have a Barbie" and similar phrases were echoed throughout the interviews. What girls learned, then, was that if you wanted to be considered a girl, you *must* have a Barbie. As the different stories illustrated, girls experienced Barbie through the production of artifacts (such as clothes), the dramatic play through which they imagined more possibilities and assumed different roles, and the interactions that went beyond the doll (such as belonging to a fan club).

Many participants also pointed out the use of pink as the main color for most items related to Barbie, which propagates the idea that in order to be feminine (and to be a girl), girls *must* like pink. This is a result of years of marketing and color gendering, establishing that pink is a feminine color while blue is a masculine one. Moreover, several participants noted that they either believed or were aware of others who believed that *every girl should have a Barbie*. The idea that to be a girl you must have Barbie turns the doll into the epitome of femininity. Many girls, however, do not identify with the ideas about femininity that Barbie presents. We saw that Lisa, Frankie, and Isabel identified at times as "tomboys," not as "girly," and as a result did not always see themselves reflected in the image of girlhood created by Barbie. Seeing themselves as "tomboys" did not deter them completely from interacting with Barbie. However, many girls reject Barbie for various reasons, but they still want to be considered girls. Indeed, there are many reasons for not closely identifying with Barbie; some prefer to engage in "tomboy" activities, some cannot access the doll because of economic circumstances, and some are simply not interested in fashion or even Barbie's culture. Yet, the perceived obligation that to be a girl you have to have Barbie can become unfavorable to girls' ideas of femininity and girlhood.

Participants raised an important aspect of gender issues when they discussed Barbie's body. In some cases, they did not receive her exaggerated body as a harmful message about their own bodies. Still, for other participants, her body was an important part of growing up with the doll, as Barbie's figure was very notable and caused tensions between the girls and the dolls. As some of the participants expressed, Barbie can promote the idea that their bodies have to look a certain way—like Barbie's body. The experiences and perspectives provided by the girls and women suggest that when girls notice such a stark contrast between Barbie's body and their own, it becomes difficult to identify with the doll. Among the girls who presently play with Barbie, this was not an issue that emerged in our conversations, with the exception of Annie's observation that if girls (and boys) think they have to look like Barbie or Ken, they may go to extreme lengths to alter their appearance. This can be very dangerous if they go through numerous surgeries that could have fatal complications. Annie brought up the example of the "real" Ken because, even though his death was not caused by his surgeries, she wanted to note how dangerous wanting to look like Barbie could be. (As mentioned in chapter 3, his Leukemia was discovered while he was being treated for infections caused by a product called "hydrogel.") Other participants, especially mothers, talked about Barbie's body as one reason they might feel apprehensive about having Barbie in their houses. They do not want their daughters to suffer problems of body image because they do not look like Barbie. At the same time, some of these participants also highlighted the importance of educating children about their bodies. As they suggested, talking to them about accepting their bodies as they are instead of seeing Barbie as a physique to emulate could greatly diminish girls' body issues.

Similarly, differences emerged among participants when discussing their own identities vis-à-vis Barbie's race and ethnicity. This was an important topic of conversation. I examined girls' and women's perspectives toward the lack of racial and ethnic variety among Barbie dolls, especially when many of my participants were growing up. Mainly, girls encountered Barbie's race or ethnicity through the color of her hair, but also through the color of her skin. Many participants complained that throughout their girlhoods there were not many options for them to choose from, and they could not find Barbie dolls that looked like them. This lack of diversity played an important role among parents who did not want their daughters to have contact with Barbie if the only option was the white and blond doll. However, participants' examples illustrated how they pushed against the continuous use of white, blond Barbie as the main representative of the brand either by altering the doll's physical appearance or assigning dolls an ethnicity closer to that of the player. Sharon, for instance, tired of blond Barbie, painted the hair of two of her dolls; Alondra assigned a different ethnicity (Puerto Rican) to all of her dolls and made the dolls of color the main characters in her play scenarios. Barbie's ethnicity was essential to girls who had experiences with Puerto Rican Barbie, a doll in whom they finally had the opportunity to see themselves reflected upon her release in 1997.

More Than a Doll:
Barbie's Significance in Girlhood and Womanhood

One theme that emerged among some participants as they examined and reflected upon their views on Barbie as adults was the realization that in some ways they did not identify with Barbie, despite having played with the doll, liking the doll when they were young, and mostly viewing their interactions with Barbie as positive. When asked about their opinions of Barbie as adults, Isabel and Frankie could not help but laugh nervously. Once I assured them that I wanted to hear any type of opinion, good or bad, they opened up to share their current perspectives on the doll:

> Isabel: I would have liked to be able to identify more [with Barbie], and now that one can see other things and understand other things, that Barbie wouldn't always be driven to everything pink, and other things. I know at least I didn't watch TV about Barbie and I didn't see the plot there used to be for Barbie. For

example, I would create my own plot. But I don't like the plot and I don't like the stereotype of Barbie that she's an airhead, that she's always beautiful, and that she's always fashionable.

[. . .]

Frankie: But now that we're adults we think differently. It used to be that Barbie was everything for us. Today it is more like, "Barbie who?" (Isabel and Frankie, Group 3 transcript)

Carla also noted that, as a girl and through her Barbie years, she "never identified with the doll" and that Barbie was her "frenemy." In some ways, Carla felt that playing with Barbie was an obligation she had because she was a girl and because family and friends continued giving her Barbie dolls. Carla stated that, during her childhood, "it was like, 'I have to play with you because you're there and because they bring so many of you, and I have to accept you, but I also accept you because everyone else does because you're pretty, because you're fun.' But it was always with some jealousy. I used Barbie, but it was always with some jealousy" (Carla, interview transcript). However, as Barbie held the status of "frenemy" through Carla's girlhood, she clarified that, as an adult, there were certain "abstract aspects" of the doll with which she identified.

Like I am independent. Barbie was independent. On that aspect, within my tastes, I am fashionable, and Barbie is fashionable. I am social. You see? In that aspect I can say that I identify with Barbie and that maybe they are personality traits that I obtained from being exposed to the doll for so long. Maybe it was from that or maybe not. (Carla, interview transcript)

Jessica viewed her years of Barbie play as a learning experience that allowed her to understand the realities of the expectations for girls and women. In some ways, having a doll that represented the cultural ideologies about female beauty resulted in a positive experience for her. At the same time, these expectations and ideologies about femininity for Jessica are points of criticism, aspects about Barbie that she would like to see changed.

Well, something positive in the sense that, speaking philosophically, it allowed me to understand and accept that not all women have the same body. You know, because you start growing up in that ideology that every woman has to be a certain way. And when you start facing reality and your daily life, you realize that not every woman is going to be blond, not all women will have perfect breasts. And that's the most positive I could have gotten from her. But if you ask me something that I could criticize, it's the illusion the doll creates, the false expectations toward people, toward girls. (Jessica, Group 3 transcript)

Interestingly, Carla, who had a very complex and multidimensional relationship with Barbie, described her overall experience with the doll as a positive one.

> Yes, yes, I remember Barbie in a positive way. I remember the game of Barbie as something, well, as an experience that a child that . . . your parents present the toy to you, and as a child you make of your toys whatever you want. So, I look back and see it as positive. Even though there were internal conflicts, she was never a trigger for something bad or something negative. Like for example, girls who have eating disorders because they see themselves in Barbie's image and they can never see themselves like her within that expectation. Or the issue about the physical appearance, or the issue about economic independence, you see, that have marked other people. Personally maybe at that point in my life, maybe I had some complex because of Barbie, but it wasn't something that transcended to my psyche, that transformed me and messed up my life. No. Because I always knew she was a doll, something to play with. [I knew] that she was too perfect and was . . . well yes, but nothing that I could tell you deeply affected me emotionally or frustrated me. No, no, no. (Carla, interview transcript)

For other participants, their childhood memories of Barbie were about the relationship they fostered with the doll and how the doll served as a companion. In the first section of this chapter, I presented Lisa's memories of Barbie play. Lisa (age forty-five), who only had a brother and did not have many friends to play with Barbie, remembered that much of her interactions with the doll took place by herself. Moreover, she pointed out that "Barbies were [her] friends." Likewise, Isabel, who was the only girl in her family, felt that Barbie became a companion and friend to her at certain points. For her, Barbie "was also company. Yes, because for example I grew up with all boys, so once in a while playing with Barbie was like there was another (girl) friend. And the fan club too because I knew there were other girls there" (Isabel, Group 3 transcript).

If certain arguments call for Barbie to be seen as just a toy whose supposed messages are actually placed upon her by adults and cultural ideologies, there is also an argument to be made that Barbie's role is more than that of just a toy or a doll in children's lives. For many girls, myself included, Barbie was a friend who invited us to her world to become all the characters we wanted to be. In these cases, Barbie's role as more than a doll was not about the messages she promoted and how girls received them but rather about the meaningful bonds that girls created with her. For some of my participants, Barbie was there when they most needed a companion. For Gabriela, beyond the connection they brought between her and her mother, Barbies were her only friends for a long time: "My Barbies fought, were friends, hung out, everything. If I didn't have any friends, Barbies were my friends" (Gabriela, Group 4 transcript). Alondra remembered Barbie as a favorite toy that kept her company during a time of health difficulties, when there were no other people with whom she could spend time:

> I spent a lot of time sick with a cardiac condition when I was little. I was an only child and did not have cousins, and that's why I did not play outside frequently and did not practice any sports. I spent much time playing passive and solitary games. I lived with my grandmother until I was seven years old, and during that time I did not have many interactions with other children. From then on, I went to live with my mother, and then I could share this and other games with other girls and boys in my new neighborhood. Barbie was my favorite toy, my most favorite. (Alondra, email interview)

When I asked fifty-nine-year-old Patricia if her daughter Gabriela created dramatic scenarios with Barbie, she remembered that she, herself, used to do some role-playing with the doll, but now as an adult, she said, "I dress them, brush their hair, bathe them, but play like before, you kind of lose that" (Patricia, Group 4 transcript). Perhaps the testimony where Barbie's influence and significance became the most notable was Patricia's.

Her story, as do those of Alondra, Lisa, Gabriela, Isabel, and me, showcases how influential Barbie can be in girls' formative years. These stories of friendship and companionship with Barbie suggest an impact on girlhood that is separate from the messages girls receive from the doll. While critics of Barbie as well as many who played with Barbie have pointed out the doll's flaws, these meaningful experiences of friendship offer an angle that highlights how important Barbie was, has been, and continues to be for many girls. Furthermore, Barbie's influence can transcend into adulthood. Despite being considered a "toy for children," Barbie can be impactful in women's lives, as she was in the cases of Carla and Jessica, who look back on their years of Barbie play and understand how the doll contributed to shaping who they are as adults.

Implications of Barbie's Transnational Presence in Puerto Rican Girlhoods

I have explored in this work how women's and girls' meaningful and complex experiences with Barbie gave way to imaginative narratives, encounters with femininity, class, body image, and race, which allowed girls to construct identities. Twenty-one participants recounted their stories of how Barbie became part of their childhoods and what meanings the doll held in their lives, showing how those experiences can be different for girls according to their contexts. It was a main goal of this study to examine women's and girls' views on Barbie and their experiences with the doll that were either currently taking place (girls) or that had taken place in the past (adults). In specifically paying attention to the experiences of Puerto Rican women and girls, I aimed to disrupt the tendency to mostly do research about girls in dominant cultures and thus extend the research on Barbie to places where the scholarship has yet to explore.

The findings of this research position girls as important critics of the artifacts of their popular culture. They were and are able to identify aspects of the objects made for them, such as Barbie, that may send problematic messages to the person interacting with it. Simultaneously, they understand that Barbie serves as an instrument they can use to construct their own meanings, where they can gain pleasure from playing with Barbie and can modify the doll or play with it in ways that create meaning to their own lived experiences. There is something to be said about how girls actually experience(d) Barbie. The participants in my research—both girls in the present and adults remembering their childhood—pointed out some of the issues about Barbie and the potential messages girls may be receiving from the doll. Yet, it is important to emphasize not only how the girls (present and past) identified those problems but also how they subverted them through their interactions with Barbie. The critical engagement with Barbie that happens alongside the pleasures of Barbie play underlines the fraught and complex relationship girls have with the doll. This constitutes an important contribution my research makes to the field of girlhood studies, for it positions girls as central critics and experts on Barbie.

Moreover, the specific context in which this research took place offers significant contributions to the study of girlhood and the study of Barbie. In addition to the issues of race, gender, and class generally identified in the scholarship about Barbie, the cultural ideologies imposed upon the participants of this study added to the complexities of said issues. This happened, for instance, when participants claimed that Barbie did not have negative influence on their body image, yet their ideas of beauty were closely tied to the ideologies and discourses of beauty and race of their culture. The context was also important in examining how Barbie's model of affluent femininity takes a different meaning when it happens in a colonial territory where wealth and progress are believed to be achieved only through mobility to the colonizing country.

Barbie's role in the Puerto Rican girlhoods depicted in *An American Icon in Puerto Rico* was complex, nuanced, and full of tensions. As stated in this book's introduction, Barbie embodies contradictions that also manifest in how girls and women relate to her. Barbie is a fraught object that comes into contact with girls at a fraught phase of life. What this research has presented illustrates the different layers of girls' experiences with Barbie. Even within the testimony of a single girl, there are multiple nuances of how she experiences and views the doll. A girl can remember Barbie in a positive way because the doll offers a space to live a dream, while the same girl can perceive Barbie as an enemy because she cannot see herself reflected in the doll. Barbie, a transnational object in a transnational context is a site of contestation. Yet, she is also a site of resistance.

As Barbie continues to manifest in girls' and women's lives, despite the introduction of other brands of fashion dolls, so should we as researchers continue the work about the meanings she carries in girls' lived experiences. As has been depicted throughout this book and stated by scholars of girlhood, childhood, and cultural studies—among other fields—dolls are not mere objects of play. Dolls' continuous contact with girls provides possibilities for insightful observations about girls' everyday lives. They carry stories, meanings, and serve as windows into girls' lived experiences. They tell us about who girls are. Through dolls we can trace a history of girls' lives. As such, dolls, and particularly Barbie, an icon of US culture that is both welcomed and contested, helps us understand, learn, and continue tracing Puerto Rican (transnational) girlhoods.

References

Abu-Lughod, Lila. 1993. *Writing Women's Worlds: Bedouin Stories.* Berkeley: University of California Press.

Adams, Annmarie. 1995. "The Eichler Home: Intention and Experience in Postwar Suburbia." *Perspectives in Vernacular Architecture* 5: 164–78.

———. 2009. "The Power of Pink: Children's Bedrooms since World War II." Children at Risk/Children Taking Risks Conference, Society for the History of Children and Youth, University of California, Berkeley, 10–12 July 2009.

———. 2010. "The Power of Pink: Children's Bedrooms and Gender Identity." *FKW// Zeitschrift Für Geschlechterforschung und Visuelle Kultur* 50: 58–69.

African American Policy Institute. 2015. *Black Girls Matter: Pushed Out, Overpoliced, and Underprotected.* New York: African American Policy Forum.

Aguilar, Louis. 1997. "New Barbie Fuels Puerto Ricans' Debate Over Identity." Philly.com, 10 November. Retrieved from http://articles.philly.com/1997-11-10/news/25542969_1_puerto-ricans-doll-51st-state.

Aguiló-Pérez, Emily R. 2014. "Barbie and Ken." In *American Childhood in 25 Artifacts.* Popular Culture Association/American Culture Association H-Net, 22 October. Retrieved from https://networks.h net.org/node/13784/discussions/49762/20-barbie-and-ken.

———. 2016. "Review of Book *Princess Cultures: Mediating Girls' Imaginations and Identities*, edited by Miriam Forman-Brunell and Rebecca C. Hains (2015)." *American Journal of Play* 8(3): 397–99.

———. 2017. "Review of Book *Dolls Studies: The Many Meanings of Girls' Toys and Play*, edited by Miriam Forman-Brunell and Jennifer Dawn Whitney (2015)." *Children & Society* 31(1): 84–85.

———. 2021. "Commodifying Culture: Mattel's and Disney's Marketing Approaches to 'Latinx' Toys and Media." In *The Marketing of Children's Toys: Critical Perspectives on Children's Consumer Culture*, edited by Rebecca. C. Hains and Nancy A. Jennings, 143–63. New York: Palgrave Macmillan.

Aldama, Frederick Luis. 2013. "Multimediated Latinos in the Twenty-First Century: An Introduction." In *Latinos and Narrative Media*, edited by F. L. Aldama, 1–30. New York: Palgrave Macmillan.

Algren de Gutierrez, Edith. 1987. *The Movement against the Teaching of English in Puerto Rico*. London: University Press of America.

The Annie E. Casey Foundation. 2015. *Kids Count 2015 Data Book: State Trends in Child Well-Being*. Baltimore, MD.

Anzaldúa, Gloria. 1987. *Borderlands/La Frontera: The New Mestiza*. San Francisco: Aunt Lute Books.

Arroyo Pizarro, Yolanda. 2018. *Pelo Bueno*. Río Piedras: Editorial EDP University of Puerto Rico.

Atia, Nandia, and Jeremy Davies. 2010. "Nostalgia and the Shapes of History: Editorial." *Memory Studies* 3(3): 181–86.

Barbie. 2015. "Imagine the Possibilities." YouTube. Retrieved from https://www.youtube.com/watch?v=l1vnsqbnAkk.

Barreto, Amílcar A. 2001. *The Politics of Language in Puerto Rico*. Gainsville: University Press of Florida.

Beck, Laura. 2012. "Human Barbie Claims She's Never Had Plastic Surgery, Thinks We're All Stupid." *Jezebel*, 21 November. Retrieved from http://jezebel.com/5962402/human-barbie-claims-shes-never-had-plastic-surgery-thinks-were-all-stupid.

Bernstein, Robin. 2011. *Racial Innocence: Performing American Childhood from Slavery to Civil Rights*. New York: New York University Press.

———. 2015. "Children's Books, Dolls, and the Performance of Race; Or, the Possibility of Children's Literature." In *Dolls Studies: The Many Meanings of Girls' Toys and Play*, edited by M. Forman-Brunell and J. D. Whitney, 3–14. New York: Peter Lang.

Bonilla-Silva, Eduardo. 2010. "Reflections about Race by a *Negrito Acomplejao*." In *The Afro-Latin@ Reader: History and Culture in the United States*, edited by M. Jiménez-Román and Juan Flores, 445–52. Durham, NC: Duke University Press.

Boyle, D. Ellen, Nancy Marshall, and Wendy W. Robeson. 2003. "Gender at Play: Fourth-Grade Girls and Boys on the Playground." *American Behavioral Scientist* 46(10): 1326–45.

Brandt, Pamela. 1999. "Barbie Buys a Bra." In *The Barbie Chronicles: A Living Doll Turns Forty*, edited by Yona Zeldis McDonough, 53–58. New York: Touchstone Press.

Brookfield, Molly. 2012. "From American Girls into American Women: A Discussion of American Girl Doll Nostalgia." *Girlhood Studies an Interdisciplinary Journal* 5(1): 57–75.

Brown, Bill. 1998. "How to Do Things with Things (a Toy Story)." *Critical Inquiry* 24(4): 935–64.

Brown, Ruth Nicole. 2009. *Black Girlhood Celebration: Toward a Hip-Hop Feminist Pedagogy*. New York: Peter Lang.

Bury, Chris. 2015. "Is this 1917 law suffocating Puerto Rico's economy?" *PBS Newshour*, 13 August. Retrieved from http://www.pbs.org/newshour/makingsense/jones-act-holding-puerto-rico-back-debt-crisis/.

Cabot, Heather. 2005. "Doll Maker Embarks on 'Save Girlhood' Campaign." *ABC News*, 14 December. Retrieved from https://abcnews.go.com/Business/story?id=1403610.

U.S. Census Bureau. 2012. *Puerto Rico: 2010 Summary Population and Housing Characteristics*. Retrieved 13 July 2021 from https://www.census.gov/prod/cen2010/cph-1-53.pdf.

Chambers, Aiden. 1996. *Tell Me: Children, Reading, and Talk*. York, ME: Stenhouse Publishers.

Chin, Elizabeth. 1999. "Ethnically Correct Dolls: Toying with the Race Industry." *American Anthropologist* 101(2): 305–21.

Christensen, Pia Haudrup. 2004. "Children's Participation in Ethnographic Research: Issues of Power and Representation." *Children and Society* 18: 165–76.

Cohen, Louis, Lawrence Manion, and Keith Morrison. 2007. *Research Methods in Education*. New York: Routledge.

Cohn, D'Vera, Eileen Patten, and Mark Hugo Lopez. 2014. "Puerto Rican Population Declines on Island, Grows on U.S. Mainland." Pew Research Center, 11 August. Retrieved from http://www.pewhispanic.org/2014/08/11/puerto-rican-population-declines-on-island-grows-on-u-s-mainland/.

Coleman, Barbara. 2001. "Barbie." In *Girlhood in America: An Encyclopedia*, edited by Miriam Forman-Brunell, 1:63–68. Santa Barbara, CA: ABC-CLIO.

Collins, Louise, April Lidinsky, Andrea Rusnock, and Rebecca Trostrick. 2012. "We're Not Barbie Girls: Tweens Transform a Feminine Icon." *Feminist Formations* 24(1): 102–26.

Colón, José. 1984. "Estado Libre Asociado: The Constitutionality of Puerto Rico's Legal Status." *Journal Chicana/o Latina/o Law Review* 7(0): 95–112.

Cordero-Guzman, Hector. 1994. "Lessons from Operation Bootstrap." *NACLA Report on the Americas* 27(3): 7–10. DOI: 10.1080/10714839.1994.11723002.

Cox, Don Richard. 1977. "Barbie and Her Playmates." *Journal of Popular Culture* 11: 303–7.

Crabtree, Benjamin, M. Kim Yanoshik, William L. Miller, and Patrick O'Connor. 1993. "Selecting Individual or Group Interviews." In *Successful Focus Groups: Advancing the State of the Art*, edited by David Morgan, 137–49. Newbury, CA: Sage.

Crawford, June, Susan Kippax, Jenny Onyx, Una Gault, and Pam Benton. 1990. "Women Theorising Their Experiences of Anger: A Study Ising Memory-Work." *Australian Psychologist* 25(3): 333–50.

———. 1992. *Emotion and Gender: Constructing Meaning from Memory.* London: Sage Publications.

Damico Amy, and Sara E. Quay. 2006. "Stories of Boy Scouts, Barbie Dolls, and Prom Dresses: Challenging College Students to Explore the Popular Culture of Their Childhood." *Teachers College Record* 108(4): 604–20.

Dávila, Arelene. M. 1997. *Sponsored Identities: Cultural Politics in Puerto Rico.* Philadelphia: Temple University Press.

De Beauvoir, Simone. [1949] 2009. *The Second Sex.* Translated by C. Borde and S. Malovaney-Chevallier. New York: Vintage.

Delgado, Richard, and Jean Stefancic. 2001. *Critical Race Theory: An Introduction.* New York: New York University Press.

Denzin, Norman, and Yvonna S. Lincoln. 2011. "Introduction: The Discipline and Practice of Qualitative Research." In *Handbook of Qualitative Research*, 4th ed., edited by Norman Denzin and Yvonna Lincoln, 1–17. Thousand Oaks, CA: Sage Publications.

Dittmar, Helga, Emma Halliwell, and Suzanne Ive. 2006. "Does Barbie Make Girls Want to Be Thin? The Effect of Experimental Exposure to Images of Dolls on the Body Image of 5- to 8-Year-Old Girls." *Developmental Psychology* 42(2): 283–92.

Driscoll, Catherine. 2002. *Girls: Feminine Adolescence in Popular Culture and Cultural Theory.* New York: Columbia University Press.

———. 2008. "Barbie Culture." In *Girl Culture: An Encyclopedia*, edited by Claudia Mitchell and Jacqueline Reid-Walsh, 1:39–47. London: Greenwood Press.

Duany, Jorge. 2002. *The Puerto Rican Nation on the Move: Identities on the Island and in the United States.* Chapel Hill: University of North Carolina Press.

duCille, Ann. 1994. "Dyes and Dolls: Multicultural Barbie and the Merchandising of Difference." *Differences: A Journal of Feminist Cultural Studies* 6(1): 47–68.

———. 1999. "Barbie in Black and White." In *The Barbie Chronicles: A Living Doll Turns Forty*, edited by Yona Zeldis McDonough, 127–42. New York: Touchstone Press.

———. 2003. "Black Barbie and the Deep Play of Difference." In *The Feminism and Visual Culture Reader*, edited by Amelia Jones, 337–48. New York: Routledge.

Engin, Hande Bilsel. 2013. "Barbied Dreams, Barbied Lives: On Our Backs, in the Attics of Our Memories, on the Shelves." *International Journal of Social Inquiry* 6(2): 18–37.

Epstein, Rebecca, Jamilia J. Blake, and Thalia González. 2017. *Girlhood Interrupted: The Erasure of Black Girls' Childhood.* Washington, DC: Center on Poverty and Inequality, Georgetown Law.

Ferrer, Dorothy Bell. 2016. "How 'Mestizaje' in Puerto Rico Makes Room for Racism to Flourish." *La Respuesta: A Magazine to (Re)Imagine the Boricua Diaspora* (8 February): 1–9. Retrieved from http://larespuestamedia.com/mestizaje-racism/.

Figueroa-Vásquez, Yomaira, and Yarimar Bonilla. 2020. "A White Scholar Pretended to be Black and Latina for Years. This Is Modern Minstrelsy." *The Guardian*, 9 September. Retrieved from https://www.theguardian.com/comment isfree/2020/sep/09/jessica-krug-white-scholar-black-latina.

Fiske, John. [1989] 1998. *Reading the Popular*. London: Unwin Hyman.

Forman-Brunell, Miriam. 2002. "What Barbie Can Tell Us about Postwar American Culture." In *Artifact and Analysis: Interpreting Objects and Writing History*. Washington DC: Smithsonian Center for Education and Museum Studies, Smithsonian. Retrieved 8 March 2020 from http://www.smithsonianeduca tion.org/idealabs/ap/artifacts/barbie.htm.

———. 2011. "The Politics of Dollhood in Nineteenth-Century America." In *The Girls' History and Culture Reader: The Nineteenth Century*, edited by Miriam Forman-Brunell and Leslie Paris, 222–41. Urbana: University of Illinois Press.

———. 2012. "Interrogating the Meanings of Dolls: New Directions in Doll Studies." *Girlhood Studies an Interdisciplinary Journal* 5(1): 3–13.

Forman-Brunell, Miriam, and Jennifer Dawn Whiteney. 2015. "Introduction." In *Dolls Studies: The Many Meanings of Girls' Toys and Play*, edited by M. Forman-Brunell and Jennifer Dawn Whitney, ix–xviii. New York: Peter Lang.

Frost, Joel L., Sue C. Wortham, and Stuart C. Reifel. 2012. *Play and Child Development*, 4th ed. Boston: Pearson.

Geertz, Clifford. 1994. "Thick Description: Towards an Interpretative Theory of Culture." In *Readings in the Philosophy of Social Science*, edited by M. Martin and L. McIntyre, 213–32. Boston: MIT Press.

Gerber, Robin. 2009. *Barbie and Ruth: The Story of the World's Most Famous Doll and the Woman Who Created Her*. New York: Collins Business.

Gilman, Susan Jane. 1998. "Klaus Barbie and Other Dolls I'd Like to See." In *Adios Barbie: Young Women Write about Body Image and Identity*, edited by Ophira Edut, 14–21. Seattle: Seal Press.

Glesne, Corrine. 2011. *Becoming Qualitative Researchers: An Introduction*, 4th ed. Boston: Allyn & Bacon.

Godreau, Isar. 2008. "Slippery Semantics: Race Talk and Everyday Uses of Racial Terminology in Puerto Rico." *El Centro Journal* 20(2): 4–33.

Gottschall, Kristina, Susanne Gannon, Jo Lampert, and Kelli McGraw. 2013. "The Cyndi Lauper Affect: Bodies, Girlhood and Popular Culture." *Girlhood Studies an Interdisciplinary Journal* 6(1): 30–45.

Grewal, Inderpal. 2005. *Transnational America: Feminisms, Diasporas, Neoliberalisms*. Durham, NC: Duke University Press.

Grosfoguel, Ramón. 2003. *Colonial Subjects: Puerto Ricans in a Global Perspective*. Berkeley: University of California Press.

Gubar, Marah. 2021. "Innocence." In *Keywords for Children's Literature*, 2nd ed., edited by Philip Nel, Lissa Paul, and Nina Christensen, 105–12. New York: New York University Press.

Guerrero, Lisa. 2009. "Can the Subaltern Shop? The Commodification of Difference in the *Bratz* Dolls." *Cultural Studies <=> Critical Methodologies* 9(2): 186–96.

Guerrilla Girls. 1995. "Guerrilla Girls Bare All: An Interview." *Guerrilla Girls Reinventing the "F" Word: Feminism.* Retrieved from http://www.guerrillagirls.com/interview/index.shtml.

Guy, Therese. 2012. "Generation Gap." In *Chicken Soup for the Soul: The Magic of Mothers and Daughters*, edited by Jack Canfield, Mark Victor Hansen, and Amy Newmark, 109–10. Cos Cob, CT: Chicken Soup for the Soul Publishing.

Hade, Daniel. 2001. "Curious George Gets Branded: Reading as Consuming." *Theory into Practice* 40(3): 158–65.

Hains, Rebecca C. 2012. "An Afternoon of Productive Play with Problematic Dolls: The Importance of Foregrounding Children's Voice in Research." *Girlhood Studies an Interdisciplinary Journal* 5(1): 121–40.

———. 2015. "If I Were a Belle: Performers' Negotiation of Feminism, Gender, and Race in Princess Culture." In *Princess Cultures: Mediating Girls' Imaginations and Identities*, edited by Miriam Forman-Brunell and Rebecca C. Hains, 209–31. New York: Peter Lang.

———. 2021. "The Politics of Barbie's Curvy New Body: Marketing Mattel's Fashionistas Line." In *The Marketing of Children's Toys: Critical Perspectives on Children's Consumer Culture*, edited by Rebecca. C. Hains and Nancy A. Jennings, 265–283. New York: Palgrave Macmillan.

Halter, Marilyn. 2000. *Shopping for Identity: The Marketing of Ethnicity.* New York: Schocken Books.

Hateley, Erica. 2011. "Gender." In *Keywords for Children's Literature*, edited by Philip Nel and Lissa Paul, 86–91. New York: New York University Press.

Haug, Frigga. 1997. "Memory-Work as a Method of Social Science Research: A Detailed Rendering of Memory-Work Method." Retrieved from http://www.friggahaug.inkrit.de/documents/ memorywork-researchguidei7.pdf.

Haug, Frigga, et al. 1987. *Female Sexualization: A Collective Work of Memory.* Translated by E. Carter. London: Verso.

Hegde, Radha S. 2001. "Global Makeovers and Maneuvers: Barbie's Presence in India." *Feminist Media Studies* 1(1): 129–33.

Hohmann, Delf Maria. 1985. "'Jennifer and Her Barbies': A Contextual Analysis of a Child Playing Barbie Dolls." *Canadian Folklore* 7(1–2): 111–20.

Hughes, Bob. 2002. *A Playworker's Taxonomy of Play Types*, 2nd ed. London: PlayLink.

Jackson, Stevi. 1998. "Telling Stories: Memory, Narrative and Experience in Feminist Research and Theory." In *Standpoints and Differences: Essays in the Practice of Feminist Psychology*, edited by Karen Henwood, Chris Griffin, and Ann Phoenix, 45–64. London: Sage.

Johnson, James E., James Christie, and Francis Wardle. 2005. *Play, Development, and Early Education*. Boston: Pearson.

Jones, Wendy Singer 1999. "Barbie's Body Project." In *The Barbie Chronicles: A Living Doll Turns Forty*, edited by Yona Zeldis McDonough, 91–107. New York: Touchstone.

Jong, Erica. 1999. "Twelve Dancing Barbies." In *The Barbie Chronicles: A Living Doll Turns Forty*, edited by Yona Zeldis McDonough, 201–6. New York: Touchstone.

Kamberelis, George, and Greg Dimitriadis. 2005. *On Qualitative Inquiry: Approaches to Language and Literacy Research*. New York: Teachers College Press.

Kearney, Mary Celeste. 2007. "Productive Spaces: Girls' Bedrooms as Sites of Cultural Production." *Journal of Children and Media* 1(2): 126–41.

———. 2009. "Coalescing: The Development of Girls' Studies." *NWSA Journal* 21(1): 1–28.

Kinsbruner, Jay. 1996. *Not of Pure Blood: The Free People of Color and Racial Prejudice in Nineteenth-Century Puerto Rico*. Durham, NC: Duke University Press.

Kolmar, Wendy, and Susan Stern. 2002. "Remembering 'Barbie Nation': An Interview with Susan Stern." *Women's Studies Quarterly* 30(1/2): 189–95.

Korrol, Virginia Sanchez. n.d. "The Story of Puerto Ricans in the U.S.—Part Four: The Great Migration at Mid-century." Centro: Center for Puerto Rican Studies. Retrieved from http://centropr.hunter.cuny.edu/education/puerto-rican-studies/story-us-puerto-ricans-part-four.

Kuther, Tara L., and Erin McDonald. 2004. "Early Adolescents' Experiences with, and Views of, Barbie." *Adolescence* 39(153): 39–52.

Leong, Deborah, and Elena Bodrova. 2012. "Assessing and Scaffolding Make-Believe Play." *Young Children* 67: 28–34.

Lichtman, Marilyn. 2009. *Qualitative Research in Education: A User's Guide*, 2nd ed. Los Angeles: Sage.

Lipkin, Elline. 2009. *Girls' Studies*. Berkeley, CA: Seal Press.

Lloréns, Hilda. 2013. "Latina Bodies in the Era of Elective Aesthetic Surgery." *Latino Studies* 11(4): 547–69.

———. 2020. "Racialization Works Differently Here in Puerto Rico, Do Not Bring Your U.S.-Centric Ideas about Race Here!" *Black Perspectives*, 3 March. Retrieved from https://www.aaihs.org/racialization-works-differently-here-in-puerto-rico-do-not-bring-your-u-s-centric-ideas-about-race-here/.

Lloyd, Alexandra. 2015. "Dolls and Play: Material Culture and Memories of Girlhood in Germany, 1933–1945." In *Dolls Studies: The Many Meanings of*

Girls' Toys and Play, edited by Miriam Forman-Brunell and Jennifer Dawn Whitney, 37–59. New York: Peter Lang.

Lobenstine, Lori, Yasmin Pereira, Jenny Whitley, Jessica Robles, Yaraliz Soto, Jeanette Sergeant et al. 2001. "Possible Selves and Pasteles: A Truly Socially Contextualized Model of Girlhood." Paper presented at A New Girl Order: Young Women and Feminist Inquiry Conference, London, England. Retrieved from http://www.whatkidscando.org/archives/shorttakes/HolyokeGirlsPaperdoc.pdf.

Lord, M. G. 1994. *Forever Barbie: The Unauthorized Biography of a Real Doll.* New York: Walker & Company.

Loveman, Mara, and Jeronimo O. Muñiz. 2007. "How Puerto Rico Became White: Boundary Dynamics and Intercensus Racial Reclassification." *American Sociological Review* 72(6): 915–39.

MacDougall, J. Paige. 2003. "Transnational Commodities as Local Cultural Icons: Barbie Dolls in Mexico." *Journal of Popular Culture* 37(2): 257–75.

Magee, Carol. 2005. "Forever in *Kente*: Ghanian Barbie and the Fashioning of Identity." *Social Identities: Journal for the Study of Race, Nation and Culture* 11(6): 589–606.

Marsh, Jackie. 2010. "Young Children's Play in Virtual Worlds." *Journal of Early Childhood Research* 8(1): 23–39.

Mattel. 2010. *Barbie: I Can Be a Computer Engineer.* New York: Random House Books for Young Readers.

Memmi, Albert. 1965. *The Colonizer and the Colonized.* Boston: Beacon Press.

McDonough, Yona Zeldis. 1999. "Sex and the Single Doll." In *The Barbie Chronicles: A Living Doll Turns Forty*, edited by Yona Zeldis McDonough, 111–13. New York: Touchstone Press.

McRobbie, Angela. 1991. "Introduction." In *Feminism and Youth Culture: From "Jackie" to "Just Seventeen,"* edited by Angela McRobbie, ix–xx. Boston: Unwin Hyman.

McRobbie, Angla, and Jenny Garber. 1991. "Girls and Subcultures." In *Feminism and Youth Culture: From "Jackie" to "Just Seventeen,"* edited by Angela McRobbie, 1–15. Boston: Unwin Hyman.

McRobbie, Angela, and Mica Nava, eds. 1984. *Gender and Generation.* London: Macmillan.

Mitchell, Claudia, and Jacqueline Reid-Walsh. 1997. "And I Want to Thank You Barbie: Barbie as a Site of Cultural Interrogation." In *Education and Cultural Studies: Toward a Performative Practice*, edited by Henry Giroux and Patrick Shannon, 87–100. New York: Routledge.

Mitchell, Claudia, and Jacqueline Reid-Walsh. 2002. *Researching Children's Popular Culture: The Cultural Spaces of Childhood.* New York: Routledge.

———. 2008. "How to Study Girl Culture." In *Girl Culture: An Encyclopedia*, edited by Claudia Mitchell and Jacqueline Reid-Walsh, 1:17–24. London: Greenwood Press.

————. 2011. *Memory and Pedagogy*. New York: Routledge.

Mohanty, Chandra T. 2003. *Feminism without Borders: Decolonizing Theory, Practicing Solidarity*. Durham, NC: Duke University Press.

Moore-Henecke, Deb. 1997. "Rethinking Barbie." *Images: A Journal of Popular Culture* 4: 1–3. Retrieved from http://www.imagesjournal.com/issue04/features/barbie.htm.

Morgan, Carol. n.d. "The Barbie Doll: Perpetuating Ideologies of a Capitalistic Society," 1–19. Retrieved from https://www.yumpu.com/en/document/view/3903443/the-barbie-doll-perpetuating-ideologies-of-a-drcarolmorgan.

Morgan, David L., and Richard A. Krueger. 1993. "When to Use Focus Groups and Why." In *Successful Focus Groups: Advancing the State of the Art*, edited by David L. Morgan, 3–19. Newbury, CA: Sage.

Muñoz, José Esteban. 1999. *Disidentifications: Queers of Color and the Performance of Politics*. Minneapolis: University of Minnesota Press.

Navarro, Mireya. 1997. "A New Barbie in Puerto Rico Divides Island and Mainland." *New York Times*, 27 December. Retrieved from http://www.nytimes.com/1997/12/27/us/a-new-barbie-in-puerto-rico-divides-island-and-mainland.html.

Negrón-Muntaner, Frances. 2002. "Barbie's Hair: Selling Out Puerto Rican Identity in the Global Market." In *Latino/a Popular Culture*, edited by M. Habell-Pallán and M. Romero, 38–60. New York: New York University Press.

————. 2004. *Boricua Pop: Puerto Ricans and the Latinization of American Culture*. New York: New York University Press.

Newmark, Amy. 2012. "Introduction." In *Chicken Soup for the Soul: The Magic of Mothers and Daughters*, edited by Jack Canfield, Mark Victor Hansen, and Amy Newmark, xi–xii. Cos Cob, CT: Chicken Soup for the Soul Publishing.

O'Reilly-Scanlon, Kathleen, and Sonya Corbin Dwyer. 2005. "Memory-Work as a (be)Tween Research Method: The Beauty, the Splendor, the Wonder of My Hair." In *Seven Going on Seventeen: Tween Studies in the Culture of Girlhood*, edited by Claudia Mitchell and Jacqueline Reid-Walsh, 79–94. New York: Peter Lang Publishing.

Onyx, Jenny, and Jennie Small. 2001. "Memory-Work: The Method." *Qualitative Inquiry* 7(6): 773–86.

Orr, Lisa. 2009. "'Difference That Is Actually Sameness Mass-Reproduced': Barbie Joins the Princess Convergence." *Jeunesse: Young People, Texts, Cultures* 1(1): 9–30.

Ortiz Cofer, Judith. 1990. *Silent Dancing: A Partial Remembrance of a Puerto Rican Childhood*. Houston, TX: Arte Público Press.

Pahl, Kate, and Jennifer Rowsell. 2010. *Artifactual Literacies: Every Object Tells a Story*. New York: Teachers College Press.

————. 2011. "Artifactual Critical Literacy: A New Perspective for Literacy Education." *Berkeley Review of Education* 2(2): 129–51.

Patton, Michael Quinn. 2001. *Qualitative Research & Evaluation Methods*, 3rd ed. Thousand Oaks, CA: Sage.

Pelletier, Caroline. 2008. "What Education Has to Teach Us about Games and Game Play." In *Play, Creativity and Digital Cultures*, edited by Rebekah Willet, Muriel Robinson, and Jackie Marsh, 166–82. New York: Taylor & Francis.

Peña-Pérez, Diana. 2016. "Understanding Ethnic Labels and Puerto Rican Identity. Yale-New Haven Teachers Institute. Retrieved from http://www.yale.edu/ynhti/curriculum/units/2000/1/00.01.05.x.html.

Picó, Fernando. 2006. *History of Puerto Rico: A Panorama of Its People*. Princeton, NJ: Markus Wiener Publishers.

Pike, Kristen. 2015. "Princess Culture in Qatar: Exploring Princess Media Narratives in the Lives of Arab Female Youth." In *Princess Cultures: Mediating Girls' Imaginations and Identities*, edited by Miriam Forman-Brunell and Rebecca C. Hains, 139–60. New York: Peter Lang.

Pousada, Alicia. 1996. "Puerto Rico: On the Horns of a Language Dilemma." *TESOL Quarterly* 30(3): 499–509.

Quindlen, Anna. 1999. "Barbie at 35." In *The Barbie Chronicles: A Living Doll Turns Forty*, edited by Yona Zeldis McDonough, 117–19. New York: Touchstone.

Rakow, Lana F., and Caitlin S. Rakow. 1999. "Educating Barbie." In *Growing Up Girls: Popular Culture and the Construction of Identity*, edited by Sharon R. Mazzarella and Norma Odom Pecora, 11–20. New York: Peter Lang.

Ramos Oliver, Gamaliel. 2017. "Puerto Rico: Niña intenta detener acoso racial y ahora enfrenta cinco cargos por agresión." *Univisión*, 31 July. Retrieved from https://www.univision.com/radio/puerto-rico-wkaq-am/puerto-rico-nina-intenta-detener-acoso-racial-y-ahora-enfrenta-cinco-cargos-por-agresion.

Rand, Erica. 1995. *Barbie's Queer Accessories*. Durham, NC: Duke University Press.

Reid-Walsh, Jacqueline. 2011. "Girlhood." In *Keywords for Children's Literature*, edited by Philip Nel and Lissa Paul, 92–95. New York: New York University Press.

———. 2013. "Artifactual Memory: Fragmentary 'Memoirs' of Three Eighteenth- and Nineteenth-Century Moveable Books about Their Child Owners." In *Productive Remembering and Social Agency*, edited by Teresa Strong-Wilson, Claudia Mitchell, Susann Allnutt, and Kathleen Pithouse-Morgan, 197–211. Rotterdam, The Netherlands: Sense Publishers.

Reid-Walsh, Jacqueline, and Claudia Mitchell. 2000. "Just a Doll? 'Liberating' Accounts of Barbie-Play." *Review of Education/Pedagogy/Cultural Studies* 22(2): 175–90.

Reyes, Alba G. 2015. "Ser Negra en Puerto Rico." *Alba Giselle Reyes* (blog), 2 November. Retrieved from https://albagisellereyes.wordpress.com/2015/11/02/ser-negra-en-puerto-rico/

Ribon, Pamela. 2014. "Barbie Fucks It Up Again." Pamie.com, 17 November. Retrieved from http://pamie.com/2014/11/barbie-fucks-it-up-again/.

Riddick, Kristin. 2001. "Barbie: The Image of Us All; Project." American Studies at the University of Virginia. Retrieved from http://xroads.virginia.edu/~class/am483_95/projects/barbie/barb.html.

Rivera-Brooks, Nancy. 1997. "Barbie's Online Critics See Guise in Dolls." *Los Angeles Times*, 21 November. Retrieved from http://articles.latimes.com/1997/nov/21/business/fi-56134.

Rivera-Hernández, Nayda, and Verónica Andino Ortiz. 2010. *Nuestros Niños Cuentan: Libro de Datos Puerto Rico*. Washington DC: National Council of La Raza- NCLR.

Rodríguez-Silva, Ileana M. 2012. *Silencing Race: Disentangling Blackness, Colonialism, and National Identities in Puerto Rico*. New York: Palgrave Macmillan.

Rodriguez-Soto, Isa, and Shir Lerman Ginzburg. 2019. "Beyond Good and Bad Fat: Understanding Puerto Rican Body Size Norms." *CENTRO: Journal of the Center for Puerto Rican Studies* 31(3): 72–92.

Rogers, Mary. 1998. *Barbie Culture*. London: Sage Publications.

Rousseau, Jean-Jacques. [1762] 1921. *Emile, or Education*. Translated by B. Foxley. New York: E. P. Dutton. Retrieved from http://oll.libertyfund.org/titles/2256.

Ryan, Frances. 1994. "If Opportunity Knocks—Let It In! Franchise Business Is a Natural for Puerto Rican Entrepreneurs." *Caribbean Business* (31 March): 1.

Santana, Déborah Berman. 1998. "Puerto Rico's Operation Bootstrap: Colonial Roots of a Persistent Model for 'Third World' Development." *Revista Geográfica* 124: 87–116. Stable URL: https://www.jstor.org/stable/40992748.

Santiago, Esmeralda. 1993. *When I Was Puerto Rican*. Reading, MA: Addison-Wesley.

———. 1999. *Almost a Woman*. New York: Vintage Books.

Sarasohn-Kahn, Jane. 1996. *Contemporary Barbie: Barbie Dolls 1980 and Beyond*. Dubuque, IA: Antique Trader Books.

Schwarz, Maureen Trudelle. 2005. "Native American Barbie: The Marketing of Euro-American Desires." *American Studies* 46 (3/4): 295–326.

Sharman, Carole, Wendy Cross, and Diana Vennis. 2004. *Observing Children: A Practical Guide*, 3rd ed. New York: Continuum.

Simmons, Lakisha Michelle. 2015. *Crescent City Girls: The Lives of Young Black Women in Segregated New Orleans*. Chapel Hill: University of North Carolina Press.

Smiley, Jane. 1999. "You Can Never Have Too Many." In *The Barbie Chronicles: A Living Doll Turns Forty*, edited by Yona Zeldis McDonough, 189–92. New York: Touchstone.

Smith, Ann. 2017. "Introduction: The Transnational Girl in the Text; Transnationalism Redefined?" In *The Girl in the Text*, edited by Ann Smith, 1–12. New York: Berghahn Books.

Sohail, Rabia, Raheela Naz, and Nazir Ahmed Malik. 2014. "A Postcolonial Study of Barbie Phenomena and Its Implication in Pakistani Urban Context." *European Academic Research* 2(5): 6949–78.

Soong, Roland. 1998. "Barbie in Latin America." Zona Latina. Retrieved from http://www.zonalatina.com/Zldata37.htm.

Sprague, Joey. 2005. *Feminist Methodologies for Critical Researchers: Bridging Differences.* Walnut Creek, CA: AltaMira Press.

Steinberg, Shirley R. 1997. "The Bitch Who Has Everything." In *Kinderculture*, edited by J. Kinchelo and S. Steinburg, 219–26. Boulder, CO: Westview Press.

Strong-Wilson, Teresa, Claudia Mitchell, Susann Allnutt, and Kathleen Pithouse-Morgan. 2013. "Productive Remembering and Social Action." In *Productive Remembering and Social Agency*, edited by Teresa Strong-Wilson, Claudia Mitchell, Susann Allnutt, and Kathleen Pithouse-Morgan, 1–16. Rotterdam, The Netherlands: Sense Publishers.

Sullivan, Megan. 2008. "The Scholar Recalls the Child: The Difference Girlhood Studies Makes." *Girlhood Studies an Interdisciplinary Journal* 1(2): 95–107.

Ticona-Vergaray, Evelyn. 2009. "Barbie's 50 Years of Beauty and Controversy." UPI Next. Retrieved from http://next.upi.com/archive/2009/11/08/Barbies-50-years-of-beauty-and-controversy/3381257729165/.

Tosa, Marco. 1998. *Barbie: Four Decades of Fashion, Fantasy, and Fun.* New York: H. N. Abrams.

Torres-Gonzalez, Roame. 2002. *Idioma, Bilinguismo y Nacionalidad: La Presencia del Inglés en Puerto Rico.* San Juan: Editorial de la Universidad de Puerto Rico.

Valdivia, Angharad N. 2016. "Contemporary Mainstream Latinidad: Disney Tales and Spitfire Endurance." *Límite: Revista Interdisciplinaria de Filosofía y Psicología* 11(37): 66–78. Retrieved from http://www.redalyc.org/articulo.oa?id=83648394007

Vincent, Roger. 2005. "Mattel Profit Down 28% as Barbie Sales Decline." *Los Angeles Times*, 16 April. Retrieved from https://www.latimes.com/archives/la-xpm-2005-apr-16-fi-mattel16-story.html.

Wagner-Ott, Anna. 2002. "Analysis of Gender Identity through Doll and Action Figure Politics in Art Education." *Studies in Art Education* 43 (3): 246–63.

Washburn, Dorothy K. 1997. "Getting Ready: Doll Play and Real Life in American Culture." In *American Material Culture: The Shape of the Field*, edited by Ann Smart Martin and J. Ritchie Garrison, 105–34. Winterthur, DE: The Henry Francis du Pont Winterthur Museum, Inc.

Weida, Courtney Lee. 2011. "Gender, Aesthetics, and Sexuality in Play: Uneasy Lessons from Girls' Dolls, Action Figures, and Television Programs." *Journal of Social Theory in Art Education* 31: 1–26. Retrieved from http://www.bluedoublewide.com/openJournal/index.php/jstae/index.

Wertheimer, Sophie. 2006. "Pretty in Panties: Moving beyond the Innocent Child Paradigm in Reading Preteen Modeling Websites." In *Girlhood: Redefin-

ing the Limits, edited by Y. Jiwani, C. Steenburgen, and C. Mitchell, 208–26. Montreal: Black Rose Press.

Whitney, Jennifer Dawn. 2012. "Some Assembly Required: Black Barbie and the Fabrication of Nicki Minaj." *Girlhood Studies an Interdisciplinary Journal* 5(1): 141–59.

Wilkinson, Sue. 1998. "Focus Groups in Feminist Research: Power, Interaction, and the Co-construction of Meaning." *Women's Studies International Forum* 21(1): 111–24.

Wohlwend, Karen E. 2009. "Damsels in Discourse: Girls Consuming and Producing Identity Texts through Disney Princess Play." *Reading Research Quarterly* 44(1): 57–83.

———. 2015. "Playing to Belong: Princesses and Peer Cultures in Preschool." In *Princess Cultures: Mediating Girls' Imaginations and Identities*, edited by Miriam Forman-Brunell and Rebecca C. Hains, 89–112. New York: Peter Lang.

Wolitzer, Meg. 1999. "Barbie as Boy Toy." In *The Barbie Chronicles: A Living Doll Turns Forty*, edited by Yona Zeldis McDonough, 207–10. New York: Touchstone.

Wright, Nazera Sadiq. 2016. *Black Girlhood in the Nineteenth Century*. Urbana: University of Illinois Press.

Zamora, Omaris. Z. 2020. "Black Latina Girlhood Poetics of the Body: Church, Sexuality and Dispossession." Post45, 21 January. Retrieved from https://post45.org/2020/01/black-latina-girlhood-poetics-of-the-body-church-sexuality-and-dispossession.

INDEX

www.ingramcontent.com/pod-product-compliance
Lightning Source LLC
Chambersburg PA
CBHW070624030426
42337CB00020B/3908